About the author

Charles Tyzack spent most of his career ⎯⎯⎯⎯⎯⎯⎯⎯ the
University of Wales (Lampeter and Cardiff). His interest in China
stemmed from his family history: his grandfather and three of his great-
uncles spent their lives in China as Quaker missionaries. He has told
their story in his earlier book *Friends to China*. Charles himself has taught
English at Chinese universities in the 1980s and 1990s, as well as
courses on Chinese History and Art back in the UK. He lives in
Oxfordshire.

All royalties for this book will be donated to the Development
Organisation of Rural Sichuan (DORS), a UK registered charity
(1061133) established in 1996. DORS runs poverty alleviation projects
in poor mountainous villages of Hanyuan County, Sichuan Province.
From their office based in the county, they work directly with community members to develop projects that bring real and lasting
improvements to people's lives. Projects include community built and
managed drinking water supplies, roads and paths, forestry, micro-
loans, education support, training and capacity building, and fuel efficient stoves. DORS needs funding support to continue their work,
please see www.dors.org.uk

By the same author

Wychwood and Cornbury (The Wychwood Press, 2003)

Friends to China: The Davidson Brothers and the Friends' Mission to China, 1886–1939 (William Sessions, The Ebor Press, 1988)

NEARLY A CHINESE

A Life of Clifford Stubbs

Charles Tyzack

Book Guild Publishing
Sussex, England

First published in Great Britain in 2013 by
The Book Guild Ltd
The Werks
45 Church Road
Hove, BN3 2BE

Typesetting in Garamond by
YHT Ltd, London

Printed and bound in Great Britain by
4edge Ltd, Hockley, Essex

A catalogue record for this book is available from
The British Library.

ISBN 978 1 84624 963 1

Contents

List of Illustrations in Plate Section
between pages 116 and 117

Preface

Ever since Clifford Stubbs was killed in 1930 the idea of a biography has been suggested. William Sewell wrote a short appreciation of his life the following year, *A Life for Many*, but Clifford's widow Margaret felt unable to write anything herself, and must in any case have been preoccupied with bringing up three children on her own. When Jean Stubbs came to teach at the Friends' School in Saffron Walden in the 1960s, and lived with her mother, the idea was revived; reminiscences were sought from those who had known Clifford, and Margaret recorded some of her memories, both on tape and on paper. After her mother's death in 1976 Jean continued to carry out research, especially in the archives of Friends' House, but felt unable to take the work further. However, she carefully preserved a mass of family letters and papers, and finally invited me to write the biography in 2005. This must have been a hard decision for her, to entrust her father's reputation to a comparative stranger, and I hope I have proved worthy of her confidence.

In the 1980s I had written an account of my own forebears' activities with Quakers in West China: *Friends to China: The Davidson Brothers and the Friends' Mission to China 1886–1939*. I was therefore familiar with the context of Clifford's work and the people he knew. Moreover this would complement my earlier book, which had little to say about the West China Union University in Chengdu, where Clifford was Professor of Chemistry. The more I read in Clifford's letters and papers, and in accounts of him by others, the greater my admiration – affection indeed – grew for a quite remarkable and lovable human being.

The main sources for information about his life are the family papers ('The Jean Stubbs Papers') which are to be deposited in the Durham University Library, and the records of the Friends' Foreign Mission

Association/Friends' Service Council in the Library of Friends' House in London. There are many gaps – the Friends' House archives were drastically weeded in the 1920s – and there are full sets of Clifford's letters only for those periods when he and Margaret were apart, in 1913–15, 1924–26, and 1927–28. But there is enough to give a good idea both of the man and the – today very alien – world in which he worked.

I am very grateful to John Lees for being an ever-cheerful and encouraging link with the Stubbs-Lees family, Helen Stubbs for providing important information about Frederick Stubbs, and Bill Willmott for researching into Clifford's college days in New Zealand. I would also like to thank Adrian Johnson for reading a draft version of the book, and for his most helpful comments. Ann Lees, Ruth Baker, Patrick Wood, Xiao Bing, Zhang Liping, and Sam Li Zhou have also helped in various ways, and I would like to thank them and the staff of the Friends' House Library, Melissa Atkinson and Josef Keith in particular, for their assistance and advice.

A Note on Chinese Names

In recent years it has become customary to use the modern 'pinyin' system of Romanisation for writing Chinese names, of people and places, in English, and I have mostly done so in this book. In the original documents the spelling is often inconsistent, and sometimes reflects Sichuan dialect pronunciation rather than Mandarin. However, when a new person is introduced into the story for the first time, I have added in brackets the name by which that person was usually referred to at the time, e.g. 'Yang Guoping (K.P. Yang)'. For two groups of names, however, I have retained the older spelling: (1) well-known places and people where the old spelling is still widely used, e.g. Peking (not Beijing), and Chiang Kaishek (not Jiang Jieshi); (2) the very few names where I have insufficient information to give the modern form, e.g. C.W. Hsiung, where the personal name represented by 'C.W.' is unknown.

Picture Acknowledgments

The following pictures are taken from *Memory of West China Union University*, published by Sichuan University in 2006: nos. 10, 13, 14, 19, 24.

No. 8 is taken from H.G. Wood, *Henry T. Hodgkin: A Memoir*, 1937.

Nos. 9, 18 and 20 appear by permission of the Friends' House Library, © Religious Society of Friends in Britain.

I am grateful to the following for permission to reproduce these pictures:

Nos. 1 and 2 – Helen Stubbs

No. 21 – Ruth Baker (This picture is in the Sewell Archives in the Library of the School of Oriental and African Studies.)

No. 28 – John Lees

Nos. 9, 16, and 22 are in my own collection.

All the other pictures come from the collection of Jean Stubbs.

The Great Wall

Peking

Yellow River

Yellow River

River Huai

Nanjing

Chengdu

Sichuan

Wanxian

Yichang

Hankou

Shanghai

Chongqing

River Yangzi

Jiangxi

Guizhou

Hunan

Fuzhou

Yunnan

Guangxi

Canton

500 Kilometres

A sketch map of
CHINA

Guanxian

Tongchuan

Wanxian

Chengdu

Suining

Yangzi River

N

Mt. Emei

Tongliang

Jiajing

Chongqing

Miles

0   100   200

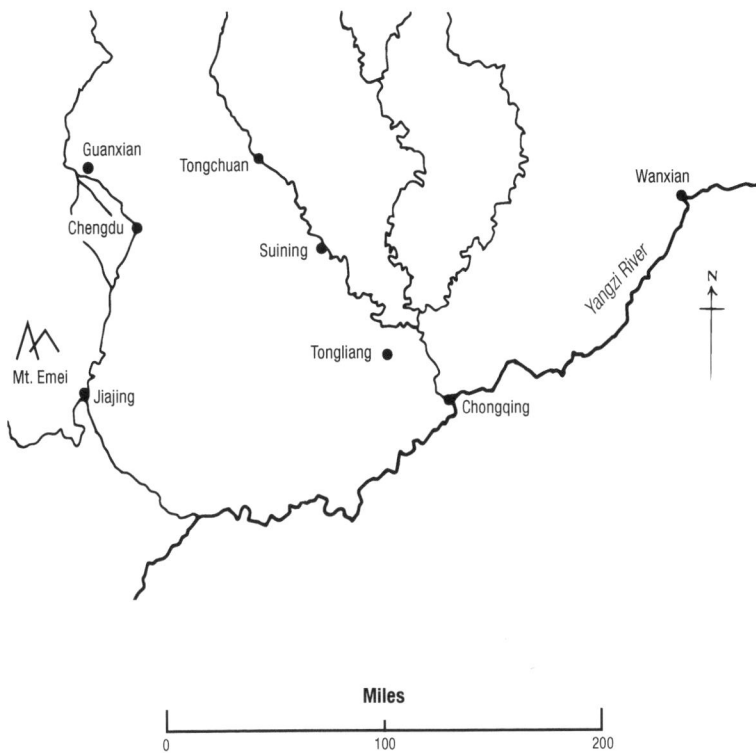

A map of
CENTRAL
SICHUAN

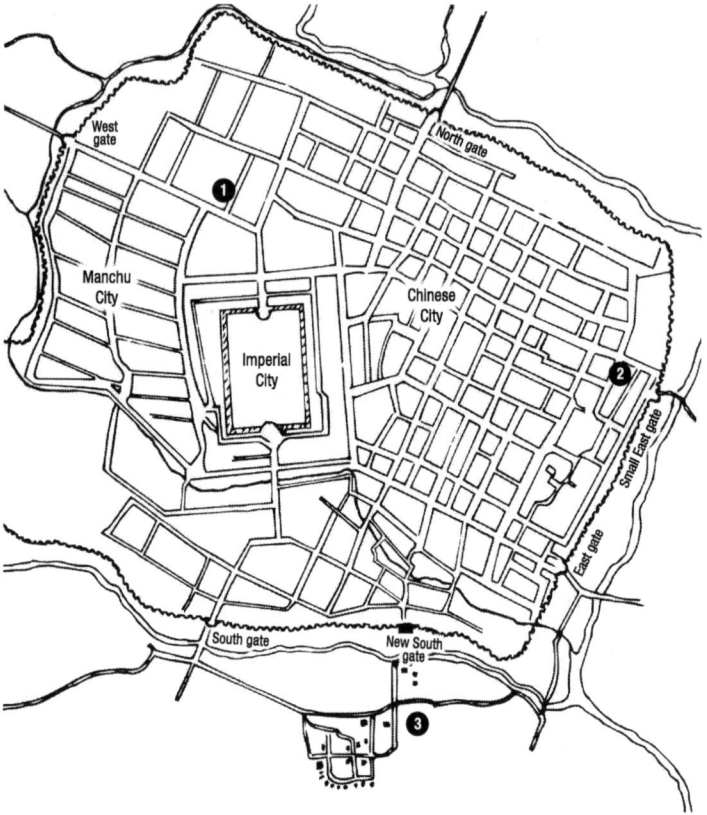

Map of
CHENGDU
c.1920

1. Friends' Compound in Qinlonggai
2. Canadian Mission Hospital, where Stubbs died
3. West China Union University

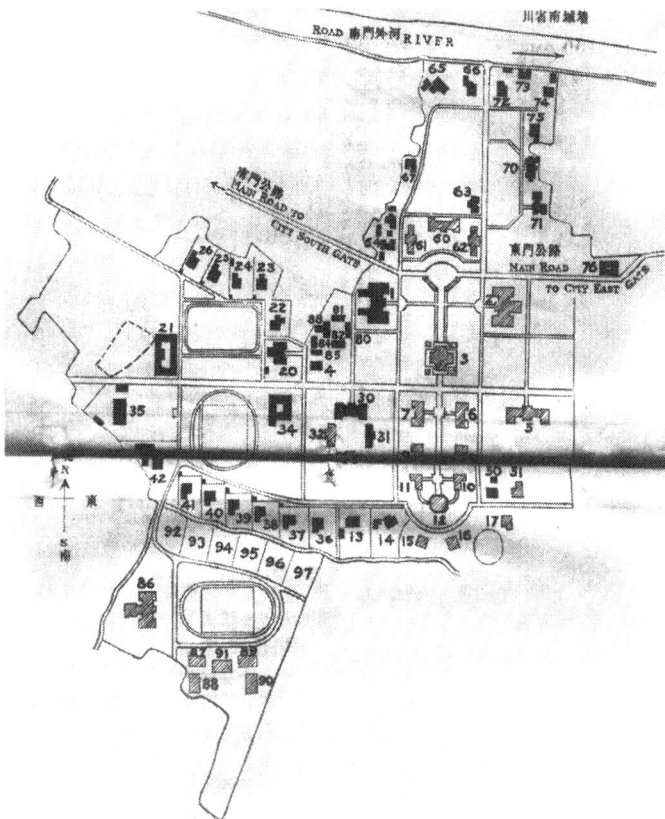

West China Union University campus

in the 1920s

1

1930, Chengdu

May 30th 1925 is an infamous date in the history of Anglo-Chinese relations. On that day an angry protest by Chinese workers and students took place in the International Settlement in Shanghai. A few days before, a worker had been killed in a Japanese factory by armed guards, which led to a series of demonstrations culminating in one outside the main police station, in Nanjing Road, the main shopping street of downtown Shanghai. This was guarded by a mixed group of Chinese and Sikh policemen, under the command of a young and inexperienced British officer. (One account suggests that his superiors had taken the day off to go to the races.) As the numbers grew, shouting angry slogans, he ordered his men to fire into the unarmed crowd. Eleven people were killed outright, and several dozen injured.

Rage against Britain spread swiftly throughout China, and furious demonstrations erupted, especially in cities where there was a large British presence. In Canton on 23rd June British and French troops opened fire on another crowd of Chinese protestors, this time killing 52. Dock workers in Canton and Hong Kong went on strike, paralysing trade. Patriotic anger continued to seethe, but helplessly, as the country was under the control of warlords who were themselves the target of nationalist anger, and in any case did not want to antagonise the foreign powers.

The dock workers' strike continued for more than a year, by which time the political situation in China was transformed, as in the summer of 1926 a joint Nationalist/Communist army, under General Chiang Kaishek, moved north from its base in Canton to take over southern and central China from the warlords. Its fiercely nationalist and socialist rhetoric caused panic in the foreign communities, and most foreigners living in south China or along the Yangzi were evacuated to Shanghai or abroad. However, in April 1927 Chiang turned on his Communist allies, killing many of them out of hand, and ruthlessly suppressing the few urban uprisings they attempted. Foreigners began to return, feeling the country to be safer once more.

Nationalist students, and workers in the communist-influenced trade unions, might be helpless but they had not lost their anger against the foreigners who continued to occupy parts of their land according to the 'unequal treaties' forced on China in the nineteenth century. As May 30th came round each year, the authorities were always on guard against trouble.

In 1930 the western province of Sichuan was not yet under Chiang Kaishek's control, but the quarrelsome cliques of warlords who ruled there were just as concerned to suppress any sign of political dissent. One of those killed in 1925 was from Sichuan, and this was not forgotten. In the provincial capital of Chengdu, a potential focus for trouble on 30th May was the West China Union University, founded twenty years before by four missionary societies from North America and Britain. Its spacious campus lay to the south of the city, outside the walls and beyond the narrow Brocade River (Jinjiang). Unusually for an institution in China it was not protected by a wall, as its missionary founders did not wish it to appear a 'foreign citadel' on Chinese soil, and its tree-lined avenues and wide open spaces had become a favourite place of resort for the people of the crowded city.

That year all seemed peaceful on 30th May; but shortly after midday a group of about a hundred young men suddenly converged from all directions on the Clock Tower, the central feature of the campus, then as quickly dispersed. Some were known radicals, and had done this on previous occasions. The gathering was little more than a ritual gesture, on a significant date, against a foreign institution on Chinese soil.[1]

The same afternoon a small boating party set out for a picnic on the river. The boat had been built by the Dean of Science, a 42-year-old English Quaker called Clifford Stubbs, and the party included his wife Margaret, and their eight-year-old son John. It was a jolly occasion, as

2

two of the party were celebrating their birthday. 'We had such a happy time,' one of them wrote, 'Clifford and Margaret singing their songs together; he was full of plans for enlarging and strengthening the Science Department.'[2] It was about eight o'clock when they got back to their house near the river-bank, and while Margaret prepared John for bed Clifford set off across the campus on his bicycle to see some colleagues on business. Two nights before had been the new moon and it was very dark on the unlighted campus paths. Shortly after nine, two students returning to their dormitory heard groaning in the dark. They flashed their torches around, and there, stretched out on the pathway, lay Clifford Stubbs. He had been hit over the head with a carrying-pole, his face had been crushed into the cinders on the path, and he had been stabbed six times in the left side of his chest. There was no sign of his bicycle. Quickly the two students called their friends; they improvised a stretcher from a bedstead and carried him to his house. By now the news had spread to other dormitories, loud cries went up around the campus, and students rushed to the Stubbs' house where they gathered in appalled silence. Three doctors were hastily fetched, and decided he should not be moved until morning. Clifford was in great pain and could hardly breathe, and at first it was not even safe to give him morphine. The students were asked to leave and return the next day for news. The doctors stayed with him all night.

Early the next day he was taken on a stretcher, with Margaret in a rickshaw, to the Canadian Mission Hospital, two or three miles away inside the city. There was an operation to clean the wounds, and he was given anti-streptococcal injections. Margaret was at his bedside; most of the time he was unconscious, but there were moments when he appeared to recognise her. The following morning, Sunday 1st June, he seemed to improve, but during the afternoon he took a sharp turn for the worse and at seven in the evening he died.

The next morning all classes were suspended. The students had handbills printed and distributed around the city, and wrote an article for one of the local newspapers describing their teacher's achievements. All day they streamed across the city to the hospital, to pass by his coffin and say farewell. Afterwards they stood in the courtyard with bowed heads, tears running down their faces. Margaret came out briefly to acknowledge their sympathy; they bowed to her, and then turned to leave. 'We Chinese feel much worse than you can,' one said to a missionary bystander. 'We are so ashamed.'[3]

The next day the students returned to the hospital to accompany their teacher on his final journey back to the University for his funeral; they were joined by boys from a Quaker Mission School in the city. The largest building on the campus was the Library, but so many wanted to be there that even this was not big enough, so two services were held, one in the morning for his fellow Quakers, and one in the afternoon for the university. The coffin was placed in the Library. The morning service was conducted by leading Chinese Friends. The afternoon ceremony was organised by the students, who had decorated the stage with flowers, including the English word VICTORY picked out in white. They wished to claim Clifford Stubbs as one of their own, and a senior student took the chair. Memorial scrolls in Chinese calligraphy were hung from the galleries above, expressing love and grief. One composed by the teachers and students of the Science Faculty read:

> In the midst of our national trouble we are full of shame
> That our war has led to the death of a foreign guest
> In the needs of our University we are full of grief
> At the loss of such high qualifications

And from the Industrial and Analytical Chemistry class:

> In recent years there have been many alarming and cruel happenings beyond expression
> This man was a peacemaker between China and foreign countries
> Is it of no concern to God that in the narrow path
> The innocent one has suffered at the hands of evil men?
> In the future it will be difficult to find another
> So ready to pour out his heart in teaching us
> We were his disciples by day and night. We mourn our loss with breaking hearts
> Where and how can we show our gratitude to you?[4]

The University President, Zhang Lingao, expressed the grief of the community, and included a Christian message of forgiveness. He asked 'why this man of all others should have been taken. Neither as individuals or as a university could we spare him. Did we wish to have the men who had wantonly taken his life killed? What advantage? He thought Dr Stubbs himself would not wish this, but would say as Jesus had done, "Father forgive them, for they know not what they do".'[5]

Other speakers included General Xiang Chuanyi, the newly appointed head of public safety in the city; but it was the Anglican Bishop Song Chengzhi, an old friend of Clifford, whose address touched the students' hearts. Hundreds will lead better lives, the bishop told them, because he lived such a life in their midst. That life will continue on in theirs. After the service the students crowded around him asking him to speak to them again that evening, to help them understand how anything positive could come out of this seemingly pointless sacrifice. 'These boys, these men,' wrote a missionary friend, 'whose whole heredity and training has not allowed or tolerated true outward expressions of grief at such times of loss, were weeping out, openly and unashamedly, their love for him and their deep sense of deprivation of a true friend and teacher.'[6]

Finally Clifford Stubbs's body was taken, accompanied by at least 500 people, to the little Christian graveyard to the south of the university. There he was interred, with readings and hymns in Chinese and English, the grave surrounded with flowers from both communities, including a wreath from a General Huang. It had been the largest funeral he had ever seen in Chengdu, wrote a close colleague, 'but it was not the tragedy but the life of the man in our midst that brought folk out to the burying.'[7] Another summed up: 'It seemed to require the entire day to express in any adequate way the deep impression of the life that has been lived among us ... a reminder of the crucifixion, for there could not have been found among us a person more fitted to give his life as a sacrifice on the altar of peace and goodwill.'[8] A pacifist and a Quaker, Clifford Stubbs had won tributes from generals and a bishop; and above all, at a time of great political and racial division, he had brought Chinese and foreigner together in an experience of shared grief. The funeral had been, to quote his colleague again, 'just what Clifford would have wished.'

A letter of sympathy to Margaret from one of his students, Wu Xuanxi, suggests how it was that Clifford Stubbs had so won their hearts: 'Dr Stubbs was my teacher and is my teacher not only in Chemistry and also in his Christian character. Besides all he is nearly a Chinese. He has the Chinese point of view in every problem.'[9]

2

1888–1913, New Zealand and Liverpool

Clifford Stubbs had not been born a Quaker. His father, Frederick Stubbs, was a Presbyterian minister in Newcastle upon Tyne when Clifford was born on 26th November 1888, and he was brought up very much within the Presbyterian faith. Frederick had been born in London in 1855, 'within the sound of Bow Bells', seventh in a family of eleven children. His father was a stationer, of Lincolnshire yeoman stock, but with many children and limited resources he could not afford Frederick more than a basic education. By the age of twelve Frederick had left school and was working as a grocer's boy. But he was intelligent and energetic, and studied on his own – getting up two hours early for this before starting work at 6 a.m. – and at the age of 20 won a scholarship to Regent's Park College, where he trained for the Baptist ministry.[1]

The Stubbs family, according to Frederick's younger son Eric, were 'people who loved goodness and were devoted to truth'. They were also 'great talkers with a distinct gift for language', and the ministry must have seemed an obvious career for a poor but able boy. In 1878, after three years of study, he was appointed minister to the Baptist Church in Studley, Warwickshire. At this period he was intensely evangelical, given to preaching hellfire sermons, and the necessity of personal conversion to avoid the torments of the damned. However, his theological position gradually softened, and his move to a Presbyterian church in Newcastle in 1882 may be an indication of this. His beliefs would continue to evolve in a liberal direction, and over time his sermons became less doctrinal, and more devoted to moral exhortation. His only extravagance in his early years was buying books; his reading was extensive,

7

and far from purely religious. Towards the end of his life, in the 1930s, he compiled a book of *'Pensees'*,[2] a collection of quotations and thoughts gathered over decades: a single page taken at random includes references to Tom Paine, Hawthorne, Ibsen, Voltaire, Borrow, Gibbon, Watts, and Omar Khayyam. His mind ranged far beyond the narrow pieties of his nonconformist upbringing, and later references to Conrad and Einstein show a mind that remained open to new ideas. He was a father who must have stimulated intelligent and enquiring minds in his children.

When Frederick arrived at Studley in 1878 the organist in his church was a young lady called Emma Morgan; they soon became engaged, and married in 1883 after Frederick's move to Newcastle. The long engagement might reflect unease on the part of the Morgan family, for John Morgan, Emma's father, was one of the richest men in Studley, owner of a needle factory which employed most of the village. Emma and her numerous younger sisters had been brought up to be young ladies, Emma played the harp as well as the organ, and the family lived in style in the Manor House. They were definitely 'carriage folk'. A minister with no wealth beyond his stipend, and from a Cockney background, might well not have been what the Morgans had in mind for their eldest daughter.[3]

But married they were, and in 1885 their daughter Winifred was born, and then Clifford in 1888. Two years later they returned to the West Midlands, to Dudley, and their last child Eric was born there in 1893. Emma's health was not good; in Dudley she suffered from repeated attacks of bronchitis and catarrh, and their doctor suggested that the climate of New Zealand would do her good. Frederick's favourite brother George, and his sister Annie, had moved there in 1877, so they would not be going to a land of strangers. They embarked in October 1895; at the age of six Clifford had left the land of his birth, and he would not return until he was 21.

So far Clifford's experience of life had been confined to the polluted cities of industrial England, and the wide spaces and clean air of New Zealand must have seemed akin to a rebirth. One of his most vivid early memories of his new home was of running naked with other boys on the beach all day, in and out of the waves; this experience of freedom in the sun and the wind created in him a joy in the natural world which he carried with him wherever he went. Later he would say that the country he would choose for his own children to grow up in would be New Zealand.

This was not just because of its natural advantages, but also its freedom from convention and traditional social divisions. By the end of the nineteenth century New Zealand had developed into a remarkable society, one of the most equal, peaceful and progressive in the world. It had been the first country in the world to give women the vote, in 1892, and this had been followed by old age pensions and progressive labour legislation: 'This amalgam of democratic and humanitarian legislation … made New Zealand for a time the most radical state in the world. French political scientists, American radicals, English statesmen and political philosophers, made pilgrimages to the distant colony. [The future Prime Minister] Asquith described it as "a laboratory in which political and social experiments are every day made for the information and instruction of the older countries of the world." '[4] The main element in the New Zealand tradition has been described as a democratic and egalitarian aspiration, a yearning for what was later called 'social justice'. Clifford grew up in a land free from the divisions of class and denomination that so marked England, and this no doubt contributed to the ease with which he later related to people from very different backgrounds. Once, in a letter[5] from China, he refers to the Maori friends of his youth; so he also acquired in New Zealand the ability to cross barriers of race and culture, which would be so important to him during his career in China.

Frederick's first church was at Fielding, a small settlement in the North Island, then after two years he moved to Cust in the South Island, another small township. In both churches Emma played the organ and ran the choir, and between them they greatly increased their congregations. At Cust the manse had two acres of land attached, and the family kept a few cows and a horse for transport. After four years there Frederick began to suffer from laryngitis, which made preaching difficult, so they moved to Christchurch, and then in 1903 Frederick spent six months in Australia 'for his throat's sake', preaching occasionally, but also writing articles for various newspapers in both New Zealand and Australia. This was the start of a new career which would occupy much of the rest of his life, as traveller and journalist. There was a restlessness in him that would never let him stay in one place for long, and an intellectual restlessness as well, that was no longer content with the life of a rural minister. His sermons began to upset some of his congregation, and Emma had to soothe their hurt feelings afterwards.[6] Eric Stubbs wrote of him in 1967, 'From his late forties onwards I am now sure that he had much less orthodox religious faith than any of his three children, but I never remember him at any time trying to lessen our orthodox beliefs. He chose to let us do our own thinking and evolve our own ultimate faith.'

Meanwhile the needs of Frederick's family brought him back to the ministry, and on his return from Australia he moved back to the North Island, to a church in Rotorua where he built the first manse. Life in rural parishes meant that Clifford had to be boarded out when he was at school, and he learned at an early stage to be self-reliant. While the family was at Cust, he attended Rangiora High School for two years (1901–02). He stayed with a family called Jennings, and quickly won their affection with his 'thoughtful acts and altogether lovable disposition'. The only anxiety the Jennings felt was that Clifford finished his homework every evening too quickly, and they wondered if he was slacking. So Mr Jennings had a word with the headmaster, and was told that, far from slacking, Clifford was the most brilliant boy in the school. 'His essays were written in a style far above any other pupils in the school, promising that he would have a distinguished career in the literary world.' Mr Jennings had a look for himself: 'I was astonished that a boy of his age could produce such work. His subjects as written abounded in original thoughts and apt illustrations, and his diction was excellent, all denoting a fine intellect and keenly observant mind.'[7] He had also inherited his mother's musical talents. He had perfect pitch, and could tune her harp from the age of seven. He could pick out tunes on the piano by ear, and improvise variations on them, playing 'Three Blind Mice' as a march, a lament, or a comic song.[8]

Clifford left Rangiora at the age of 14 with the Headmaster's Special Prize, and went on to Canterbury Boys' High School, where his career was also marked by a succession of prizes, especially in mathematics and science. In a letter of August 1904 he tells his father how he is doing: 'In Mathematics and Chemistry I have a long lead, from 8 to 10%. If you think I am working too hard, let me off cadets next term. It means a lot of extra work besides the drill. Whenever we have a dress parade there are buttons to brighten, leggings to black, clothes to clean, also rifles, all of which means at least an hour's work.'[9] It would be unwise to see in his dislike of the cadets an early tendency towards pacifism; it is probably more a case of a typical teenage boy trying to wriggle out of something he does not enjoy.

The young Clifford was a promising scholar but he also loved the opportunities the wide spaces of New Zealand gave for the outdoor life. The happiest memories of his boyhood were of long days spent roaming the hills and beaches with his friends. To his father again: 'Yesterday was a whole holiday, so I went with a chum to the Waimakariri riverbed. We had an all right time. Part of the day we wore nothing at all; most of the day we wore a shirt only; for a short time we also wore a hat. It was very hot, but we didn't mind so much, because when we felt warm we could jump into the river without bothering to undress. As a result I am most fearfully sunburnt – my neck has swollen so I can't do up my shirt; but what is that to the joys of living for a day in a primeval condition?'[10]

Frederick Stubbs wrote that Clifford's outstanding quality as a child was 'his entire fearlessness, amounting almost to recklessness, a quality which twenty years after made me tremble for his safety in China. He was a thorough boy, fond of mischief, especially fond of experimenting in physics, chemistry, etc., to his mother's terror (one day the boys set a room on fire) thus early indicating a scientific bias.'[11] Another episode, or a different account of the same one, has Clifford experimenting with gunpowder, putting it in a biscuit tin, getting Eric to sit on it, and setting fire to it to see if it would explode. Fortunately it only jumped. Other examples of his early sense of mischief, playful and never malicious, have him as a small boy sitting under the dining table and tying together the shoelaces of the adults as they ate; and protesting at what he considered an unjust punishment from his father by climbing a fir tree near the church and bombarding the congregation with fir-cones as they arrived for service. But he was also a reliable and responsible boy, always trusted to carry out such basic family duties as cleaning boots and chopping wood.[12]

Clifford's mother Emma's death from typhoid in 1905, while he was at school in Canterbury, must have left him desolate, and led to a great change in their family life. 'We had a wonderful mother, and her mantle fell most of all on Clifford,' wrote his sister Winifred after Clifford's death.[13] Two years later Winifred went to work as a nurse, and Eric joined Clifford at school in Christchurch where Clifford, four years older, took on the responsibility of looking after his brother. Frederick, meanwhile, travelled for six months in the South Pacific, the first of the many journeys which would occupy his later years. Never again did the Stubbs have a family home. While Clifford was naturally sociable, he seems to have had few close personal relationships, and must have learned to be very reliant on his inner resources. When he moved to England in 1910 he would discover many aunts and cousins, but home life was something he would not know again until his own marriage. During his first months in China, at the age of 24, he attended a missionary wedding, and noted that he had never been to a wedding before: 'I really feel quite an ignoramus on matters matrimonial.'[14]

Without Emma's help, Frederick found it hard to carry out the work of a minister, and a small inheritance from her gave him the freedom to travel. Given the growing liberalism of his beliefs, release from a regular ministry was probably a relief. He supplemented his income with preaching, lecturing and writing travel articles, which were widely syndicated. In 1911 he was appointed special correspondent for several Australian and New Zealand newspapers at George V's Coronation Durbar in Delhi. There he was treated virtually as a representative of New Zealand and was given the Durbar medal. This led to many useful contacts on his later travels, and in 1913 he was elected a Fellow of the Royal Geographical Society, sponsored by Sir Thomas Mackenzie and Sir John Harris.

As for Clifford, in 1906 he was awarded a Junior Scholarship and entered Canterbury College in Christchurch, where he specialised in mathematics and chemistry, gaining his B.A. in 1909, and M.A. with double First Class Honours in these two subjects in 1910. During his summer holidays he would go camping, and roaming over wide expanses of the country, also working on farms, 'to get to know human nature thoroughly', he told his father. Among the practical skills he acquired on the farm was bee-keeping. He was fit and athletic, played tennis, and practised running, boxing and single-stick. Most of all, it was in his college days that his deep religious commitment became apparent. He was a leader in the Christian Endeavour movement, and in 1909 was President of the Students' Christian Union. On Sundays, wearing his boater with the college ribbon, he would go down with his fellows to Cathedral Square in Christchurch, to preach the Word. A listener commented, 'I remember how I said to myself, "There is a man who really believes what he says he does." '[15] In August that year the Christian Union hosted Rev. W. Mawson, from the New Zealand Presbyterian Mission, who was recruiting for the Student Volunteer Movement, and it seems likely that this encounter led Clifford to consider a missionary career in China.[16]

In 1910 he won the 1851 Exhibition Scholarship to study in England for three years, and left for Liverpool University to take a doctorate in Chemistry. Before leaving New Zealand he went to see his old friend Mr Jennings in Rangiora, who asked what profession he was going to take up. 'I met with a great surprise when he replied very quietly "I am going to be a missionary." I had not for a moment thought that one so talented to succeed in almost any of the learned professions would decide to enter the mission field.'[17] Clifford added that China was his chosen destination. His mathematics tutor in Christchurch also had no doubt that he could have a glowing career ahead of him: 'If he had applied his high talents to commercial purposes, he might have looked forward to great wealth and position, as the world counts such things; but he chose the better part.'[18]

Clifford did not go alone to England. Eric and Winifred went with him, Eric to study medicine in Liverpool. Winifred kept house, on £1 a week, and occasionally their father visited in intervals from his travels. Sadly there is no record of how the young Kiwi responded to the narrow smoky streets of a great English city, and the equal narrowness of a class-bound Edwardian society. It was a great contrast to the wide spaces and social equality that he had known hitherto. But he devoted himself to his chemistry, and to church activities, with the same commitment that he had shown in Christchurch. A fellow student, who also went to China as a missionary, recalled him as a leader of the Liverpool University Christian Union, and 'one of those who most helped me to realise what an attractive person a real Christian could be'. She also remembered his preaching at the Presbyterian Church when his father was visiting. 'His quiet sincerity appealed to us younger folks particularly. At the end of the service we were waiting with his father at the church door to say good night to him, but after waiting some time we realised he had slipped out by a side door!'[19] This was characteristic modesty.

The church was in Princes Street, and it was the Young Men's Bible Class at that church which took the initiative in 1911 in founding the Liverpool Presbyterian Young Men's Bible Class Union. Since Clifford was to be its founding Secretary/Treasurer one can assume he was a leading figure in the enterprise. Starting with six classes from different churches, after only a year the number had increased to twenty-four. Its first Annual Report, written by Clifford, notes that they were unanimous about accepting groups from 'Mission' (i.e. working class) churches – 'we have no time for snobbishness'. The Kiwi egalitarian spirit was to apply in Liverpool. The Union not only encouraged groups to visit each other, supported the weaker ones by supplying speakers, and encouraged the creation of new groups in churches without one, but also organised rambles and a weekend summer camp, inter-class football matches, and debates. In the light of Clifford's later pacifism, it is interesting to note that the Princes Street group won a debate by supporting the motion that 'war had retarded civilisation rather than advanced it.'[20] The only other record we have of Clifford's debating skills is his successfully opposing the proposition 'That war has advanced the cause of civilisation' at the Canterbury College Dialectic

Society in 1910. It is as though the ground was being prepared for his becoming a Quaker.[21]

Another recollection of the young Clifford by a fellow student, also a New Zealander, is placed in the Muspratt Laboratory at the university. 'The most striking characteristic was his earnestness. The next was his quiet reasonableness. He was never tired with serious conversation. One evening I was working in the Muspratt ... when Clifford came in. We embarked on a discussion of fundamental issues and continued it till eleven o'clock that evening, finishing up under a lamppost near his lodging. It was commonly said in the Muspratt that Clifford was the most careful experimenter who had ever worked there. Whatever he did, he did well ...' The same writer also felt that Clifford applied his scientific principles to his faith: 'This same careful testing he applied to his religion. He tested and retested his principles, both by individual study and by serious conversation with others; and having finally found a sure foundation, he went out to put his faith into practice where he thought his work was most wanted.'[22]

There would be no conflict between science and religion for Clifford; he was not a Biblical Fundamentalist, and when, on the voyage out to China, he encountered a fellow missionary who was, he was sharply critical: 'Believing as I do, I feel it is a pity that the converts he wins should have one day to undergo the exhausting struggles of reconciling such a belief with modern science and historical criticism – perhaps losing their faith altogether as so many have similarly done in Christian lands. It is *not* a matter of indifference to us who believe otherwise, whether or not the doctrine of verbal inspiration should be preached to the East.'[23]

Clifford developed into a very able chemist, specialising in inorganic chemistry. The Department was a distinguished one. The head of his laboratory, Professor Frederick Donnan, and his supervisor Miles Walker, would both become Fellows of the Royal Society. While still in New Zealand Clifford had published his M.A. paper in the *Transactions* of the New Zealand Institute (1910); his work at Liverpool led to two articles in the *Proceedings of the Royal Society* (1912 and 1913), and two in *Transactions of the Chemical Society* (1911 and 1913).[24] There is little doubt that he could have gone on to a distinguished career in academic research or in industry, and that he was torn between this and his calling to be a missionary. Were he to adopt the latter career his three years research experience would have gone for nothing, and he would be wasting the exceptional talent he had been granted. The answer to his dilemma came – and it must have seemed providential – at a conference of the Student Christian Movement in Liverpool in January 1912. One of the speakers was Henry Hodgkin, Secretary of the Friends' Foreign Mission Association (FFMA), which had been working in the western Chinese province of Sichuan for over 20 years. Two years earlier, in 1910, the FFMA, together with three other missionary societies, had opened a Christian university in Chengdu, the provincial capital of Sichuan. Hodgkin, from a famous family of Quaker intellectuals, and himself a double first in Natural Sciences from Cambridge, was the driving force behind the foundation of the University, and determined that the West China Union University (WCUU) should provide China with the best the West had to offer. The Chinese themselves were interested most of all in Western science and technology, and Hodgkin wanted to recruit able teachers to go out to Chengdu with the FFMA.

One wonders who was the more delighted at their encounter, Clifford or Hodgkin. For Clifford it was the answer to his dilemma; for Hodgkin, Clifford must have seemed the ideal candidate to give the embryo university a solid academic basis. That Clifford was not a Quaker was unimportant; soon Hodgkin introduced him to the only current FFMA teacher on the University's staff, who was fortunately on leave in England at the time. This was Harry Silcock, an Oxford B.A., who was a Congregationalist. Friends were not strictly sectarian: provided candidates were not unsympathetic to Quaker principles, what mattered were their intellectual calibre and their personal qualities.

By the end of January Clifford had 'provisionally' applied to join the FFMA in China, and had a long talk with the pioneer Quaker missionary in China, Robert Davidson, who was passing through Liverpool.[25] It was not until December that he was interviewed by the Friends' China Committee in London, when he formally expressed his 'readiness to take his place in loyalty to the Committee of Missionaries in China', and they swiftly approved his candidature. However, he could not leave until sufficient funds for his support had been raised. Silcock promised to devote himself to a 'Campaign in the Interests of China', and approaches were made to, among others, the Presbyterian Church of Scotland, but by the following April only £30 had been promised. Hodgkin grew anxious, and persuaded the FFMA Board to sanction his departure that autumn whether funds were forthcoming or not. It would be a keynote of Clifford's career, and indeed of missionary life – urgent needs met with good intentions, and few resources to carry them out. [26]

1913 was an intensely busy year. Clifford had to complete and present his D.Sc. dissertation; he received the degree at a University Congregation on 5th July. He spent several months during the summer at Kingsmead College in Birmingham, jointly run by Friends and Methodists, studying in preparation for a missionary career. A large outfit had to be bought, to equip him for at least five years in China. The list of things he should buy stretched over 25 typed pages – missionaries were expected to maintain in China as close a lifestyle as they could to that at home. Knowing that the practical application of chemistry would be an important aspect of his work, he fitted in a meeting of the Society of the Chemical Industry, and associated factory visits. A mere couple of weeks before his departure he made further visits to a glassworks and match factory.[27] The family household in Liverpool had to be closed down and their chattels disposed of. Eric would remain in Liverpool studying medicine; Winifred would go to China at the same time as Clifford, but to Canton rather than Chengdu, as a missionary nurse. That summer Frederick Stubbs, (always referred to as 'the Pater') was in England, though rarely in one place for long; one evening in August all four ate together, and Clifford realised, rightly, that it was the last time they would ever do so.[28] Separation from family was a part of the missionary life. Later he would say a final farewell to his Stubbs grandmother, now 90 years old. The problems of maintaining a normal family life as a missionary would be even more acute when he had one of his own. And this would also be on his mind, as over and above everything else that summer he was wooing a wife.

One of Clifford's closest family connections in England was his mother's younger sister, Jessie Silk, who lived in the prosperous Birmingham suburb of Moseley. Like the rest of her family she was a Baptist; one of the leading members of her local church was Antony Lees, a banker originally from Scotland, who was for many years Secretary of the Birmingham City Water Department, in which role he was responsible for the building of the Elan Valley Reservoirs. The Lees' eldest child, Margaret, was the same age as Clifford, and it seems that Aunt Jessie felt that Margaret would be a suitable wife for him, and quietly did what she could to bring the two together.

After leaving school Margaret had spent a year at home, then in 1908 was sent by her father to study for a year at Woodbrooke, the Quaker College in Selly Oak. Although Mr Lees was a leading Baptist, it was typical of his breadth of mind, Margaret said later, that he should take an interest in Friends; that Woodbrooke was only a few miles from home would also have been an attraction. So, though remaining a Baptist, Margaret had spent a year in a Quaker community, and had more experience than Clifford of Friends' ways of thinking and acting. While at Woodbrooke she followed courses in comparative religion, social and biblical studies, logic, and beginners' Greek. Her teachers included two of the most distinguished Quaker thinkers of the day, H.G. Wood and Rendel Harris.[29]

After her year at Woodbrooke she was still uncertain of her future, hovering between social and religious work. To help her decide, her father suggested she go to his old homeland and study at the Women's Missionary College in Edinburgh. This understandably led her towards considering a missionary career, with China specifically in mind. So it was natural that Aunt Jessie should think of her as a suitable bride for her nephew, but with one of them in Edinburgh and the other in Liverpool, matchmaking was not going to be easy.

It seems that they first met at Aunt Jessie's house in Birmingham in 1910, but all Clifford recalled of that occasion was that she was remarkably quiet. There is no record of a further meeting until January

1912, when he and Winifred invited her to Liverpool for the SCM conference at which Hodgkin had spoken. From then on they corresponded, and he kept all her letters (many of which have not survived).[30] It was another year before she began to keep his. In the first of them he daringly addresses her for the first time as 'Margaret': 'I like the Quakers' practice in this regard, if not in all their ideas.' His courtship, as Margaret later recalled, was 'shy, modest, but steadfast'; as the year progressed, and the date of his departure in September grew nearer, it also became more urgent. It had to be carried on mainly by letter, and he did not find it easy to express his feelings in writing. For one thing, humour kept breaking in ('These are not tears: the paper got on to some wet photographic plates which are drying on my table.'); but by late May we have what can fairly be called a love letter, and by June he is using the term 'life-partnership' in a letter which is effectively a proposal. Margaret seems to have been reluctant to commit herself by post, and it was only when they were able to meet in Birmingham in mid-July that all was settled. Margaret's parents must have felt concern at the prospect of their daughter going off to as distant and dangerous a place as China, but in other respects Clifford would have seemed a most suitable husband. It was agreed that Margaret should stay in England for a further year, and that their marriage would take place in China.

Meanwhile, Clifford was asked to join the Lees family for a week at the end of August during their holiday in Switzerland. This gave them for the first time a chance to relax in each other's company, and really get to know each other without any of the external pressures of work and travel. It was an interlude of never-to-be-forgotten happiness during a hectic summer: when they built their first home in Chengdu they would call it 'Marécottes' after the village where they stayed. Margaret's memories of that week include watching in shared awe and delight as thunderstorms rolled along the valley, of sheltering under a rock in the rain, and a last outing in a rowing boat on Lake Geneva before Clifford took the train back to England. They would not meet again for nearly eighteen months and that would also be on a boat, but on the Yangzi, not Lake Geneva.

Immediately on his return Clifford attended a formal Farewell

Meeting given by the FFMA for him and others going out or returning to China (including Harry and Margaret Silcock). Then he went to mid-Wales and Shrewsbury for family farewells, some to cousins whom he was meeting for the first time. Then it was back to Liverpool, a farewell address at the Princes Street church, more shopping – buying a type-writer, being measured for a new suit, arranging life insurance – before sailing on the P&O steamship *Sunda* from Tilbury on 20th September. Winifred was sailing with him, and the Pater was on the quayside to see his two eldest children depart.

3

1913, Voyage Out

For the next year and a quarter, until Margaret joined him early in 1915, Clifford wrote to her every few days, and also wrote a journal for circulation to his family and friends. These describe the voyage out and his early impressions of China, and allow us to get close to the man Clifford was at the age of 25.

Descriptions of shipboard life reveal a sociable man, able and ready to get on with all kinds of people. He was serious but also playful, and any account of him has to emphasise his sense of fun and how delightful a companion he was. According to Margaret, the crow's-feet that appeared early in the corners of his eyes came from laughing so much. He readily joined in the on-board larks of his young male contemporaries going out to make their fortune as businessmen or engineers. 'Pillow-fighting went on for half-an-hour on deck last night – great sport.' He was a member of the passengers' sports committee, won the egg-and-spoon race (and Winifred won the potato-and-bucket race), on the fancy dress night he appeared as 'a sort of mix-up between a bandit and a Welsh countrywoman', and enjoyed 'great old sing-songs lately in the evenings roaring out all the old songs from the University Song-Book and elsewhere.' The only activity he declined, as courteously as he could, was whist: 'I do feel one's influence would have gone down a peg if one had done it merely to be popular and "one of the bhoys".' [1]

Perhaps these young men responded to him as a chemist, rather than as a missionary. They certainly let him know what they really felt about missionaries, including some of their fellow passengers. Probably hoping for a bit of on-board flirtation, they were particularly indignant about the stand-offishness of eleven young women of the strictly evangelical China Inland Mission. Clifford had some sympathy with this criticism: 'Most of the C.I.M. people [were] very absorbed in study or each other's company. One can well imagine how such a thing may bring missionaries into bad odour, and as far as conscience permits it should be guarded against.'[2] He was himself at odds with their theological 'narrowness': their faith in the literal verbal inspiration of the Bible was alien to his scientific beliefs. But he got on well enough with them (Winifred of course would have been close to them), joining them each morning for an hour's prayer and Bible study, and escorting them on outings at their ports of call. There was an increasingly wide variety of theological opinion in the missionary world, and the divisions between liberal and fundamentalist Christians would grow ever more acute during his years in China. While he himself moved ever further towards the liberal end of the spectrum, he always managed to retain the affection and trust of all those he worked with.

Before the First World War, Doctors of Science were rare beings, and for one to go to China as a missionary would have been almost unheard of. It made him something of a 'star' on board, although Clifford would be the last person to see himself in this light. Despite the presence of older missionaries, most Sundays it was he who led a nonconformist service in the second-class saloon (an Anglican service was held in the first class), and the title of his first sermon – 'Experiment in the Life of the Soul' – clearly played on his double role. Afterwards he heard that the Anglican parson, 'fortunately unbeknownst to me', had slipped down from first class to listen. Though still a Presbyterian rather than a Friend, he turned the final Sunday service into a Quakers' Meeting, 'which was to me, and as several said afterwards, one of the most helpful we have had on board. I do think the Friends teach us something in their idea of silent worship, and waiting on the Spirit. Things don't seem so man-made and worked up somehow.'[3]

Clifford was of course devout, and committed to his missionary vocation. The six weeks it took to reach Hong Kong gave him plenty of time for reading, and this included the Edinburgh Conference Report on the preparation of missionaries, and books on mission work in China, in addition to his Chinese Language primer, which he studied for one hour a day. His view of his vocation was characteristically modest and down-played: 'I feel more deeply my unfitness of mind for the work of witnessing to which I go: unfitness of mind and of spirit. Otherwise I take things pretty phlegmatically, though naturally one feels glad that one is at last to get to grips with one's life-work, and that the waiting-time is over. I may not feel strongly enough the special privilege and responsibility of being a missionary – I am rather accustomed to regard it as simply one's Christian duty, and in that sense no higher than any other Christian's.'[4] He had a similarly modest view of his doctorate, and had been amused by his relatives' wish for photos of him 'swanking' in his doctoral robes. 'I do feel not to have deserved it – but there it is, and perhaps such consciousness will keep me a little humbler in the face of what men count as a great honour. I hope it will be used to His glory. After all, there are greater things in life than degrees, aren't there?'[5]

His reading on the voyage also shows that he had inherited his father's wide-ranging mind. It extended well beyond chemistry, religion, and Chinese; he mentions reading various novels, and articles on Maeterlinck, and the philosophy of Bergson, in the *Fortnightly Review*. Keen as ever to find out how things worked, he talked his way into the wireless operator's cabin and had the new apparatus explained to him.

His journal also shows an informed interest in current politics, unusual for a missionary. Nothing indicates a particular political allegiance, but as a nonconformist he was probably of a Liberal inclination, like his future in-laws, the Lees. He found it frustrating being cut off from the news while he was at sea, and in Colombo and Singapore he 'luxuriated' in several weeks' newspapers, with the latest on the American Tariff Bill, and how 'old Winston was stirring up the Home Rule issue.' Later, in China, he would ask Margaret to send him newspaper cuttings, especially of 'big political speeches'. In Singapore he also read an article on the recently founded Hong Kong University, which after only one year, it was said, had 'taken highest place among Far Eastern Universities'. But the writer 'seemed to me to write too much from the Britisher's top-dog standpoint: I don't believe China could ever settle down permanently to send her students to be taught in a foreign tongue and in a foreign possession!' Even before he arrived in China he could use his imagination to see things from the Chinese point of view. This political awareness would help equip him to face the intensely political atmosphere of China in the 1920s.[6]

His brief outings on shore gave him his first encounters with alien religious traditions. A Hindu temple in Colombo appalled him: 'A disgusting introduction to heathen idolatry. In one place was a shrine at which one of the natives informed us propitiatory sacrifices were made to some devil or other; there was a good deal of coagulated blood about, with insects swarming – pretty putrid in more senses than one. ... A true idea of God seemed so lacking that one cannot wonder many see in all this a diabolical influence, and not the groping of man after God. No doubt however this is a debased form of the original Hinduism ...' On the other hand, a mosque in Port Said was impressive in its simplicity: 'Turkish rugs on the floor – a marble arch on the side towards Mecca etc. One cannot wonder at the Moslem's sense of superiority when he beholds the gaudy interiors, candles, incense, etc., etc., of the Christian churches which mostly represent Christianity to him in the East.' An unusually open-minded Anglican chaplain from Penang, who was on board, also thought there was much to be learned from Muslims, especially in their attitude towards death.[7]

It was in Penang that he encountered a Chinese community for the first time and, apart from a 'deadly dull' Chinese opera performance, his impressions were very positive. 'That they are a *great* race came home to me at once: there is something capable and highly intelligent in them which at once awakens a respect due to ones who in many ways are our equals in civilisation. One feels quite differently towards them and say the Malays or Sinhalese. I was forcibly struck by their industry – working in their well-organised shops until late into the evening, and giving a great impression of *efficiency* ... They seemed pretty clean – perhaps a few sensitive noses have over-emphasised the other side. As a crowd they were much more well-behaved and orderly than most similar English crowds would be.' Then, later in the same letter, it is as if he recalls his vocation, and what he ought to feel about the heathen Chinese: 'the people are interesting, but the sense of them as so ignorant and degraded in their knowledge of the higher and true life comes to me. What might they be with a knowledge of God and Christ – but they are without Him, and the missionary can but touch the fringe of the work in his parish of tens of thousands.' Missionary pre-conceptions seem to be at war with Clifford's instinctive openness, and respect for other races and traditions. For example he noticed on the ship 'how the coloured stewards *do* get bullied. It is a shame the white man cannot rid himself of the pride of race.'[8]

On arriving off Hong Kong, Winifred was met by a Scottish doctor, Edward Kirk, who had come to escort her to her work in Canton – four years later they would be married. Clifford accompanied them to Canton, where he was delighted to meet some Presbyterian missionaries from New Zealand, and experienced his first Chinese service, a Communion. 'I had the privilege on my first Sunday in China of keeping the memorial of a common Lord with Chinese fellow-Christians ... altogether the service was inspiring to me, and a foretaste of the Kingdom which we seek to bring to China.' This all helped him feel at home – he wrote of 'the tremendous magnitude of the Christian task, and the oneness of China with us in the great things – Nature and Human Nature. I don't somehow feel a stranger here.'[9]

In Canton he said goodbye to Winifred – although they were both in China they were so far apart that their chances of meeting in the future would be very few. He also visited the Christian College and saw the work they were doing in chemistry – the lab facilities struck him as very elementary. Then in Hong Kong he visited the new university, before taking a coastal steamer for Shanghai. It stopped briefly at Shantou, Xiamen, and Fuzhou; forgoing any sightseeing he took the chance to visit other Christian colleges, to find out more about the state of chemistry teaching in China and its problems.

It took Clifford nearly two months to reach Shanghai from London; he still had more than two months' travelling before him until he would reach his destination in Chengdu.

Here in Shanghai he joined some of his new colleagues in the Friends' Mission. Harry and Margaret Silcock he already knew; the three would travel upriver together with Leonard Wigham – who after twenty years in China was now returning for the first time without his family – and another newcomer, Irene Hutchinson, who would become a close friend, and who would stay in China, a much-loved figure, until the Communist victory in 1949. Clifford only had a few days in Shanghai, just enough time to enquire about chemistry equipment and books, and that essential luxury, a piano. Good ones were available, designed to cope with the climate, for between £45 and £70. When Margaret came he would buy one, and somehow get it to Chengdu. With Silcock he visited two of the best mission colleges in China – St John's College in Shanghai, and Nanjing University in their first port of call on the river. These were more advanced than those he had seen on the coast, and set a standard for what he hoped to achieve in West China.

For the first 800 miles up the Yangzi, to Yichang at the entrance to the famous Gorges, they went by steamboat. A single small steamboat, the *Shutung*, plied upriver from Yichang to Chongqing, the great trading port of Sichuan Province, but only in the summer months when the water level was high. It was now November so they had to move to a Chinese houseboat for the rest of the river journey. The last 150 miles from Chongqing to Chengdu would be overland, on foot or by sedan chair. This brings home how remote Chengdu was – 'How hard is the way to Sichuan, as hard as the way to Heaven', a Chinese poet had written over a thousand years before. Sichuan was a wealthy and densely populated province, but was surrounded by mountains and still without any form of modern transport. All Clifford's goods, all he needed for his work – books, chemical equipment and supplies – would have to take this route, through the hazards of shipwreck, theft and, increasingly, banditry and war.

The houseboats were about 60 feet long and 10 broad, with a roofed section from amidships, where the passenger cabins were, to the stern, where the captain, the cook and their families lived. The forward section was open, though covered with mats at night. This was for the crew who would row or haul the boat upstream unless there was a favourable wind. Here the several dozen men would eat, sleep, and defecate over the side – passengers soon learned not to trail their hands in the water. The boats usually travelled in groups, accompanied by a smaller one, a *wuban*, to take the men to and from the shore when the boat had to be pulled upstream. There was also a 'red boat' provided by the local authorities as a guardship and lifeboat. The sailors on these were 'very obliging', and essential in the case of shipwreck.

As the boats set off to the accompaniment of gongs and firecrackers to appease the river god, Clifford left all traces of the familiar modern world behind. The journey through the Gorges satisfied all his taste for natural beauty. Since the waters were low at this season – perhaps 200 feet lower than in the summer – the cliffs past which the yellow-brown river snaked were higher and more majestic, beyond anything he had expected. In the distance mountains were already sprinkled with snow; closer at hand the autumn leaves blazed in red and gold. The river itself was 'beautiful, dark and deep and swirling and eddying with the undercurrents, with now and then a rapid making billows on the surface – one is roaring outside the window as I write. It is simply great, and one of the experiences of a lifetime to be making this trip.'[10]

When he could, he would get the *wuban* to take him ashore, and walk for several miles along the bank. Adventure in spectacular countryside was something he had relished in his New Zealand days, and he would get plenty of it in China. He was fascinated by the boatmen's work, and spent hours watching them. 'They row or scull or tow or do almost anything else to the accompaniment of a kind of rhythmic chanting, mostly just cries with no meaning – e.g. Hey-ah, Hey-o, o-ah, i-ah, etc, etc. It sounds great at times, especially when they are doing a bit of specially stiff rowing when they shout and stamp like demons. There is a chap who does nothing else but urge them on with weird and frantic cries, and probably a good flow of bad language, and now and then goes for anyone he thinks is slacking. But our boatmen are willing workers...'[11]

The hazards of river travel became clear as they passed several wrecked boats beached on the river bank, with their cargoes spread out to dry. The rapids were the most dangerous spots, where the boats had to be hauled by a rope attached to the mast over what were effectively small waterfalls. Clifford himself had a narrow escape on this first journey. 'We were ascending the Chin-tan rapids, and had got to the middle of the third and highest one, when suddenly the current swung the boat's head out into the stream, beyond control, and we were in danger of capsize by the tension of the tow-rope broadside on the mast. Two axe-blows sounded (they seem to produce an axe at a moment's notice) and the ropes were cut through, leaving us in mid-current, at the top of the rapids, and with only a few men on board, the others having been tracking [hauling]. These set to work to row vigorously, and by a very skilful bit of navigation the captain just managed to get us across to still waters on the other side.'[12] Otherwise they would have gone back down over the two lower rapids, in danger of capsize on each.

With only a minimal knowledge of Chinese he could not communicate much with the crew, but entertained them on the Jew's Harp (the only musical instrument he had) to their great delight; and when crowds gathered on shore he found 'a broad grin puts us all at our ease'. A shared sense of humour created friendly feelings in the absence of language. 'While waiting to come aboard I entered into conversation with the boatmen – a very fluent one it may be imagined. We passed a few remarks about the boat, regarding its qualities of goodness or otherwise ... I was then instructed in the art of counting to twenty, which I pretty well knew already. One of them then asked if I had three cash I could pass on to him. At first I didn't understand the word he used for cash, and replied with the familiar formula "bu dong" – don't understand. At last I saw what he meant, but by this time there was a great joke among the men, in which I shared – "He can count one, two, three, up to twenty, but when ask three cash, bu dong, bu dong!" We parted the best of friends.'[13]

Many of his observations on the river were scientific – noting the geology of the rocks, timing the echo between the cliffs to measure the breadth of the river, visiting a salt-works with brine-wells and evaporating pans – but he was also gaining some insight into the problems of preaching Christianity. On Sundays they would have a short service for the crew; although Clifford could not understand anything that was said he observed the men's reactions. 'All sorts of different receptions are given to the Message: some didn't care, or wouldn't bother to come to

Worship at all: others looked on curiously: others found material for jokes which in very audible tones they communicated to bystanders: others gave occasional comments of approval, or explained the meaning of some phrase to their neighbours: a very few seemed to drink it all in intensely.'[14] The Parable of the Sower, he wrote later, had a new force to him now.

One form of Christian witness, which could be made at any time, was the medical. Basic first-aid was part of the missionary's training, and both Clifford and Irene Hutchinson, while unable to talk with the crew, could at least help with their various injuries and ailments. 'I set to work for a couple of hours tying up smashed fingers, anointing all kinds of cuts and sores, dispensing stomach medicine etc. It was the first time I had tackled such a job, so was a bit slow, but sent them away comfortable and happy ... The man I dosed the other night I am proud to say announced himself better next day.'[15] But Clifford, young and inexperienced in missionary work, wanted to make a point of telling the men that it was the love of God that led the missionaries to help them, not the desire to heap up merit for themselves. 'I feel that with all true humility we should thus witness to the power and love of Christ our Master, and let our light *so* shine that men may see *and glorify* our Father.'[16] Leonard Wigham, however, with twenty years' experience, felt this would do little good.

On this occasion Clifford seems gauche and dogmatic, but on the matter of travelling on the Sabbath he was the more flexible of the two. Wigham was all for staying put on Sundays, 'as a testimony of Christian sincerity to the Chinese'. Clifford was more aware of how the crew might actually feel if they missed a day's travel when there was a good wind, and then were faced with additional labour of rowing and hauling to make up the lost time. 'It is a ticklish question,' thought Clifford, 'how far we are right in forcing our Christian customs on heathen employés ... I feel personally that a voyage such as ours has special circumstances such as the liability to enforced rest on other days so that there is special reason for taking advantage of fair conditions on the Sabbath..'[17]

Apart from their scare on the Chin-tan rapids they continued without serious upset, and reached Chongqing on the last day of 1913. The Silcocks had left them at Wanxian, some 200 miles downriver: Margaret Silcock was a highly strung woman with a particular fear of water, and the houseboat journey was agony to her, especially on the rapids. She was also six months pregnant. So they decided on the long overland journey from Wanxian to Chengdu, over the mountains in wintertime, rather than have another two weeks on the river. Missionaries in West China had to be tough when it came to travelling, and Clifford hoped his Margaret would be made of sterner stuff.

On arrival in Chongqing he was warmly greeted by the seven Quaker missionaries working there, and immediately enjoyed a warm bath and a delayed Christmas dinner with plum pudding. 'I like the Chongqing missionaries immensely, they seem a fine and able lot of people, and have been very hospitable to me.'[18] He stayed at the Friends' High School for boys on a hilltop outside the city, and was impressed. It was the most important single piece of educational work undertaken by Friends in Sichuan and was run by Ernest and Margaret Sawdon, both with B.Sc. degrees from London University. There were 40 boys there at that time, within a year there would be 55. It continued to grow, in numbers and reputation, over the coming years, and would become an important source of students for the West China Union University; by the 1930s it was recognised as the best secondary school in the whole province.

On 3rd January, after only two days in Chongqing, Clifford set out with several colleagues to experience for the first time what it was like to travel overland in Sichuan. Heavy goods would be taken on to Chengdu by river, but that was a long and roundabout journey. There were no roads as Westerners knew them, merely paths a few feet wide, between rice fields and over hillsides, sometimes but not always paved with slabs of stone. A sedan chair was essential, and was 'my private possession, a very swank affair, for four bearers, comfortably fitted up and roofed over – all for a cost of not much over £1.'[19] People varied in their responses to being carried in a chair; some felt seasick, others found they could read or write without difficulty while travelling. Clifford found it rather pleasant: 'The bearers keep in step, two before you and two behind. The usual stage is from 25 to 30 miles a day. Chinese coolies must have great physical endurance.'[20] Once one of the bearers lost his footing, and Clifford and his luggage were tipped into a muddy rice-field. Much of the time, though, he walked, and delighted in the beauty of the fertile and densely cultivated countryside, with its terraced hills, flooded rice-fields and wooded gorges. The area they travelled through was one where Quakers were the only Christian presence, and they slept in local temples, or sometimes in street chapels that missionaries had rented for preaching.

After two days they reached Tongliang, a small city with a resident missionary couple, Ben and Florence Jackson. They were the most isolated members of the Friends' Mission – it was three months since they had seen another Westerner, and they did not expect to see another until the summer. Florence 'was telling me that the work and good friendships with the Christian women prevent her from feeling the loneliness. Mr J. is a great wit, and was evidently delighted by such an opportunity of telling his vast fund of funny yarns, for a good part of our time there was spent enjoying his wit.' It was a happy coincidence that the travellers had arrived on the Saturday, and they could avoid Sabbath travel as well as relieving the Jacksons' loneliness. The dangers of life in rural Sichuan, as law and order decayed after the collapse of the Chinese Empire in the 1911 Revolution, were brought vividly home by a walk around the city walls. 'Every four yards along the wall a man's name is written in characters to show the place each citizen must occupy in case of an assault by robbers etc. Our host made us avoid the part of the wall overlooking the execution ground, where even that day nine had been beheaded and left lying. This is almost a daily occurrence, and anyone who cares may be a spectator.' On the Monday the travellers set out again, and after another two days arrived in Suining, where the annual meetings of the Mission were about to start.[21]

The Friends' Mission in Sichuan had been established in the province since 1890, when Robert and Mary-Jane Davidson had opened the first Meeting House in Chongqing.[22] Others had come to join them and by 1904, when the Davidsons moved to Chengdu, it was established in five centres – the two large cities just mentioned, and the smaller cities of

Tongchuan (today known as Santai), Suining and Tongliang. Around each of these smaller places there was a network of 'out-stations' in market towns and villages, which missionaries would visit as often as they could. Often a shop was rented there, and converted into a street chapel in charge of a convert-evangelist. These also provided welcome accommodation for a travelling missionary – anything was preferable to the discomforts of a Chinese inn.

By 1915, the year after Clifford's arrival, the number of Quaker missionaries in Sichuan would reach its maximum of 39. Their work was threefold – medical, educational, and evangelistic. A small hospital had been opened in Tongchuan in 1904, and a second was now being built in Suining. The Mission also ran primary schools for boys, and sometimes girls, in all five centres and in some of the out-stations, and secondary schools for boys in Chongqing and Tongchuan. And at the heart of the Mission's work was preaching the Word, seeking to win converts for Christ. They preached in market places and temple courtyards, wherever an audience could be found; they travelled from village to village hoping to collect groups of the interested; they distributed tracts and New Testaments, and placarded walls. The FFMA had grown out of the evangelical strand in the Society of Friends, which had been very strong in the mid-nineteenth century, and to start with there was little difference between the message preached by Friends, and their methods, from those of the other missionary societies in Sichuan. Services included hymns, prayers, sermons and Bible readings, and silent worship 'after the manner of Friends' was very rare.

A church organisation had been created on the model of Friends in Britain; there were five Monthly Meetings in the five centres of Friends' work, and these had been brought together as the Sichuan Yearly Meeting (YM) in 1904. Yearly Meeting was held in one of the five centres on or near the Chinese New Year holiday, and included both Chinese and missionaries. Attending YM meant several days' journey, in winter and often in danger from bandits, and at a season where tradition would have them stay with their families; this says something about the commitment of the Chinese members. A Yearly Meeting is normally the main decision-making authority for Friends, but in the mission field it was felt by most to be too immature to play this role, and real power rested with the Committee of Missionaries (COM), held at the same time. Funding came almost entirely from the FFMA in London, which wanted, through its missionaries, to ensure it was well spent. The ideal of a self-supporting church was present, but only as a faint hope for the future. Since the YM conducted its business in Chinese, Clifford would probably not have attended, but it is interesting that he does not even mention it in his journal.

Apart from being a time for debates and decisions, the COM was a very important occasion for bonding, the only time in the year when most of the members of the Mission could gather together. Some wives might be detained at home by children, but for those like the Jacksons, alone in Tongliang, it provided a wonderful few days of contact. As a newcomer Clifford would not take part in the discussions, but could observe the variety of opinions and personalities displayed, and learn about every aspect of the work. He would have known from Hodgkin that, ten years before, the Mission had nearly been destroyed by clashes of personality, and that it was still wise to station certain missionaries several days' journey from certain other missionaries. Now he could put faces to names and discreetly form his own judgements. But to keep him occupied he was given the task of typing up the minutes. He was not an experienced typist, and it was an unfamiliar machine; it kept him up late every night, and this section of his journal comes to an abrupt end. But the ten days of meetings could not have provided a better introduction to his new life.

Finally the meetings were over, and then he was off on another four days' travel to Chengdu. On the last morning they came down into the wide Chengdu plain, stretching for thirty miles or so around the city. The size of Chengdu, the capital of Sichuan, was striking: after entering the city it took a further hour to reach the Quaker compound in Qinlonggai (Green Dragon Street) in the north-west quarter. On 27th January, more than four months after he had left England, Clifford wrote to Margaret: 'Here I am at last writing to you from the place that, if God will, is to be Home to us for most of the years we share together on earth ... I am afraid my nature is not thrilled by such arrivals, as yours perhaps would be; but it certainly is interesting, to say the least, to have come to one's desired haven.'[23] Emotional display was not in Clifford's line.

4

1914–1919, Chengdu

Before following Clifford's career further it would be as well to take a
look at the world in which he now found himself. The province of
Sichuan, of which Chengdu was the capital, was one of the largest in
China, and enjoyed great wealth from its natural resources. The land is
very fertile, especially round the capital where it is irrigated by a canal
system over two thousand years old. It regularly produces three cereal
crops a year – wheat in the winter, and rice in summer and autumn –in
addition to sugarcane, tea and fruit. Other products included silk, salt
and opium. Yet Sichuan is isolated from the rest of China by a ring of
mountains, and it was still virtually untouched by the modern industrial
world. Chengdu was utterly unlike the great cities of the China coast;
while there was some rudimentary street lighting, the streets themselves
were narrow, unevenly paved, and teeming with pedlars, night-soil carts
and swarms of children. It was still traditional China.

Yet it was Sichuan that had provided the spark for the 'Revolution' of
1911 and the end of the Qing Dynasty and the Chinese Empire. The
government had awarded a contract to a foreign company to build a
railway into the province; this provoked anger from local gentry who
had hoped for the contract themselves, and in collusion with the ubi-
quitous secret societies they provoked disturbances throughout the
province during the summer of 1911. The Imperial Government sent
an army from Wuhan in central China to suppress the troubles, and it
was there, in a city denuded of loyal troops, that a rising took place on
10th October. As the news spread, cities throughout central, south and
west China rose against the Qing regime. It was unexpected and
unplanned; a revolutionary movement, the Tongmenghui, led by Sun

Yatsen, had members throughout the country, but they were as taken aback as everyone else. It was less a revolution than a collapse: the imperial government disintegrated, but no one knew what to put in its place. As time passed it became clear that all it had brought about was a mixture of military dictatorship and anarchy.

Officially China was now a republic, and in 1913 its president was an old imperial general, Yuan Shikai, who controlled the north and was seeking to confirm his power over the rest of the country. In Sichuan itself at the end of 1911 separate 'revolutionary governments' had sprouted up in many cities, but after a few months of negotiation they had given way to a local army officer called Hu Jingyi, who was now governor of the province, and at least nominally loyal to President Yuan. Hu was 36, from a local gentry background, and had studied in a Japanese military academy. But he had also, for a few months in 1898, studied with Robert Davidson at the Friends' School in Chongqing, and the link thus formed now seemed extraordinarily useful to them both. Hu, like most of the new leaders, wanted to modernise China; this meant learning from the West, and in Sichuan most Westerners were missionaries. The missionary community, meanwhile, was delighted at having for the first time active support from Chinese authorities; Americans in particular were enthralled by China having become a republic like themselves. Sichuan appeared, as Clifford wrote, 'the quietest part of China just now,'[1] and the future looked promising.

Hu Jingyi's support was especially useful to the new West China Union University. Robert Davidson was one of the founders, and was now Secretary of the Senate; his closeness to Hu earned a warning from the resident British consul against any close political contacts. More politically aware than the missionaries, he knew that Hu's position was insecure, and that 'any suspicion that foreigners were no longer disinterested spectators of political events in China ... might lead to unfortunate and possible disastrous consequences.'[2] The consul was right, in that in 1915 Hu was replaced; but his successors followed his example in supporting the University as the main source in the province of the 'Western Learning' which China so needed.

36

In 1905 the Qing Dynasty had abolished the civil service examinations, which had dominated Chinese education and thought for over a millennium. The idea was that the Confucian syllabus on which they were based would be replaced by 'Western Learning', but nothing was, or could be, done to bring this about. China had hardly any teachers or institutions capable of providing what was needed. For many centuries the examination system had provided the only career path for educated young Chinese, the only means to social prestige and success; their lives and hopes had revolved around this to a quite extraordinary extent. Now, suddenly, it was not there. The only approximation to an alternative career path was the army, studying in a Japanese military school, or one of their Chinese imitators, and this goes some way to explaining the pattern of Chinese history in the early twentieth century.

Military schools did actually provide some access to Western learning, and to the practical applications of science. But China needed its own modern universities, and a schools system that would prepare students for them, and this would take many years to develop. The situation created an opening for missionaries, and since the turn of the century Protestant missions in the great cities of east China had been developing institutions of higher education; Clifford had visited some of them on his journey out. Recently a number of these colleges had merged to create 'Union' institutions, involving missions of different denominations. But West China was the first to be a Union University from the outset. In 1905 four mission societies in Sichuan had agreed to work together in its foundation: the Canadian Methodist Mission (CMM), the American Methodist Episcopal Mission (AMEM), the American Baptist Missionary Union (ABMU), and the FFMA.

This had been made possible because missions in West China had advanced further down the path of ecumenical collaboration than anywhere else in the mission world. Friends had played an important role in this.[3] In 1898 an Advisory Board had been set up to help coordinate the educational work of the various missions; and this led in 1904 to the founding of the West China Christian Education Union, to create a common syllabus and examinations for all Christian schools, to enhance their efficiency and standing in the eyes of the community. It was at this point that the proposal to found a university was first mooted. The following year Henry Hodgkin arrived in Sichuan. With a forceful personality, and his Cambridge double first in the natural sciences, he towered over a missionary community whose academic background was mostly modest or non-existent, and he did more than anyone to push the proposal forward both in China and in the home countries. He was seen by many as the obvious candidate to be the university's first president, a man who would give it a high standing from the outset. But the sudden death of the FFMA's secretary in 1910 meant that he was summoned back to London to take over.

Because it was a 'Union University' its system of government was extraordinarily unwieldy. The missionaries in the field had become accustomed to working together in harmony, but this was far from the case with their governing bodies in the US, Canada and Britain, where ecumenism was a concept that had scarcely impinged. And money was involved – few missions wanted the funds they had spent so much effort raising to be placed under the control of another, perhaps heretical, denomination. The presence of Friends, with their denial of the sacraments, made this example of collaboration particularly challenging. To make the scheme more acceptable, Hodgkin proposed that each mission should have its own college, effectively a hall of residence, to ensure that students under its aegis would receive the right kind of religious instruction; this pattern owed something to the model of Oxbridge and allowed missions to work together without betraying their own separate insights.

The supreme authority for the University was the Board of Governors, with an office in New York, and representatives from each of the four missions. But these missions' headquarters were located in three countries, one of which was separated by the Atlantic Ocean from the other two. Board meetings were difficult to organise and infrequent. Correspondence was subject to all sorts of delays – proposals from Chengdu would go to the Board, and then be referred to London, New York or Toronto, be considered by the mission boards there, and their opinions, after discussion which was often of a dilatory nature, would be passed back to the Board of Governors. None of the Board (bar

38

Hodgkin after 1910) had any experience of China. Few people at home had the sense of urgency that prompted those in Chengdu.

The opening of the University in 1910 illustrates the difficulties. The Board of Governors had not yet been formally set up, and there had not even been any informal meetings between the home boards of the four missions since September 1908. No constitution had been written, no president appointed. But in Chengdu immediate action was required. Sixty acres of land had been bought, mostly of paddy-fields and burial sites; this would gradually expand, to 120 acres by 1918, and over 150 acres by the mid-1930s. In 1908 the four missions had opened a 'Union Middle School', with Robert Davidson as its head, to give a better quality of secondary education than any of them could provide separately. By the end of 1909 it was clear that students completing their courses would move on to a Chinese college and be lost to missionary influence, unless higher education courses could be provided for them. So, regardless of what people at home thought, and despite the lack of a president, a senate, or a constitution, the West China Union University was opened on 11th March 1910, with a modest ceremony in a lath-and-plaster temporary science building. There were ten teachers, two of whom were Chinese; Harry Silcock, whose task was to develop teacher training, was the only FFMA member. And there were eleven students, four of whom would drop out during the first year. The teachers did most of their work in the Middle School, and also had responsibilities to their missions, teaching in primary schools or engaging in evangelism. This dual loyalty would cause continual difficulties in staffing, especially when medical courses began, and teachers were suddenly removed to solve a staffing crisis in a mission hospital.

The home boards might be slow off the mark, but they had great plans for the future. An architect was appointed in October 1912, after a competition, to design the whole campus, and the central university buildings. One of the key criteria in the competition was 'respect for Chinese feeling', although none of the judges was Chinese; but in 1913 the plans, with two others for comparison, were presented to a committee of Chinese in Chengdu and approved.[4] The winner was an

Englishman from one of the great Quaker families, Frederick Rowntree. His plans show buildings widely separated from each other, linked by tree-lined avenues, with land set aside for the individual missions to put up their own colleges. For years the buildings were almost lost in expanses of grassland, and the campus became a popular resort for city-dwellers seeking fresh air. The main buildings were long and low, with curving roofs and eaves in the Chinese style. The designs were sufficiently impressive to be exhibited at the Royal Academy's Summer Exhibition in 1924.[5]

The University had opened in the autumn of 1910. Its title in English, West China Union University, was rendered in Chinese as *Huaxi Xiehe Daxue*. In the Chinese way it was colloquially referred to by the first two syllables, 'Huaxi', and has been called this for most of its subsequent history. For brevity's sake this name will be used in this book. A year later came the Revolution, whose immediate effect in Chengdu was to force the evacuation of missionaries and the closure of the University; it had only reopened in the spring of 1913, a year before Clifford's arrival. At that point there were fifteen staff and twenty-five students, but over 160 boys in the thriving Middle School. After Hodgkin's departure there were attempts to entice a distinguished American or British scholar to Chengdu, but they came to nothing. The search for an outside scholar having failed, one of the resident staff, the 36-year-old Joseph Beech of the AMEM, was appointed President. He was a fundraiser and entrepreneur rather than a scholar; his stated policy was to buy the land first, then concentrate on buildings, and leave 'academic efficiency' till later.[6] Clifford was initially less than impressed: 'He is a regular man of all trades, being originally an engineer, then graduating a Doctor of Divinity, and now turning architect and builder. He is great on hustle, and, to my mind, some abominable American educational ideas.'[7] He does not enlarge on the latter, but it is likely that Beech had a strongly vocational view of education, which clashed with Clifford's more scholarly and humanistic attitude. However, this did not prevent them working harmoniously together in future years.

The day after his arrival Clifford was taken from Qinlonggai to the University, which was two and a half miles away, going through the city to the South Gate, then across the Jinjiang river. In the future he would normally travel there by bicycle, taking over half an hour to negotiate the narrow, unpaved and densely crowded streets. The campus was outside the walls, on the south bank of the river that bounded the city at this point. Clifford knew the University was in its very early stages, but it still came as a shock to see how little had been built. Some of the colleges were under construction, but the university builder had not yet arrived from America, and teaching was being carried on in temporary lath-and-plaster buildings. Some chemistry was being taught, at a very elementary level, but Clifford found the lab 'a very primitive affair indeed, a single room with tables, and a lecture table and blackboard, and all the apparatus locked away in a small store-room.'[8] The apparatus itself was deficient, and cared for by an uneducated coolie; when later in the year Clifford attempted to put on some experiments he also found the chemicals had deteriorated and were useless. A visit to the library was also instructive and depressing, not just because of the lack of books, but also for what it told him of his new colleagues' attitude. 'The Senate had not yet seen its way to take in any of the learned periodicals and journals, because they thought there were no students fit to use them. I hope this rather amazing decision for a university will soon be revised.'[9] He wondered if Margaret's father could help: did he know anyone who subscribed to *Nature, Proceedings of the Royal Society, Journal of the Chemical Society* and could pass them on to the University?[10] Chengdu was a long way from Liverpool, and the absence of a highly-qualified scholar in the post of president had its effects at many levels.

For his first few months in Chengdu Clifford would live with the Davidsons at the Friends' compound in Qinlonggai. Robert Davidson, the founder of the Mission, referred to by everyone (and from now on in this book) as RJD, was a great contrast to the quiet, unexcitable, intellectual Clifford. He was an ebullient, sociable, impulsive, warm-hearted Ulsterman, who had left school at fourteen to work in a linen factory but had since followed a remarkable course of self-education, mostly in China. His range of interests was wide, and he had the instinctive teacher's skill in communicating his knowledge and enthu-siasm to others. Clifford was delighted to find that he had a large

41

library, and RJD doubtless looked forward to long conversations with a young guest with an open and enquiring mind and from such a different background. RJD was responsible for all the mission work in Chengdu, but he was also closely involved with the University, as the first head of the Union Middle School, and as secretary of the Senate. But much as he would have liked to teach there – his special subject was geography – he knew it was impossible: to ensure that the University had a good academic standing it was essential that all its staff should have proper qualifications.

Robert's wife Mary-Jane, seventeen years older, was now in her mid-sixties; she had found it difficult mastering Chinese, which had hampered her work as a missionary, but she had built up for herself a great position in the wider missionary community, especially in ecumenical work, as a committee secretary, founding editor of the *West China Missionary News*, and as a kind of universal aunt. Clifford's first reference to her, writing to Margaret, gives something of the flavour of this: 'Mrs Davidson congratulated me on having *you*, and said she approved of engagements made at home. That is the utterance of a very weighty friend, for she has won a great place for herself here by her talents.'[11]

The Friends' compound on Qinlonggai was a remarkably large piece of land, in which you could forget you were in the city at all. It had been bought in 1904 when the Davidsons had moved from Chongqing. It contained a meeting house, primary school, buildings for Chinese staff and servants, and two rather grand residences for missionaries. These houses with their decorated roofs and curving eaves look at first sight quintessentially Chinese. They were nothing of the sort. The house of a prosperous Chinese normally consisted of ranges of single-storey buildings grouped around courtyards and gardens, looking inwards; these houses were three-storey square blocks with verandahs, looking outwards, surrounded by extensive gardens, rose pergolas and tennis courts. The roofs alone were Chinese. So unusual were they in a Chinese context that when they were being built in 1905 the Viceroy of Sichuan himself had come to scramble over the scaffolding and inspect them. They reveal how missionaries imported a whole style of life along with their faith, instead of blending in to a Chinese context. The founder of the China Inland Mission, Hudson Taylor, had insisted fifty years before that its missionaries should all wear Chinese clothes and follow a Chinese way of life – in their early years RJD and Mary-Jane had done this, and some rural missionaries in the twentieth century still did – but most missions eschewed this austerity. A justification for the grandeur of the Qinlonggai houses was that Friends' aim in coming to Chengdu had been to make contact with gentry and officials in the hope of influencing them – this involved a lot of socialising, and you needed an appropriate place to receive people of importance. But they also represented assumptions, about the relationship of Chinese and Westerner, which Clifford would soon come to question.

The houses were European, and within them missionaries tried to reproduce the way of life they were used to at home, and this required a massive importation of domestic goods across the oceans and up the Yangzi. This explains why the FFMA luggage allowance for single missionaries was three tons, and for married couples five. The aim was to make a home in China as close as possible to what one might have in England, in order to preserve one's own health, and especially that of one's children. Mary-Jane plied Clifford with advice about what Margaret should bring with her to furnish their own house (as yet unbuilt). His early letters to Margaret are full of lists of things to purchase in England, and others she must buy in Shanghai. Bedding, curtains, mosquito netting – not furniture, as the Chinese could make it very well, but furniture catalogues so the carpenters could copy Western styles. No wallpaper, as Chinese couldn't hang it. Lamps of all kinds, upholstered sofa and chairs, mattresses. Upholstered seats for dining room chairs, picture hooks, bedroom and hat hooks, curtain fixings, knobs or handles for drawers. Plate glass for mirrors, a primus stove, linoleum, a preserving pan, a hammock, tennis racquets, tin kettles.[12] Then there were bicycles, both for getting around the campus and for riding in the countryside, and goods that related more directly to Clifford's work. Margaret was asked to bring out a supply of chemicals, to be bought by the FFMA, typing paper and carbons, photographic goods, clinical thermometers, fountain pen ink, and Keating's powder for fleas. Then his personal enthusiasms had to be satisfied. He had experience of bee-keeping in New Zealand, and 'I find there are bees to be got out here. Will you bring a small bee-keeping handbook out for us? Very few keep them, and there are lots of flowers. If you can get (e.g. in the book) full measurements of the standard kind of bee-box, don't bother to bring one, but otherwise I should be glad if you would order for me a specimen (lower storey, comb section, box storey and roof) also bellows, hive inside fittings, and any absolute essential.'[13]

Some outside observers were very critical of this missionary lifestyle – for example the British Consul H.H. Fox, who returned to Chengdu in 1914 after some years' absence. The Canadians, particularly numerous in the University, he described as enthusiastic, kindly, energetic, but of limited intellectual attainments, who did not identify with Chinese life, took a three-month summer holiday, and believed in making themselves as comfortable as possible. One consular wife (whose husband had a first-class degree from Cambridge) disliked being invited to missionaries' At Homes, because they lived in a style far above what she herself could afford.[14]

By the end of April Clifford was beginning to share this view, and expresses a desire for 'as simple comfort as possible, [otherwise] one is inclined to get everything that might possibly be wanted, and thus get a lot of lumber on one's hands, or needless luxury in the house.' A few days later he writes: 'I sometimes feel there is a little too much made of style and comfort (or rather luxury) in missionary houses. We are not here for *that*, and the trouble is that to a Chinese they appear almost what a palace does to us!' And at the end of May he writes to Margaret with (for him) unusual vehemence, on hearing that an official request has gone to the FFMA for £600 to build their house on the campus. 'I feel a *bit* myself that we might do with less – other houses out here don't cost quite that, I think. I want to live in such a house that I can come home and not be ashamed to face Mary-Ann who washes the door-step and puts her 3d into the mission box. And I should like to remember that I am a steward for Some One Else, too. And I want to have some of the spirit of Paul, who gave up his rights and worked with his hands rather than let any have occasion of reviling his Master, or of stumbling – and I don't suppose the double job was *too* good for his

44

health, either. You feel with me, don't you, dearest? I am thinking of writing to Hodgkin soon, and saying that I (and I am sure you too) are glad to live simply (if it could even be called that!), and while the Mission will rightly decide what it considers best for its work, we don't want them to consider us as factors because we want to live in as fine a house as other missionaries do. I think you see the idea, and I believe you will be of one mind with me, so I am presuming to write as above. As a matter of fact it may make little difference, I fear.'[15] The vehemence seems partly to come from his uncertainty about Margaret's (or her parents') feelings on the question. He knew that he had not had a normal family home since his mother died when he was sixteen, while Margaret was used to all the comforts of Moseley. How would she react to a simpler Chinese life? As it happened he need not have worried.

But before he could turn his mind seriously to setting up house, or teaching chemistry, he had to revert to being a student beginner, and for nearly two years his main work would be mastering Chinese. The day after his visit to the University he had his first meeting with Mr Sa, a middle-aged man with the reputation of being a capable teacher. 'He will be with me several hours a day. So far we work by his giving me the pronunciation of words or sentences out of my books, which I endeavour to twist my tongue round and repeat after him, so as to get the exact tones, etc. ... Sometimes we attempt to indulge in a little general conversation for practice, which I am afraid is rather of a desultory order at present, though doubtless very amusing to him. I got out of him yesterday that he had four small children, 2 boys and 2 girls, that there were 70 million people in Sichuan, and other equally interesting facts.'[16] That was in the morning; in the afternoons Clifford would go across the city to a missionary language school run by the Canadians. He found their course 'helpful ... especially so for getting the common expressions of everyday life'; but as in his schooldays he was soon outstripping the rest of the class, and was busy acquiring more Chinese characters than the course had to offer.[17]

It was around this time that Clifford was rechristened, being given a Chinese name – Su Daopu (苏道仆). This was – and still is – necessary for all foreigners in China, so that their name can be written in Chinese characters. The aim is usually to find a name that sounds somewhat similar, provided that it begins with a recognised Chinese surname, in this case Su.

Within a few days of arrival Clifford found an outlet for his scientific and improvisatory skills. Although missionaries all had watches or clocks, there was no standard by which to correct them, and clocks in different houses varied by up to an hour. This was very inconvenient for teaching according to a timetable, or organising the frequent meetings. 'I have invented a wondrous apparatus out of a kerosene tin, some bits of thread etc., for getting solar time. Now I am waiting for a fine day to try it.'[18] He may have had to wait some time: Sichuan is renowned for its continuous grey cloud cover, which rarely breaks to let the sun through. Sichuanese have a proverb that when the sun shines, all the dogs bark. When the dogs next barked, Clifford would establish Chengdu Standard Time. It is notable that no one else in the University had thought of this, or knew how to do it. Within a few years the whole city would recognise the Chemistry Department's scientific leadership by using Clifford's calculations.[19]

He also made a formal visit to the British Consul, 'a rather pleasant fellow'. This had an interesting follow-up, when the consul asked him to play at the Tennis Club and invited him to join.[20] One of the rules of the club was that missionaries could not be members. It existed mainly to allow the small number of foreign officials, teachers and traders to socialise without the dampening effect of missionary presence. They must have felt from the start that Clifford was different, and would not be a spoilsport – although perhaps his doctorate helped. He did not join – the subscription was too high – but he regretted this; he always wanted to reach out to all sections of the society in which he lived.

Although his main role in Chengdu was to teach chemistry at the University, Clifford was also expected to play as large a part as he could in the life of the church, and to be familiar with all that the Friends' Mission was doing. So in April he spent a week in Tongchuan, three days' journey from Chengdu. This was the oldest Friends' Mission station apart from Chongqing, and ran a hospital, and primary and middle schools. The latter would be one of the feeder schools for the

University and so was of particular interest. He also met the head of the main government school, gave a lecture on chemistry and attempted some experiments; but the lack of equipment and the need for translation made him feel it was hardly worthwhile.

The more he saw of the Mission's work, and the more colleagues he met, the more critical he became. The divisions that had so damaged the Mission ten years before had not gone away, and were merely eased by people living several days' journey from each other, and only meeting once a year at the Committee of Missionaries. At other times decisions had to be reached by correspondence, without the discussion which might lead to greater understanding. Above all there seemed to be no leadership. Clifford as a Presbyterian was accustomed to a more formal way of doing business than that of Friends. Friends do not take votes, but progress through discussion, 'reasoning together', and ascertaining the 'spirit of the meeting', but this was hardly enough when they only met once a year. Discussions were interminable, and rarely led to clear decisions. Leadership might have been given by a Friend with the strength of personality to win agreement from the rest, known as a 'weighty Friend'. Henry Hodgkin, that weightiest of Friends, had given such a lead during his few years in Chengdu. But no one had replaced him. RJD was the senior missionary, but while he was enthusiastic, inspirational and had a wonderful gift for friendship with the Chinese, he was too excitable, impulsive and sometimes lacking in judgement to provide a clear sense of direction to his colleagues. 'As a mission we suffer from individualism and lack of an executive or of a clear policy, a result being that each man confronted with his own clear and pressing problems tends to let all his enthusiasm run to them alone.' They lacked any 'considered and adhered-to plan of campaign for our work as a whole.'[21] Those not involved in the University showed little interest in it, or saw it as a distraction from their own work. The Mission had embarked on too many enterprises without sufficient resources, and the lack of personnel was made worse by people going home every six years or so on furlough, leaving their work, hopefully to be covered by others.

During 1914 Clifford was still learning the language, and it would take time before he could get to know the Chinese around him and form his own opinion about them. In his early letters and journal he tends to repeat the commonplaces of the missionary community, and one suspects that if he ever reread his journal in later years he would often have winced. Comments on 'the Chinese' are generally critical, and follow a familiar pattern. They are like children, they are materialistic, dishonest, self-seeking, with no concept of loyalty to an abstract principle, etc. Such judgements were partly a result of the nature of the Chinese church: Christianity for the most part found a response only among the poorest, and inevitably attracted those who hoped to gain some benefit from missionaries who possessed what seemed endless sources of wealth, and who, as foreigners, could very easily be deceived. So missionaries were only too frequently cheated and misled by those they had eagerly welcomed into fellowship, and adopted attitudes in response which were distrustful and patronising. Even if not directly dishonest, many converts entered the church hoping for employment – the so-called rice Christians – and they could be naively open about this: once they had learned the doctrine would they be employed as evangelists? Those few educated Chinese who responded with interest might not see the point of joining a church at all. There was no equivalent to this in Chinese tradition, any more than there was to regular Sunday morning services. They might read the Bible, have a genuine interest in Christian ideas, a degree of conviction about their truth – but to join in with a group of lower-class, uneducated people was unthinkable; and they would be more alert than any foreigner could be to the insincerity or dishonesty of so many of these converts.

Much of this comes across in a journal entry in April: 'I wonder if people at home [i.e. Clifford in 1913] realise what kind of problems the church has to face out here ... These problems emerge in a very crude and direct fashion. In China the whole spirit is one of self-assertion, however disguised by various forms of politeness, and it is difficult for the cultured and educated to take a humble place alongside the brethren of the coolie class, even when the latter show the fruit of Christianity as some do in real goodness. Another question is that of the "rice Christian" – not so much I think that many get into the church from that motive, as that it is so ingrained in the Chinese to take advantage of every opportunity of a material kind, as that the degree of Christianity of many never lifts them above it. Then this again leads to harsh and bitter and outspoken accusations by other Christians. Some would say that the Chinese are very like children in these ways, and perhaps it is partially true of the coolie class. But much must be put down to an environment and hereditary ideals which make pride, and face-saving, and wealth and show, the all-important ends of life. Whatever ideals may be expressed in the Chinese classics, the fact remains that as a nation, from the President down, there are few indeed who are exempt from self-seeking or that seem to have that unselfish concern for the good of all which is not seldom met with in England.'[22]

There were, however, two outstanding Chinese Quakers whom he met not long after his arrival. One was Yang Shaoquan (S.C. Yang), a third-generation Christian from central China, son and grandson of Anglican priests, who had come to Sichuan at the beginning of the century to work for the Post Office. He then went to teach in a school where a younger colleague was a Friend, Yang Guoping (K.P. Yang), who introduced him to Hodgkin and RJD. Soon Yang Shaoquan had joined Friends himself, and became a teacher at the Qinlonggai primary school.[23] He was the first chairman of the YMCA when it opened in 1910, and was frequently presiding clerk of the Sichuan Yearly Meeting. Even more, he enjoyed huge prestige in the local community: before 1911 he had been a member of the revolutionary organisation, the Tongmenghui, and immediately after the Revolution had become Commissioner of Foreign Affairs in the new provincial government. RJD would later refer to him as 'one of the most, if not the most, influential churchmen in West China.' Yet there was some reluctance to trust even a Chinese of his standing. He had just been appointed principal of the University Union Middle School, but this was described nervously as an 'experiment'.[24] The second outstanding figure was Yang Guoping himself, one of the original pupils of the Friends' High School in Chongqing, a key figure in the Sichuan YM, and 'the most eloquent and persuasive speaker of all Chinese Friends'.[25] It would be he who would open and bring to a close Clifford's funeral service in 1930.

Although the pressures of day-to-day life might be irksome, and lead him to repeat many of the everyday criticisms of the 'heathen' Chinese he heard around him, from a broader perspective Clifford's intelligence and reflectiveness made him aware of how missionaries unthinkingly imported a range of Western cultural practices as a package along with Christianity, and he was concerned from the start that his work should not add to the 'denationalising' of the Chinese. He was quick to note how missionaries made no effort to adapt their worship to a Chinese context. In this the Quakers were no better than others. Services followed the pattern of nonconformist worship in England – a mixture of prayers, readings, preaching and hymns – sung of course to Western tunes which the Chinese could not get their voices round, for which they were mocked behind their backs. Clifford felt the inappropriateness the very first time he attended worship at the Meeting House in Qinlonggai: 'It struck me during the service that it was rather a pity that the building, order of service, tunes etc, are not more truly native in style, and a little less obtrusively foreign. Perhaps the Native church has not yet got sufficient initiative or wisdom, but we foreigners should at least aim at welcoming the native element and being willing to give up the ideas we have come out with.'[26]

From the very start of Christian mission work in China there had been those who believed that the Chinese language could never be a true medium for Christian ideas. The earliest Catholic missionaries in sixteenth-century Macao made a knowledge of Portuguese a necessary condition of baptism, and if Chinese settlers were converted by the Spanish in the Philippines they had to cut their hair in a Western style and wear beaver hats. Hudson Taylor and the China Inland Mission had bravely gone in the other direction by wearing Chinese clothes, but that was the limit of their respect for the Chinese, whom they excluded from any positions of authority in the churches they founded. In 1913 an American missionary in Canton, Herbert E. House, published a leaflet, 'The Tragedy and Imperative of Christian Education in China', in which the 'imperative' was to teach through the medium of English.[27] 'It takes time and hard labour,' House wrote, 'to make a man of the modern type out of a crude Chinese boy, and English is the best medium through which to effect the transformation. The very language itself alters the mind of the person who learns it ... The English language has developed with the mind and spirit of Christianity, it has its very being in them. Christian civilisation is the very breath of life within our English speech, and cannot be put into another language except by some fashion of slow growth.'

It is no wonder the Chinese had a saying, 'One more Christian, one fewer Chinese'. House's views are as far as possible from Clifford's. But the aspect of the question which affected him most directly was whether the teaching of scientific subjects should be done through the medium of English or Chinese. This was discussed in the Senate (of which he was not yet a member) at the end of May. It was a major issue in missionary colleges throughout China, and the arguments for teaching science in English were strong ones. The students were willing to learn English, a knowledge of which might secure them lucrative posts in foreign businesses. The career benefits of science were much harder to discern. In terms of their studies, English gave them immediate access to scientific literature. Most importantly, it made it possible for well-qualified teachers from the West to come to China on short-term contracts and start teaching immediately, without having to spend two years learning the language as Clifford had to. Few like him were prepared to devote their lives to teaching science in China. In this way teaching in English would strengthen the academic basis of science teaching in missionary colleges, and nearly all of them would in fact follow this path. But Clifford was sure that this was wrong. Despite all the problems (absence of a Chinese scientific vocabulary, etc.), China could never develop science for itself unless it could be done in Chinese. 'There are enough tendencies already to denationalise the Chinese, and either students would not understand, or else would have to give so much time to English studies that other subjects would suffer. Of course higher students should be able to read English books, but that is not the same as following an English address in a higher subject. Chemistry students do well to read German books, but fancy an English University giving its Chemical lectures in German!'[28] This commitment, from the start, to teaching chemistry in Chinese was one

51

of the most important of Clifford's life. Huaxi was the only Christian university where all the teaching would be carried on in Chinese, and in the sciences this was quite exceptional. Clifford's later colleague William Sewell commented in the late 1920s, as he struggled with finding Chinese equivalents for terminology to teach advanced organic chemistry, that this was the first time such a course had been given in Chinese anywhere; even Chinese universities taught such courses in English.[29]

At the end of May Clifford moved to the University to stay with the Silcocks. Their house was on the northern edge of the campus, just by the river bank – 'handy for bathing!' Not far away were two fifty-foot bamboo water-wheels, groaning twenty-four hours a day as they raised water to supply the city. Across the river was a strip of trees and grass, and then the city wall. It was a quiet rural spot, where the only disadvantage was the mosquitoes from the river, very active every evening. The neighbouring plot had already been earmarked for building a home for Clifford and Margaret.

His journal entries during the summer suggest a degree of delayed culture shock, as he becomes more critical of the Chinese and of his fellow missionaries. The excitement of arrival had worn off, the slog of daily language study was unrelenting, and the steamy heat of a Chengdu summer – with its mosquitoes – may also have affected him. He may have upset some people with his criticism, as he writes to Margaret: 'Do you realise you have taken to yourself one who is not very lovable, and who will never be generally popular?'[30] One distressing episode within a week of his move to the campus certainly upset him. Some of the Middle School boys had gone bathing in a pool nearby, one had got into difficulties, none of the others could swim enough to help, and the boy drowned. Clifford was first on the scene and dived in and recovered the body, but two hours of artificial respiration had no effect. Meanwhile someone stole his purse. He felt numb and without feeling after the event itself, and his distress projected itself on to the very alien funeral ceremonies the following day. The boy and his mother were Christian, but the funeral was very different from anything he had ever encountered before. 'First was a short service in the school, then a great, long (in space and time) procession to the grave. The school band played

"Men of Harlech"; they hadn't got any other funeral music. At the head were a number of large banners bearing various inscriptions, including warnings against rash bathing. They were carried, as was usual in China, by a disreputable looking lot of hired coolies off the street. The procession went about twelve times as far as it need ... this of course for show purposes. It would scarcely be a funeral without parading a main street and holding up the traffic. The coffin was carried by eight coolies, these men also looking pretty disreputable and grunting and shouting as they went along. At length, wearied out, we arrived at the grave, where were already gathered a great press of curious neighbours, scores of children, sellers of sweetmeats, bent on seeing the sights. With a great lot of shouting and I suspect swearing the heavy coffin was lifted into the grave ... After a while we sang another hymn, prayed, and the service was over. It was a Christian burial, and very different from what a heathen one would be – what a difference the Christian hope makes – and yet one could not but feel what a gulf there was between it and the comparative quiet and reverence of a western burial.' Yet Yang Shao-quan 'seemed to think it was quite the thing.'[31]

With the Silcocks, Clifford saw more of the problems of domestic life with servants, handled by those with less experience than the Davidsons. Servants, essential for daily life in China, were the greatest test of a missionary's cultural sensitivity. It was in the home that two ways of living came into the most direct and intimate contact. They needed to combine kindness with discipline, and hopefully also lead their servants towards a faith in Jesus. If they could not influence them, what hope would they have with others? And a failure in human relations in the domestic scene would swiftly become known in the wider Chinese community. Margaret Silcock clearly had problems in this area: 'The plots, quarrelling, suspicions, thefts, and continual tendency to slackness and imposition which one has to look out for among one's servants make a very difficult and often trying problem out here. They are very much like children in some ways, and the ones that become really tried and trusty in the good old English sense are few. There is no doubt that through them our influence is extended to a remarkable degree either for or against our Message. One of our biggest tasks is to look after them aright.'[32] This was partly, of course, a warning to his own Margaret, who would also have to manage a household.

As a contrast, it was interesting to observe how Yang Shaoquan questioned the Middle School servants when there had been some thefts in the student dormitory: 'It was really great to see the way in which he tackled them, an object lesson in the relations which exist between a good Chinese master and his servants.'[33] In the autumn Clifford would acquire his own personal servant, called Leng Jiaxin. It was probably his first experience of a master–servant relationship, and he looked on it with some trepidation. 'On Monday I took the momentous step of engaging my first servant – a youth of nineteen, quite raw (amusingly so at times), never with foreigners before, but apparently good-tempered and willing, and of no more than average intelligence, the sort that often turns out to be the most faithful and dependable of servants. So I have been busy this week, among other things, giving lessons in bed-making, boot-blacking, where to lay forks at table, and such matters.' After a couple of months Leng was caught out in a petty theft. 'I had him in and exhorted him. Poor lad, he was soon in tears, and was upset all the day, but I hope it did him good, and I am glad we had it out with him. He is rather under the thumb of a bad cook we have, and is very like a child (he is only 18 or thereabouts).'[34] Clifford must have got the balance right, between kindness and strictness. Leng stayed with him for the rest of his life as a most faithful friend, accompanying him on all his journeys. When he married, his family became an important part of the Stubbs household, and Margaret saw to it that he was one of the pallbearers at Clifford's funeral.

By midsummer Clifford would have been ready for a break; the weather was becoming intolerable, steamy heat punctuated by violent thunderstorms (eight inches of rain in five hours). This was the time when most foreigners headed for the cool of the hills, and little imitations of the colonial hill-towns of India sprang up around China. The most popular sites in Sichuan were the Buddhist holy mountain, Emeishan, Bailudin to the north of Chengdu, and Guanxian to the north west. Initially rooms were rented in Buddhist temples, but gradually settlements of bungalows developed, with tennis courts and other amenities. These were little Western communities full of gossip and tea-parties, where they could forget for a while the noise, crowds, smells and tensions of the cities. Clifford's first experience of this life was with the Silcocks at Guanxian, in a temple complex where a large group of forty to fifty foreigners, mostly missionaries, had rented space. It was 1300 feet above the level of the plain (Clifford measured it with his barometer) on the edge of the great mountain ranges stretching into Tibet. He had two little rooms, one shared with a 'small and rather respectable idol'. The monks were welcoming and tolerant, but it was an odd place for Christian missionaries to be living. 'Though we do not show any desecrating attitude towards their worship, the Chinese are clear enough what we think,' he wrote, and attributed the monks' tolerance to the lifeless and decadent state of their faith.[35]

'I am really having a jolly good time,' he wrote in his next entry. It was cooler, there were tennis courts, and someone had a gramophone. Behind the temple was an almost perpendicular forested hill; Clifford's reaction on seeing any hill was to climb it, and he dragged Silcock with him. They got to the top, then it began to rain, they missed the route back amongst the thick undergrowth, the slope 'got steeper and steeper, and slippery with the rain, and soon we were having to cling on to the growth and let ourselves down, fearing to let go and slide, lest there should be a cliff underneath.' It was growing dark, and panthers and leopards were said to be roaming. But they finally got safely down, with scratched hands and torn clothes. It was a typical Clifford adventure. But he also put in the usual daily hours of language study, and started – after only six months study! – putting together a chemistry textbook in Chinese with the help of a student. There were several Chinese students there, and he found the opportunity for conversational practice and developing friendships invaluable.[36]

The mood changed in early August when news came of the outbreak of the Great War. 'We here are simply appalled by the news; it seems such a senseless needless thing, and Britain had no quarrel with Germany. One can hardly dare to look into the future. After all, the saddest thing about this whole business is not this sudden flare-up, but the greed, suspicion, envy, pride, racial hatred and misunderstanding, the misfortunes, lacks and sin of man which is there all the time, whether in outward peace or war. One part of our work here is to help this nation to imbibe the Christian spirit more than we in the West seem yet to have done.'[37] It was clear that their work would be affected. In practical terms missions would suffer from reduced income and a shortage of recruits – this would affect the fledgling University especially. China itself would not escape, as a cut-off in Western investment damaged its precarious stability, and Japan was poised to take advantage in ways yet unknown. But more significantly the supposed superiority of the Christian West was cast into question, and the Chinese were not slow to point this out. A Christian teacher at the Boys' High School in Chongqing was later quoted as saying that in the past foreigners had called the Chinese barbarians. 'Now, where are their civilisation, their virtue and their love, but all only words and their own countries are now become barbarous.'[38] And for Clifford there was a more personal and pressing concern: Margaret had been due to join him that autumn, in preparation for their wedding the following year. Would it be safe for her to travel, and would her parents allow her?

By September he was back in Chengdu. Whatever effects the war might have in the future, on the campus things were going well. About 40 students enrolled that autumn, including a dozen in the new Medical School. The first university building to be completed, the American Methodist College, which would also house the Theology Department for the time being, was formally opened at the beginning of October. The ceremony was performed by the Military Governor, Hu Jingyi, and the British and German Consuls both made speeches, though otherwise ignoring each other's presence. The Military and Civil Governors each gave a surprise and unsolicited gift of $300 to demonstrate their support of the University. Later Joseph Beech, on his way to America, had a meeting in Peking with President Yuan Shikai, who gave a further £400 to show his strong support.[39]

Clifford's Chinese was now sufficiently good for him to take charge for a while of the Friends' dormitory. This was for university and, mainly, middle school students who had moved on from Friends' primary schools. It was his first real opportunity to engage with them.

On their own initiative the boys ran an English Club, and asked him to give an impromptu speech in English about the war, in which they were intensely interested. He joined them on the football field. 'On Wednesday afternoon I sallied forth for the first time to kick a football about with the boys, with the result that within a minute the captain had neatly placed a good stiff one fair in my eye. I retired with glory and a half bunged-up ocular.' Every morning he supervised drill – 'great sport. I get them into all kinds of queer contortions' – and led the boys in prayers in his uncertain Chinese. The first morning one of the boys got such a fit of the giggles that he had to be sent out.[40]

His Chinese was also good enough to make the students laugh deliberately, with his skill in comic turns and party games. In the absence of a piano he could do wonders on the Jew's harp, performed Maori war dances, and had a recitation routine involving a squeaky arm; he entertained the chemistry students in December with 'an evening's jollification ... games, music and much hilarity. I have got to know them a great deal better through this affair.'[41] Other missionaries, too, could let their hair down at parties which shows that they were not always as solemn as one might think. 'We had a delightfully hilarious time. People wore labels and paired off as Punch and Judy, the Spider and the Fly, Adam and Eve and Pinch-me and the like, which provided a fair amount of sport; and the mad games we had after supper made people laugh till their aching diaphragms hove groans instead.'[42]

At the end of the year he faced an examination in Chinese at the Language School. 'Dear me, I have been a year on this task, and how little of the language has soaked into my so-called brain!' His modesty always made him downplay his achievement. He was intensely committed to language study and took every chance to practise his Chinese with people of all classes – students, teachers, soldiers and boatmen. He also plagued his older colleagues with endless questions on language, and tells Margaret how they have teased him, 'all saying how sorry they are for you, and vowing to expose my character when you arrive ... I have got a bad name for always asking questions and talking about Chinese ... whenever I pull out a notebook or ask any small question I am set on and as often as not sat on ...'[43]

Very much in Clifford's mind throughout this autumn was if or when Margaret would set out to join him. Turkey's entry into the war on the side of Germany might close the Suez Canal route, and attacks by the German battle-cruiser *Emden* on British shipping in the Indian Ocean were another worry. Twice her departure was delayed; but the canal remained open, the *Emden* was destroyed on 9th November, and on 16th November he received a cable to say that she had set sail. Margaret's letters to Clifford have not survived, so we know little of her life during this year of separation; but like him she had spent several months studying at Kingsmead, and then was required by the FFMA to work at the Salvation Army Hospital in Clapton, east London, for three months.[44] The reasoning behind this is not clear, but perhaps it was felt that someone from such a comfortable background needed to be tested. Clearly she passed the test successfully.

In January it was back to Suining for the Yearly Meeting, and the Committee of Missionaries. Some 60 or 70 Chinese were there, including a few women, and this time Clifford could at least partly follow what was said, and get to know some of them. On the whole he was impressed: 'I was much struck by the spirit of independence and earnest thought in it, and also by the (growing) grasp of the spiritual, and once or twice one was glad to see how the vigour of a difficult discussion would be complemented by the quiet and brotherly atmosphere of an ensuing few minutes of devotion.' A long-term aim of the Mission was to hand over control of all the work to the Meeting, and this year it was openly discussed for the first time. Clifford, as he always would, thought the Chinese should be trusted. 'Though some think we should go very gingerly in delegating our powers and responsibilities to them, I feel it is worth taking risks in order to give them the stimulus and interest which come from bearing the burdens of counsel and decision. It may be lack of faith on our part that we do not place our mission work more fully in their hands.'[45]

As always he did all he could to get to know some of them personally. 'There are a number of very nice Chinese fellows about and I get walks and talks with them, which is of great value to Chinese language as well as to friendship.' His time in Suining also saw his first attempt at open-air preaching, outside the Meeting House, to a crowd that soon gathered, and 'listen with the good breeding inborn in Chinese. But it is hard to make them realise what it is we are really talking about.'[46]

He was much less impressed by the COM. Seven days of discussion – which even squeezed out any time for worshipping together – produced a mere twenty pages of minutes (which he once again typed out). 'Missionaries like ministers seem constitutionally unbusinesslike – I include myself. One can easily waste a lot of time in a large committee discussing some small point that a small committee ought to have settled. The Friends' principles of full freedom and no voting perhaps militate against efficiency.'[47] One important matter had been how to respond to a request from the FFMA to cut their financial estimates by 20%, or by over 40% if missionaries' allowances (i.e. their salaries) remained unchanged. The COM felt that the allowances should not be cut. Clifford was not happy with this. 'I am not sure myself that this is, all considered, the best plan, but there it is, one way of dealing with the situation.' While he could not speak for Margaret before they were married, he felt they should offer to take a cut of 20% in their own allowance, especially since missionaries usually had an easier time financially in the first two years. 'Of course it must mean that we really live on a less luxurious scale – not merely make it up from resources we have and others may not.'[48] His urge towards a simpler way of life, appropriate to the Chinese context, was strong, and put him at odds with his colleagues on the delicate matter of allowances for many years.

After the meetings were over he stayed on in Suining, taking a break to get quietly on with language study, before going on to Chongqing to meet Margaret. One day he got seven letters from her all at once, posted from various places from Port Said to Hankou; the excitement was so great that he could do little work that day. Already she was half way through the Yangzi Gorges, getting nearer every day. 'Do you know, I sometimes get almost a shock to realise how deeply I am in love – terribly deeply, Sweetheart. This plain, matter-of-fact I – I can't imagine it, until I think of you again.'[49] At the beginning of February he took a boat downriver to Chongqing, the only foreigner on board, sharing the life of the Chinese crew and passengers. The experience was 'enlightening but saddening ... I found the chance to tell the gospel in outline to pretty well all on board the other day – after much funky feeling and very faulty language. Some of them *did* listen – really delightfully – but how much they understood and what they were really interested in is hard to say.' He became 'great chums' with the captain's five-year-old son.[50] The journey was not without risk, as several boats ahead were robbed, but they got through safely, in seven days instead of the expected five. In Chongqing he found a strong upriver wind blowing his Margaret towards him.

She was coming upriver on a houseboat, as Clifford had a year before. Escorting her was Alice Deane, a veteran FFMA missionary returning after several years at home. The problem of an escort had been another reason delaying her departure, as there was no way a single young woman without a word of Chinese could get to Sichuan. But there was no anxiety over two women travelling together, provided one had the language and the experience, although British Consuls disapproved. This is an indication of how safe missionaries felt themselves to be in China, despite the growing problems of banditry and violence. Having a white face gave them security. The boat journey itself was unusually hazardous, as Alice Deane wrote to Mrs Lees later: 'She was the brave one as I don't think she realised the dangers of the river. I was very nervous, and *never* want another journey by river.'[51] As they approached Chongqing Margaret spotted one of the 'red boats' of the official lifeboat service coming down towards them on the swift-flowing stream. It grew closer, and she suddenly recognised a familiar figure standing on the prow. Clifford's Chinese had been good enough to persuade the crew to take him on board. The last day they had been together they had gone rowing on Lake Geneva, nearly eighteen months before; now, in a romantic gesture both playful and serious, it was on the water that they met again.[52]

Now that Margaret and Clifford were reunited, his letters to her come to an end, and if he continued writing a journal it has not survived. He would have written official letters to Hodgkin in London, but they were destroyed with most of the FFMA archives in the 1920s. For the next few years we can only glimpse fragments of their life, and yet these years, up to their first furlough in 1919, were important ones for them, as Clifford set up the Chemistry Department at the University, and their first two children, Ruth and Jean, were born.

They returned together to Chengdu at the end of February 1915, and Margaret went to live with the Davidsons at Qinlonggai, while Clifford returned to the Silcocks on the campus. This was far enough apart to satisfy propriety, although not those who had thought Margaret should be in Tongchuan, three days' rather than thirty minutes' journey away. Margaret was not entirely among strangers, as the Davidsons had been joined by their son Robin, born in China twenty-five years before, and dedicated to mission work in his cradle. With him had come his new bride Kathleen, who had been a fellow student with Margaret at Kingsmead. Margaret settled down at once to language study, reading St John's Gospel with a private teacher in the mornings, and walking alone through the city to the Language School in the afternoon. As a foreign woman walking alone she felt 'rather special', and found herself the focus of some attention, especially from children who 'made remarks', but generally she felt people were friendly.[53]

Her fellow missionaries also liked what they saw of her. 'A lot of people have sung her praises and said how fortunate we are in our Mission,' Margaret Silcock wrote to Mrs Lees. 'I am not saying this as flattery – just to tell your mother-heart that others besides Dr Stubbs are sharing in the gift you have given to him and us in West China.'[54] The wedding day was 2nd June. Clifford had wanted to keep it simple, but was to some extent overruled. The ceremony, in both languages, took place in the Meeting House in Qinlonggai, which had been pre-pared and decorated by students from the University. There was a large attendance of missionaries and Chinese. RJD gave away the bride, and presided together with Margaret Silcock and Yang Shaoquan. The Sil-cocks' two small boys were pages. To the accompaniment of fire-crackers they left for a civil ceremony at the British Consulate, after which came both a Chinese Feast and an 'English Dinner for the Mission Circle'[55]. Mary-Jane Davidson could not be prevented from making a three-tier wedding cake, although a 90°F temperature made it less than a success. This was in addition to an equally unseasonal plum pudding prepared by Mrs Lees and brought out by Margaret. Even allowing for the emotion of the occasion, Margaret Silcock's letter to Mrs Lees, written the same evening, suggests something of the impact the bridal couple had made on the Chengdu community. 'Dr Stubbs though he is very quiet has won some real true friends, and Margaret has taken our hearts by storm.'[56]

That evening the Stubbs set out in a small houseboat for their honeymoon on the Buddhist holy mountain of Emeishan. Over half a century later Margaret could recall it all vividly.[57] It took them four days by boat to Jiajing (now Leshan), where they disembarked, and travelled by chair for two days to the foot of the mountain. After a few days in a temple on the lower slopes they set out for the summit, which reaches a height of over 10,000 feet. Margaret showed herself Clifford's equal in a climb that took several days. They had three carriers to bring their bedding and food, and stayed overnight in small pilgrimage temples. Most of the way was paved with steps. At the summit there was a flat, grassy area, and low, black, wooden buildings – temples and hostels. From there, if you were lucky, you could see the mountains of Tibet. These were usually obscured by clouds, but one morning at sunrise they had a glorious view of glittering snowy peaks. There was not a foreigner to be seen, and the only inhabitants were some monks. Clifford struck up a conversation about science with one old monk, and amazed him by igniting some marsh gas collected from a pool. Later he found some waterlogged planks, made a raft, and they took to the pool – great fun, but 'scary' because its depth was unknown.

After two weeks at the summit their supplies were running out. Ever the man of science, Clifford had arranged to flash Morse code messages to some friends staying near the foot of the mountain, using a hurricane lamp, and shielding it with the lid of a packing basket. But every evening clouds covered the peak, and only at the last attempt did he get a message through asking for bread, carriers, money and letters. After descending they spent a further two months on the lower slopes of the mountain with other missionaries, studying Chinese in the mornings, playing tennis in the afternoons, and exploring the spectacular surroundings. 'Trip to Si Dji Pin with Davidsons. Had a wonderful dew bath (there is a deep cleft with a river at the bottom and on the other side a towering cliff rising sheer to the Golden Summit. Made stern resolve to camp at Si Dji Pin – which we did next year.'[58]

That autumn of 1915 Clifford found himself, earlier than expected, setting up the Chemistry Department, and undertaking a full teaching load. This meant he had to break off studying at the Language School, and so missed the final term, devoted to the Chinese classics; he always regretted missing this introduction to the foundations of Chinese ideas and beliefs.[59] But the demands of the University, even more urgent with the founding of the Medical School, made it impossible. He was the only qualified teacher of chemistry, and the syllabus could not be delivered without his full participation.

His teaching load was over nineteen hours a week – 'too big a one in a foreign language and with work of an advanced kind'[60] – and this illustrates how limited the University's resources were, in personnel as well as in funding. And university work was not his only responsibility. The Senate Minutes for July 1913[61] noted that, in addition to their university courses, staff were also responsible for the Union Middle School, most mission primary schools in Chengdu, also evangelistic and medical work, the West China Education Union, and the Language School. Clifford taught in the Middle School, helped with services at Qinlonggai (especially with the music), and his mission duties took him several times a year to Tongchuan or Suining (three days' travel in each direction), for meetings of the Northern District Committee of the COM.

Clifford was not the only Friend teaching at Huaxi. There was of course Harry Silcock, who had been at the University from the start, and was successfully building up an Education Department. There was also an American Friend, Robert Simkin, who had been with the FFMA in Sichuan since 1906, initially as a missionary; but he would become increasingly involved with the University as a teacher of theology, both to full-time students and on the summer Bible schools for Chinese evangelists. He and Clifford would be recognised as two of the most fluent Chinese-speakers on the staff, but in many respects he was Clifford's opposite – very tall, humourless and long-winded, 'rigid and unadaptable, unable to see others' point of view',[62] he had difficulty in working with his colleagues, which he attributed to a natural inability of English and Americans to collaborate. But he was equally firm in upholding Quaker principles: when in 1911 missionaries were ordered to leave Chengdu under armed escort because of the Revolution, Simkin made his own way across country and was robbed and beaten by bandits on the way. He was also notable for loyally accepting his colleagues' decisions about the work he should do, despite disagreeing with them. For many years he argued that he should leave the FFMA, and work instead for the American Friends' Board of Foreign Missions, despite the opposition of both bodies; his obstinacy was such that he finally won his case, and in 1920 became a one-man mission in Chengdu, teaching at Huaxi and running a primary school in the city. His unhappiness had been made worse by the sickness and death of his wife; he would return from furlough in 1922 having remarried and in a much more relaxed frame of mind. He remained an important figure in the Yearly Meeting, and a powerful ally for Clifford during the 1920s, in fighting for Quaker Principles at Huaxi.[63]

Clifford was of course not the first person to teach modern chemistry in China, and it is worth having a look at what had already been done over the previous fifty years or so. One of the enigmas of history, called the 'Needham Question' after the British scholar Joseph Needham, is why China, despite its astonishing record of creativity and invention, never developed modern science. It was not until the second half of the nineteenth century, in response to the shock of defeat in the second Opium War of 1857–60, that some Chinese officials, known as the 'Self-Strengtheners', saw the need for China to learn from the West to protect herself from further humiliation. Their aims were primarily military, to develop modern armaments and a modern fleet, but they understood that science was an essential tool for this work. They built arsenals and shipyards, and sent students abroad to study. But the 'Self-Strengtheners' were a small, if influential, minority. The dominant attitude of the Qing dynasty remained as it had been throughout the nineteenth century: to maintain their traditional Confucian ideals and to resist all foreign ideologies. Western science was not included in the traditional civil service examinations by which all officials were selected, whose syllabus was exclusively based on Chinese philosophical and literary classics. So few educated Chinese had any understanding of or interest in what science might have to offer, apart from a few eccentrics who had failed the examinations and took up an interest in nature studies. It was a small number of missionaries, especially doctors, who first introduced science teaching to China in the nineteenth century, and developed a new Chinese vocabulary in which to communicate the substances, processes and equipment involved in scientific activity. It was a missionary, Benjamin Hobson, who in 1857 coined the term for chemistry itself – *huaxue*, the study of change – by which it has been known ever since.[64]

One of the best known of those who helped introduce modern science was John Fryer, an Englishman who had come to China in 1861, initially as a mission teacher, and who was later employed for over 20 years at the Jiangnan Arsenal near Shanghai. There he collaborated with a remarkable Chinese scholar, Xu Shou. Since neither of them was a scientist by training, a good number of misunderstandings crept into their translations; but their achievement was to show that 'the Chinese language could be adapted to the needs of modern science.'[65] They invented Chinese terms for the elements, for inorganic compounds, and for chemical reactions. This sometimes required them to create new characters, although they tried wherever possible to use ones that were fairly obscure, and whose meanings could not be confused with the new ones. They were successful enough for 5000 of the terms they invented to remain in use today. They also published magazines to popularise ideas about science and technology for a wider Chinese audience.

But Fryer and Xu were not the only translators of works of chemistry into Chinese. Another educational missionary, the American W.A.P. Martin, was doing similar work at a college in Peking, and in Canton J.G. Kerr ran what was in the late nineteenth century the best medical college in the country, combining basic science with its clinical application.[66] But there was no means of standardising their work; these translators, living hundreds of miles apart, often chose quite different Chinese words to translate the Western ones, and those who had studied medicine might use quite different terms again from a non-medic, for the same substances or processes. In addition, Chinese merchants who were in contact with Westerners in the port cities had also invented their own words for various chemical substances – acids, medicines – that they encountered in the course of trade. The China Medical Missionary Association in the 1880s did its best to produce standard vocabularies, but these were only used in the context of missionary education. There would be no national organisation in China with the power to harmonise and impose standard terminology until the 1930s. Clifford, remote in Chengdu, would produce teaching materials and write textbooks without being sure if his words would have meaning in south or east China.

These early textbooks were also written in classical Chinese, as every literary production on a serious subject had to be, before the 1920s brought a great cultural change. This was rather as if all scientific works in Europe had been written in Latin, and thus excluded anyone without a classical education. Clifford had his first encounter with a Chinese chemistry textbook with his teacher in July 1914 – 'My word, it is stiff!' – yet only a month later he wrote, 'It is surprising how often difficulties vanish when one comes to them. I had been expecting a great task learning the names and characters for the elements, but after all it is comparatively easy, with much to connect them in the mind with their English equivalents, so that in one morning I have really got off the most important ones.'[67] This is a tribute to the translator's skill, but also reveals the swiftness of Clifford's intelligence.

The obstacles in the way of developing modern science in China were immense. In the nineteenth century only a tiny minority of missionaries had any interest in teaching it, or the ability to do so; while educated Chinese needed to acquire a whole new way of thinking which, convinced of the superiority of Chinese ways, they were loath to do. James Reardon-Anderson writes of 'how difficult it was for scholars reared in the classics to break loose from the traditional mental framework and accept new categories of thought. The notion of a special method of enquiry that posits testable hypotheses, subjects them to experimentation and observation, and expresses the findings in measurable mathematical terms, that maintains that knowledge susceptible to such methods is impermanent and certain to be replaced by something better, and that distinguishes this type of knowledge from others, not susceptible to the methods described – this notion is nowhere evident in the writings of late Qing literati.'[68] The idea of science as an autonomous intellectual activity, to which the world of politics was irrelevant, was also alien to the Confucian ethos, which taught that government was the central human concern, and that nothing could be 'outside politics'.

By the time Clifford arrived in China, although the 1911 Revolution had created a much stronger and more widespread urge to understand 'Western Learning', things were not that much better. True, there had been an increase in the number of Chinese studying abroad and returning with Western degrees, the development of Chinese industry was creating a demand for scientific skills, and missionary colleges had grown in size and number; but these three factors were tiny, and quite unconnected with each other, in a vast country increasingly wracked by political turbulence and civil war.

Another difficulty in the way of teaching chemistry in China was the lack of apparatus and materials, all of which had to be imported. China had no chemical industry, apart from the manufacture of gunpowder, though one would begin to develop during the war as imports of industrial chemicals were sharply reduced. The low level of industrial development meant that job opportunities for chemical graduates were few; chemistry teachers like Clifford responded by stressing the application of chemistry to traditional agriculture-related activities like sugar refining and tanning.

But one of the most serious problems related to student attitudes. Not only was a scientific habit of thought absent, but traditionally a scholar was a gentleman, who did not engage in physical activity, or get his hands dirty. Study involved the reading and memorising of literary texts, and since a knowledge of science had come to China by means of translated texts, it was natural to apply this same method to science. They did not see the need for laboratory work, and carrying out experiments. There were several government colleges in Chengdu where science was taught, but the students refused to do experimental work. An American observer in the 1920s, George Twiss, summed up the problem: 'These college students are not only deficient in knowledge of the elementary scientific facts and theories, but they are also lacking in the habits of accuracy, the ideals of thoroughness and exactitude, and the appreciation of careful and methodical observation, experimenting and thinking that are the very essence and foundation of scientific study. Furthermore they lack this knowledge and these qualities to such an extent that *they are not even aware of their deficiencies*.'[69] One should add that some Chinese observers made similar comments; the weight of the Chinese educational tradition of memorisation and rote repetition was not easily cast off.

Most of these problems, common to China as a whole, were greater in Sichuan due to its remoteness and the difficulties of transport. Most chemical materials and equipment had to be imported from Europe, and were especially hard to obtain during the war. Then they had to be hauled up through the Yangzi Gorges. For the same reasons few entrepreneurs wanted to set up modern industries there, and not many students returning from study abroad would head for Sichuan to find work. The government colleges in Chengdu referred to were often better equipped than Huaxi, but they were headed by traditional scholars with no understanding of the Western ideas they were meant to teach, discipline was very poor, and the students did more or less what they liked. The situation was ironic: the government colleges had poor staff, good equipment, and plenty of students, while Huaxi had better-qualified staff, little equipment, and few students.[70]

Clifford had to start teaching full-time in the autumn term of 1915 because it had become necessary to deliver a full curriculum in chemistry with the opening of medical courses at Huaxi the previous year. He had taken a few laboratory classes already. During the summer of 1914 he had done some work with three students in the existing lab, but it was hopelessly inadequate, with no water, gas or electricity. In the autumn, when the Medical School opened with a doctor teaching elementary chemistry, Clifford helped out for two hours in the lab each week. He also supervised a two-hour lab class in the Middle School. 'It is good practice for me and not at all bad sport. The students are mostly pretty green, many never having done chemistry before, and their work tends to be slow and inaccurate. Our lab accommodation and apparatus is very inadequate however ... Some of the recent first-year meds., especially those from Govt. schools, are fearfully bumble-footed specimens. Many seem to have little idea of how to study, the old Chinese idea that it consists in attending so many classes being still quite prevalent. I am sure my laboratory class will be a great advantage not only from the point of view of chemical vocabulary, but from understanding the capacities and needs of the student material. It is also a training in running an experimental course, which I have never done before.'[71]

Sadly we have no account from Clifford of his early days of full-time teaching, but the gap is partly filled by a later account of his work by his colleague William Sewell.[72] Initially Clifford taught in a lath-and-plaster hut with broken floorboards and rickety tables, which made accurate experiments impossible. In 1918 he was allocated part of the new Administration Building, and here he improvised an approximation to a proper laboratory. Although it was a new building (designed by Frederick Rowntree) it had not been intended for a laboratory, and had no plumbing, drainage, gas or electricity. Clifford designed benches and had them built by local carpenters and covered with black lacquer, which would be unaffected by heat, acids or alkalis. Then he personally plumbed in a water system, which was dependent on coolies filling small tanks with water from a nearby well. The water pipes and the drains were made of bamboos, skilfully linked to each other, which proved leakproof and indestructible. He got a local tinsmith to make a still, so that alcohol could be distilled from local rice wine, to be used for burners, and to supply local hospitals. He persuaded the University Board to buy an apparatus for aerating petrol, to supply modified Bunsen burners made by local craftsmen, which worked well as long as the coolies remembered to wind up the stone whose weight drove the drum. In 1920 Clifford's old doctoral supervisor, Professor Miles Walker, donated a three-quarter-kilowatt petrol–electric generator, and Metropolitan Vickers a small 110V DC generator;[73] but otherwise he depended as far as possible on local materials and skills. This was not just because of transport problems, or the cost of imported goods, but from the belief that if Chinese chemistry was to develop it had to be dependent on its own resources. Likewise, students' work was directed towards traditional local industries – sugar refining, paper-making, silk dyeing, salt manufacture – so that its usefulness was immediately apparent.

Chinese students' capacity for patience and hard work could make them rewarding to teach. 'The students exhibited a placid temperament in the laboratory, the heritage of submission by the young, which helped to produce painstaking analysts and routine workers. There was an amazing capacity for unwearying attention to detail, and an ability to obtain results from apparatus so simple that many Westerners might consider it rudimentary.' But there were also cultural problems to be overcome. A common Chinese expression is *cha bu duo* – 'not much out', 'more or less right' – and students had to learn that this was not good enough when it came to measuring out chemicals for an experiment. Then there was the matter of the lab assistant, who refused to take responsibility for the chemical apparatus, as he would in a Western laboratory.[74] Because he was socially inferior to the students he could not refuse any requests from them, or report any breakages. So this was another responsibility for Clifford to take on himself, in addition to his teaching load – and the many hours of preparation needed when the courses were being given for the first time.

Gradually he acquired some assistance in the teaching, mostly from senior students. Initially his most important colleague was Shi Rucong, from a local gentry family, who had worked as a chemist in a government department in Chengdu.[75] He worked closely with Clifford as a chemical technician and assistant throughout the 1920s, and almost certainly before then, although without a degree he could not become a teacher. A loyal colleague and a good friend, he could also be feckless and absent-minded – on one occasion he was taking to the printers the manuscript of a textbook Clifford had been working on all summer, and, distracted by meeting a friend, left it behind in the rickshaw. Clifford had to rewrite the book.[76] Shi and his brother – the family as a whole – were unusually open to contacts with foreigners, and welcomed foreign guests in their home. They even invited one Friend, Leonard Walker, to live with them for several months to improve his Chinese – an almost unheard-of thing. His was the first Chinese home in which Clifford would stay overnight, in 1925. It was a traditional courtyard house with portraits of ancestors in official robes in the reception room. Shi was perhaps typical of those educated Chinese who were very sympathetic to Christianity – even ready to call themselves Christians, yet unwilling to commit themselves to church membership. The two brothers were especially drawn towards the pacifist message and in 1921 founded a local group on the lines of the Fellowship of Reconciliation. But although Shi worked with Clifford for many years he never joined any branch of the church.[77]

Clifford and Margaret settled down to domestic life, and their family soon grew. Their eldest daughter Ruth was born in 1916, followed by Jean in 1918. Initially their home was two rooms and a kitchen attached to the Middle School dormitory. The building of their new house was delayed until the end of 1915 as the FFMA had suspended all new expenditure on the outbreak of the war, and they did not move in until the spring of 1917. From then on the nearby river was a fine spot for an early-morning dip; and Clifford also designed his own boat for outings, a high point of which was shooting the rapids downstream. The house, which they named 'Marécottes' in memory of their Swiss holiday in 1913, was built of grey brick, with two storeys and an attic, a Chinese-style roof, and verandas framed by red-painted pillars with lattice work of blue, red, green and yellow. But inside it was an English home, with a fireplace and a piano.[78] Adjoining was a separate lath-and-plaster kitchen and servants' annex. The household included Leng Jiaxin and his family, and a cook called Pen Si. Pen was a vivid and contentious personality, but his skills and loyalty in the end outweighed the problems he caused, and he worked for various Quaker families for many years.

Pen would have had to learn to prepare food in the English style, food he and Leng would never think of touching. Missionaries treated Chinese food – and Sichuan cuisine is one of the finest – as something to be avoided, and never served in their own homes. As far as possible they lived off food brought upriver from Shanghai – bags of flour, tins of milk and butter and jam, bully beef, etc. When RJD invited Chinese friends and students to Qinlonggai to eat – he enjoyed doing this and was a marvellous host – they had to cope with knives, forks and finger-bowls, which cannot have helped them relax. Clifford and Margaret shared this distaste and fear – though Clifford did have genuine problems in digesting Chinese food. Within a few days of arriving in Sichuan he records eating 'a Chinese-style dinner – chopsticks and all – which led to subsequent unrest of my digestive apparatus.'[79] This was but the first of many similar accounts. It was another year before he went to his first 'Chinese feast', given by Yang Shaoquan; which he called 'enjoyable – for once in a blue moon'. By early 1915 he was 'getting quite to like it, including snake and long-buried eggs'.[80] But ten years later he would still complain in a letter: '2 Chinese meals in one day! I come back and help myself to the biscuit barrel.'[81] After his death a colleague would consider the number of Chinese meals he had to eat as one of the sacrifices he made to the cause.

Chinese food could not be avoided when travelling, or when mixing with Chinese outside the home, but at home Pen Si had to do his best to concoct a simulacrum of English middle-class cuisine. What this meant can be seen from the menu which survives from an occasion when Clifford entertained the warlord Yang Sen in 1925: soup, omelette, meat balls, jelly and custard, fruit, and cake and coffee.[82] However, the missionary community soon found that tinned milk did not provide adequate nourishment for their children, so each family took to keeping one or two cows. The empty spaces of the campus provided plenty of room for grazing, and the habit eventually led to the founding of a Department of Agriculture in the University, and a cattle-breeding station.[83] Pen Si took with enthusiasm to cow-keeping, and soon set up a small dairy sideline. When the Stubbs went camping on Mount Emei in 1917, Pen Si and a cow went with them.[84]

In 1914 Clifford had written to his future parents-in-law to assure them that their daughter would not run any risks in coming to China. 'You must not be anxious about dangers from robbers etc. here. Matters are really very quiet in China as a whole, and Sichuan is a well-ordered province, not to be compared with the mountain fastnesses in other provinces where the bandits have their homes.'[85] This was about to change, mainly as a result of events elsewhere in China. In 1915 President Yuan Shikai had dismissed Sichuan's governor Hu Jingyi and summoned him to Peking. His replacement, Chen Yi, came from the province of Hubei; this signified a return to the old imperial practice of appointing outsiders to important provincial posts. Chen Yi brought with him an army of 10,000 northern soldiers. It was becoming clear that Yuan's intention was to restore the old imperial order, and on 1st January 1916 he proclaimed himself Emperor. This provoked widespread opposition, especially among military leaders, several of whom rose in rebellion. In March Yuan withdrew his claim to the throne, and then, in June, he died. His nominal successor, Li Yuanhong, was a nonentity, and China was left effectively without a functioning central government. This was the start of what is known as the Warlord Era, as local generals struggled for supremacy. Generals in eastern and southern China might rule a whole province, or even several; there was a broad division between the conservative north, and the radical, nationalist south, but the generals' personal ambitions were mainly paramount. Sichuan reflected this on a smaller scale; some generals had, or at least proclaimed, northern or southern allegiances, but to this was added the hostility of Sichuanese armies to those from other provinces. A series of fluctuating alliances and betrayals followed, incomprehensible to outsiders, as the province was fought over and bled white by predatory militarists. This would be the condition of Sichuan for the rest of Clifford's life.

The first general to rise against Yuan was Cai E, a much respected commander from Yunnan to the south west. He invaded Sichuan in January 1916, gained the support of several local generals, and by July was in Chengdu. However, fighting continued in various parts of the province, as local juntas competed for power, and this affected both Tongchuan and Suining, where Friends' missions were located. Cai's prestige and personal qualities might have enabled him to establish a sound government in the province, but unfortunately he was dying of throat cancer, and was replaced by a much less admired Yunnanese general. Over the following months the Yunnanese, supported by other outsiders from Guizhou, set up garrisons in all the main cities of the province, provoking intense hostility from the locals. Yunnan and Guizhou were mountainous, poor and backward provinces, and produced fierce and ruthless soldiers. Their interest in Sichuan had little to do with national politics, but lay more in Sichuan's wealth, which they proceeded to loot. Tensions between the Sichuanese and the outsiders grew over the following months, and came to a head in April 1917, when the Yunnanese were attacked within the walls of Chengdu, at the very gate of the Friends' compound in Qinlonggai. This led to a week of slaughter and destruction before a truce was negotiated, during which whole sections of the city were burned to the ground. In July fighting began again and went on for three weeks, before the outsiders were expelled.

Throughout this turmoil missionaries, and foreigners generally, seemed to lead a charmed life. No side wished to harm them, for fear of provoking intervention from foreign countries, although it is hard to see how any country could have intervened to much effect in Sichuan. They had no enemies, their persons and property were treated as sacrosanct, and they were able to play a useful role as neutral intermediaries. The British Consul, Meyrick Hewlett, helped negotiate the truce in April, and Quaker missionaries performed a similar role as peacemakers in Tongchuan and Suining, earning themselves the gratitude of the townspeople. But when the fighting began on the Davidsons' doorstep they had a terrifying experience, as bullets whistled past and shells exploded all around. They spent the night lying on the dining room floor as bullets came through the lath-and-plaster walls, and they could hear the screams of the dying in the burning houses nearby. Every quarter of an hour RJD went out to see if the flames were spreading and they would be forced to flee. But they survived the night, and the next day the women were evacuated to the University, where they lodged for a week with the Stubbs.[86]

Although they were in extreme danger, this was because they were in the line of fire between the two sides. No one fired deliberately on the compound, and refugees scrambled in over the walls to what they saw as a place of safety. Soldiers of both sides let the Davidsons pass through their lines to the West Gate. Foreigners could pass through the gate, or climb the city wall, but no Chinese could do so. Even foreigners' servants, who had consular passports, could move through the streets with only minimal harassment. The University was likewise a safe area, although during the fighting in July many shells exploded on the campus, and the doctors had their hands full treating the wounded. The student dormitories were filled with refugees, and the students themselves were 'horribly frightened yet keeping up a brave front', as just over the narrow river the smoke poured from the burning city, and they wondered what was happening to their families.[87]

Much missionary work went on as usual – with even better results as, in their distress and despair, many turned to see if Christianity had anything to offer them. The Gospel was preached to the refugees on the campus. 'The conditions politically may be bad, but from a missionary point of view they were never better,' stated *The Friend* in 1916,[88] and the FFMA *Annual Report* for 1917 declared, 'It is wonderful how little political disturbance and even civil war have interrupted the quiet steady work of our missionaries.' Such comments bring home the extent to which missionaries were in China, but not of it. They were not unmoved by the suffering around them and did what little they could to alleviate it, but apart from occasional scares they remained comfortable and secure. Secure enough, indeed, to take their usual holidays in the mountains. When fighting broke out again in Qinlonggai in July 1917 the Davidsons were away in a temple resort at Bailudin. Clifford and Margaret, having missed their holiday the previous year because of the birth of Ruth, went camping on Mount Emei for several weeks, on a high meadowland which reminded them of Switzerland.[89] The sufferings of China, in the end, were not theirs.

By the end of 1917 the University had 77 students, with just over 200 in the Middle School. It had been feared that the autumn enrolment would be reduced by the political violence of the summer, and a temporary closure was seriously considered, but numbers were even greater than before, with more students than ever from high-status families. In 1918 the University instituted an annual 'University Day', with feasts, ceremonial, speeches and demonstrations, which attracted the elite of Chengdu, both traditional and modern – scholars, chairmen of guilds, generals, businessmen and college principals. The students lined up in white uniforms, the faculty processed in academic robes. The Chinese National Anthem was sung. The next day local newspapers reported favourably and at some length, noting the absence of tobacco and alcohol, and praising the patriotism implied by the singing of the Anthem. After a mere eight years the University was accepted as a major presence in the life of Chengdu.[90]

Clifford's official report for 1917[91] makes little reference to political events, and is rather reticent about his teaching. 'Chemistry teaching is absorbingly interesting, not least so when one has to struggle with the Chinese language and the Chinese students' constitutional difficulties in grasping an exact science. It is not, however, first-class material for a missionary report.' All his teaching was in Chinese. He had also written, in Chinese, 'A Laboratory Manual in Junior College Chemistry', one of the first five publications by WCUU. He was sufficiently pleased with it to indulge in a rare example of self-congratulation: 'we think [it] is the best on its subject we have seen in Chinese (we have seen one other).' Two years later his 'Handbook of Experimental Chemistry' came out. This offered a course 'in simple practical work, including an elementary study of the metals and acid radicals, their properties and tests.'[92] His teaching always emphasised the need for practical experiment in the laboratory, to develop a proper scientific habit of mind. His report on teaching concludes, 'There have been no fatal accidents this year.' This is presumably a Stubbsian joke – there is no record at any time of fatal accidents in the laboratory.

'We have three courses to teach,' his report continued, 'and find it leaves little time for much else ... the need for better lab. accommodation is more and more felt.' In 1918 he got this, when he moved from his lath-and-plaster 'laboratory' to the Administration Building.

Although these were still temporary quarters, and in some ways not very suitable, 'one feels that there is at last a real laboratory which is a credit to the University.' There were now 10 students doing advanced work, several of whom were doing 'good analytical work (qualitative) which may be of assistance in studying the mineral resources of the province.' His teaching in the Middle School was even more fulfilling. 'One enjoys no teaching more than that spent in leading a score and a half of boys in the MS through the door of personal investigation into the study of some of the great facts and ideas of science.'[93]

Increasingly the University was looking to supply the immediate needs of China, and already the Chemistry Department was considering the industrial applications of chemistry. Before the war, soda, used in a wide range of Chinese industries – paper, dyeing, textiles – had all been imported, mainly from Britain. The war forced China to develop its own production, and in 1919 Clifford's students began to play a part in this, starting up a soda factory and putting a 'patriotic soap' on the market.[94] The term reflects the growing nationalism of the period, and shows how even manufacturing soap could be seen as a contribution to China's self-esteem.

Even if chemistry teaching left 'little time for much else', Clifford crammed a lot into that little time. He had taken over from Silcock, who was now vice-president of the university, as principal of the Friends' dormitory, in charge of thirteen university students and thirty middle school boys. This was the 'missionary' side of his work, and it was less encouraging than chemistry. 'Except in the case of three or four, there is little evidence of much spiritual advance in most of the students. In both terms the dormitory has been filled to its utmost capacity, the great majority being self-supporting students, about half being previously not under Christian influence.'[95] Those not from a Christian background might well have resented the regime of compulsory prayers and Bible study, but he won their confidence by joining with them in their sports, including 'hare and hounds' in the open countryside and, with Margaret, extending an open invitation to them in their home every Sunday. In the dormitory he was helped by a senior student, Fang Shuxuan (S.H. Fong), in the role of 'Chinese Proctor'. A promising young man from a prosperous family, Fang was seen even before his graduation as a potential Quaker leader, and he eventually became president of the University.

In addition Clifford was much involved with the local Meeting. He ran two Bible classes at Qinlonggai, preparing weekly lists of daily readings in a consecutive study of the life of Christ. He was a member of the Chengdu Monthly Meeting Finance Committee, and Auditor and Report Secretary of the COM. Margaret meanwhile was teaching English in the Union Middle School, and taking Sunday School classes at Qinlonggai. 'We have much to learn,' she wrote, 'but there are moments which make one very happy. Such are the times when the children are clustered in 6 or 7 little groups about their teachers and there is a gentle murmur of the story being told to the eager little listeners. Again, when the children are kneeling by their sandtrays, intent on making the town, road, cave etc where the story has taken place.' She was helped by some Christian students from the university and middle school, meeting them for preparation each week. 'We have had afternoons of games with teachers and scholars and this has helped towards a friendly intimacy.'[96]

Clifford had also to attend meetings of the Northern District Committee of the COM, at which the missionaries from Chengdu, Tongchuan and Suining met every few months to discuss mission affairs. For most of these he would have to take a three-day journey, spending the nights in an inn or, if he was lucky, on the floor of a local mission *Fuyintang* (Gospel Hall). He travelled by bicycle along the narrow paths between rice fields, which was still all that Sichuan had in the way of roads. The alternative form of transport was sedan chair, which was much more expensive, and it may be that he had come to feel uncomfortable, as a few other missionaries did, at being carried by fellow human beings. However, when the path went uphill, and was replaced by stone steps, Leng Jiaxin, who always accompanied him, would find someone to carry the bike for him in exchange for a few 'cash' – the smallest Chinese coins. The bicycle itself was an object of great curiosity. There were only a few 'foreign horses' in the province; they evoked a fascinated interest, and soon a little jingle was composed about them: *'Yang ma qu de hao, Yang ma bu chi cao!* – The foreign horse goes well, the foreign horse doesn't eat grass.'[97]

The annual Meetings (YM and COM) in January 1919 were dominated by a rather ill-tempered debate on the devolution of power from the (foreign) COM to the (largely Chinese) Yearly Meeting. Even among Quakers there was a spectrum of views on missionary relations with their Chinese members. Clifford's contacts in Chengdu were mainly with educated people, and trust was central to his approach. But converts in, for example, Tongchuan were mostly from a poor and uneducated background; the district had been run in a rather paternalistic way for years, but there were understandable doubts about the wisdom of allowing financial control to be transferred to the members. At the other extreme were some young men from the Chongqing Monthly Meeting, influenced by the radical atmosphere of a commercial city in close touch with events elsewhere in China, who were inclined to see missionary control as imperialistic, and wanted all power transferred directly to the Monthly Meetings. This year the meetings were held in Chongqing, and so their views were strongly represented.

The discussion was very tense, and RJD grew increasingly upset. He had put forward a scheme for devolution, but could not reconcile the opposing parties. Eventually he burst into tears, and the meeting was shocked into agreement.[98] His proposal, accepted in such emotional circumstances, was that the Mission's evangelistic and educational work, and the buildings associated with them, should henceforth be under the authority of a central executive committee of sixteen members – eight Chinese chosen by the Yearly Meeting, and eight foreigners chosen by the COM. The executive would determine appointments and salaries (excluding those of missionaries), and could apply directly to the FFMA for funds. Within two years the medical work would also be placed under the executive, and little other than the work and locations of missionaries themselves remained under the COM.

Clifford felt that missionaries had contributed to the 'unharmony – I am afraid it almost amounted to that … Those days we all felt to be ones of considerable strain … I think we were reaping the fruit of having in former years set up some form of collaboration without (unintentionally largely) attaching great weight to its results.'[99] It illustrated the lack of planning and coordination which he had long felt to be a major weakness of the Friends' Mission. The new executive might help to remedy that, and he was happy enough with the result, unlike the missionary in charge of Tongchuan, who resigned in protest. Clifford, despite his comparatively junior status, was immediately chosen as a member of the new executive.[100]

In the summer of 1919 Clifford, Margaret and their children returned to England for their first furlough, a time for renewing family ties, but by no means just a holiday. Clifford had to get up to date with developments in chemistry, and would also be expected to carry out 'deputation work', visiting Friends' Meetings around the country to publicise the work of the Mission and hopefully to raise funds or even recruits. They left in June, preceded by a glowing testimonial from RJD: 'Dr Stubbs and family leave us this week – we will miss them very much. He has done excellent work for the University and the Church while he has been here. His interest in the work of the FFMA could not have been keener if he had been born a Friend. He is a member of the Society here, and that is the only Church association he at present holds, not having kept up his church membership in England. He holds higher degrees than anyone in the University, but there is not a humbler man associated with it. He has been keen in his own subject, he writes the notes of his lectures on the blackboard in Chinese characters, but he has also taken a most active part in everything that affects the Church and Mission. He gave valued help in connection with collaboration at last YM, and has locally taken his full share in the responsibilities of Monthly Meeting. I think you ought to know these facts, he won't tell you himself.'[101]

Clifford's modesty gets in the way of understanding all he had done during the years since 1913, but no similar tribute from the Mission's senior member about any other colleague survives. The reference to his writing Chinese characters on the blackboard suggests that few of his colleagues could do this, and it is likely that many missionaries' command of Chinese was actually quite limited. Among Clifford's papers is a test paper from the Language School in 1914.[102] This reveals that students were expected to understand Chinese characters, but it was sufficient to write Chinese in a Romanised form, although bonus marks could be earned for writing the characters. It is interesting that Harry Silcock, when back in England, tells a Chinese correspondent how nice it is to receive a letter in Chinese, and apologises for not being able to reciprocate.[103] Clifford's command of written and spoken Chinese was perhaps the greatest achievement of his first tour of duty in China, a result not only of hard work but of a commitment to making friends, and spending time, with Chinese of all backgrounds. It was in this way that he laid the groundwork for the rest of his career.

5

1919–1920, England

Clifford, Margaret and their two little girls arrived in Southampton on
2nd August 1919, having travelled via Canada, and went straight to the
Lees' home in Birmingham. Their plan was to spend two months
resting and seeing family – Eric Stubbs and his new wife Kathleen, and
the numerous aunts and cousins. Clifford then hoped to spend three
months catching up on developments in chemistry. Before leaving
China they had offered to return via New Zealand and Australia, to
carry out 'Deputation Work' – publicising their work, among Friends
especially, and hopefully finding recruits and funding. It would also be a
rare opportunity for Clifford to see old friends there. The intention was
to leave in March, giving them more than two months in each country,
but in the event it would be June 1920 before they left Britain, greatly
shortening their stay in the Antipodes.[1]

They had returned to an England traumatised and transformed by
the war. It was a very different country from the essentially Edwardian
England that Clifford had left in 1913, and it must have taken them
some time to realise and absorb the social and mental changes that had
taken place. Some of these changes would seriously affect the work of
the Friends' Mission in China, and during his stay Clifford was closely
involved in debates in the FFMA China Committee and elsewhere.

To start with, Friends in Britain with a concern for overseas work
were concentrating on relief work in Germany and Russia, which were
suffering the terrible after-effects of war and revolution. In addition the
majority of Friends who had opposed the war and conscription,
sometimes suffering imprisonment in the cause, had turned away from
the whole idea of missionary work, seeing in it a reflection of the

imperialism that had led the world to war in the first place. 'The very word "missionary", long under scrutiny by some Quakers, now became to many almost unbearable.'[2] Europeans no longer had any moral right to preach to the heathen. These factors exacerbated the always difficult problem of funding the Mission's work. Then the general economic effects of the war caused further difficulties. The pound sterling had slumped in value against the Mexican dollar (universally used in China), which meant that each pound raised in England went much less far in China. For example, the estimated cost of building one wing of the proposed Friends' College on the WCUU campus was $50,000. Before the war this had been the equivalent of £2500; now it was £12,500.[3] And this was only the cost of one wing. The whole college would cost over £40,000. This was a matter of immediate concern to Clifford – other missions' colleges were almost finished, yet the Friends' College now looked like being postponed endlessly into the future. It was essential to go ahead if Friends were to maintain their position in the University. In December he persuaded the China Committee to agree to raise the money by a loan in China – this could be done at a reasonable interest rate, and would avoid the problem of the adverse exchange rate for the pound.[4] But this decision was overruled by the more cautious Finance Committee, who would not borrow money unless they knew for sure how it would be repaid. By June 1920 £6000 was available, and the builder, Harold Morrison, was told he could start on the first half of one wing of the college.[5] Further funding would take several more years.

The FFMA's financial problems were certainly making them into poor relations in the University. Their transatlantic colleagues had all kinds of plans for expansion, and when President Joseph Beech, on a visit to England, attended a China Committee meeting in December 1919 he brought with him the Board of Governors' request that each mission board should provide an extra $15,000 for the purchase of further land in Chengdu. They also asked the two British missions (the Church Missionary Society had recently joined the University) to provide an extra five teachers between them. The China Committee's response was something of a humiliation: 'We are a small missionary society … the European War has seriously affected our financial position … the Governors will have to consider the different size and ability of missions.' The days when all missions could contribute equally to the University had passed and Friends could only be junior partners from now on. At this stage, in 1920, the only Quaker missionary actually in the University was Robert Simkin, who was on the point of leaving the FFMA to put himself under the American Board. Clifford was in England; Silcock was on his way home and would not return to China. Friends could not expect to have much influence on University policy.

Another financial matter that was under discussion by the China Committee was that of missionary 'allowances' – i.e. salaries. This was an issue over which Clifford usually found himself at odds with colleagues in China and at home. We know that even before his marriage he was embarrassed by the comfortable life-style of the missionary community in comparison with that of his Chinese colleagues and friends, and wanted a simpler way of life. Now the China Committee and the Committee of Missionaries were considering increases in allowances which Clifford thought excessive, and he expressed himself on the matter at length in a letter to Hodgkin.[6] Missionaries, he felt, had to express their faith through their lives as well as their teaching, and their apparent prosperity had the effect of encouraging Chinese to join the church in order to share in it. 'I have been almost oppressed with the thought of the difficulty which our way of life must be to their conception of a fundamental part of our message, the pure gladness of unselfish service, free from any thought of personal gain. Our scale and style of living must be a constant set-back to our message. They know our salaries (I have several times been asked, and have given a frank reply – they would know anyhow) – they see our style of living; and I feel many must conclude that it is a beautiful combination of serving our fellows with a "good thing" (materially) for ourselves. And it is true that our lives as missionaries are, on the whole, *very* comfortable.

'What is the way out? … The heroic [way] would be to embrace lady poverty, and live so as to identify ourselves unquestionably with the Chinese standards. One might use the argument that it is impossible to conceive the idea of Christ going as a missionary to China, and living in the houses, and with the retinue of servants etc. that we do. The [other] course, than which I cannot yet see a better, is to acknowledge that our lives must be on a different material scale from the Chinese, and even need a different degree of plenty and of amenities which many of us would not have in England – and yet to so order them in simplicity and giving up all unnecessary luxury and display, that the least possible stumbling block may be placed in others' way, and the motive of our service most clearly shine forth.'

The reason for not 'embracing lady poverty' was the effect on their children, who should not have to suffer for their parents' principles. 'If missionaries' lives are anywhere to feel hardship, let it not be through economic pressure on their children. Clothing, medical expenses, insurance, and in later years the expense of education and upkeep in England, are some heavy items of expense. I have heard the remark made that the policy of the FFMA has been to discourage families. The two outstanding cases of financial stress in our mission ... are cases of people with large families.'

So he was not in sympathy with current plans to increase allowances. There were two proposals, one from the Committee of Missionaries in China and another, much more generous, from the FFMA in London. If allowances were increased, the FFMA under current conditions would have to reduce the number of missionaries. 'Yet the present is a situation where one longs for *more* workers, to occupy our present stations efficiently, and relieve the load of overwork falling on others.'

He then – insisting on confidentiality – writes about his own circumstances over the past few years, showing that by living plainly he had even been able to return part of his allowance. 'First I may say that during the War we tried to go on the principle of bearing some share in the material sacrifice all at home were making, and by living simply managing to return a portion of our income to the Mission. And yet I do not feel we denied ourselves anything necessary, or much even of legitimate amenity – in fact we had a lovely home and a jolly good time. Our current expenses in the field were for three years as follows: 1916 – $1280; 1917 – $1460; 1918 – $1370. These amounts included one or two quite exceptional large items of expense. Of course, one has to put by for expenses in England – insurance, stores and furlough time – we reckoned about $350 annually for this. The total would thus be about $1720 per annum. Of course we lived fairly simply – we had less entertaining than some (mainly students who do not need elaborate dinners etc) though quite a good deal; and it is only fair to say that I think we temperamentally find it easier to do on a small income than many, or most, would. Living at Chengdu I should think cost more than country stations, rather less than Chongqing. For our family, last COM's proposal would be $2256 p.a. – a margin of $536, but the China Committee's proposal would be $2912!'

In 1922, when the Mission was faced with further cuts in funding, he would write: 'My own feeling is that before drastic cuts are made in grants for work, missionaries should at least be given the opportunity to accept less allowances. I believe it is easy for us to live too comfortably in some ways – habits of life inherited from past years are difficult to break. Personally I am sorry that last year we asked for an increase, though we agreed to what was definitely the genuine feeling of most out here. We felt ourselves no need for such an increase, and indeed find we can live on the old scale and have a balance.'[7]

One of the most important results of this furlough period in England, although there is no direct record of it, is a change in Clifford's attitude towards Quakerism. He had been accepted by the FFMA in 1912, and he had spent a few months at Kingsmead, but what with completing his doctorate, getting engaged to Margaret, and preparing for his journey out East, he had had little time to acquire any more than a superficial acquaintance with Friends. Margaret, having spent a year at Wood-brooke, was probably more familiar with Quakerism than he was. His church connections at that time were still with Presbyterians. These had formally lapsed, and his only church membership was with the Sichuan Yearly Meeting. But while, as RJD had testified, he was a devoted and conscientious member of this, and of the Committee of Missionaries, in his day-to-day life at the University he had little contact with Friends. Most of his colleagues were Baptists and Methodists. Harry Silcock belonged like himself to the FFMA, but was still a Congregationalist. Clifford would see the Davidsons at Qinlonggai at least once a week, but he was hardly part of a Quaker community.

Denominational differences mattered little to him, and for as long as he was in China he had no problems with this situation. But as his return to England approached he wondered how he would fit in back at home. He wrote to Hodgkin about his 'hitherto very loose connection with English Friends, and indeed the fact that in some things I do not altogether share Friends' views e.g. about the Lord's Supper. I feel it best to describe myself as a member of the Sichuan Society of Friends; though of course I am quite in harmony with the basic principles of Friends, I doubt if I should ever have felt it necessary to break with the Christian body I was connected with in order to join the Society in England. It is a Christianity which includes the principles of Quakerism that I wish to proclaim here, not Quakerism per se.'[8]

He does not mention the very topical question of pacifism, but a letter from Irene Hutchinson suggests that he was not sound on this subject either. She lamented that the Peace Testimony was little heard in the University: 'I often wish we had more Friends out here in the University – only Simkin sticks to his peace principles but he is rather alone I think. It cannot be expected I suppose that Dr Stubbs and HTS[ilcock] should uphold our peace views, or at least as far as we do, but it is very disappointing, I think, that our mission is not taking the part that it might in influencing these students towards peace views.'[9]

Most British and Canadian missionaries were strongly patriotic, and some of the younger ones were put under pressure by their elders to volunteer for military service.[10] Clifford's responses to the outbreak of the war in his letters to Margaret express concern but not any commitment to pacifism. Clifford and Silcock both attended a meeting in support of the war in 1916 at the British Consulate, organised by the Patriotic League of Britons Overseas, at which Clifford spoke on behalf of New Zealand. The League in Chengdu was mainly a social and fundraising body, and held regular meetings at which 'fun and frolic was the order of the day'. The Stubbs are recorded as giving $50 to their collection for the Red Cross; only the consul and the Anglican bishop gave more.[11] Silcock was far from wholly opposed to the war: when some war newsreels were shown in Chengdu he thought their effects were very positive, and demonstrated 'the high principles underlying the war'.[12] In 1917 he went further and offered to serve with the Chinese Labour Battalions in France, which horrified the China Committee in London. Fortunately the British Consul in Chengdu issued a certificate to say that his work there was of such national importance that he should not be subject to call-up.[13]

It was, then, only during his first furlough that Clifford had any real opportunity to get to know the Society of Friends, whose interests he had been serving in China for the past six years. The Quakerism he now found was very different from what it had been in 1913.[14] It had been both shattered and rebuilt by the experience of the First World War, when Quakers had confronted, resisted and been imprisoned by the State, as had not happened since the seventeenth century. It had been a wounding and divisive experience: many who had been born into the Society, and had accepted its teachings on peace without ever needing to think about them deeply, had found themselves in 1914 faced with a conflict between their Quakerism and their patriotism, and for a significant number patriotism had proved the stronger. As many as a third of Friends of military age took up arms, some older ones even involved themselves in recruiting. But these 'War Friends' had little influence on the collective voice of the Society, as expressed in London Yearly Meeting, and its standing committee, still known by its traditional name as the 'Meeting for Sufferings'. These bodies refused all compromise with the State, especially when conscription was introduced in 1916. The government offered to exempt all members of the Society of Friends from military service, but the Society refused this privilege, unless it was extended to all others who objected to serving on grounds of conscience.

Opposition to the war involved more than just a refusal to bear arms. Friends became actively involved in anti-war bodies such as the No-Conscription Fellowship, and this brought them into close contact with other opponents of the war, many of whom were socialist and not necessarily pacifist. Opposition to the war also led to a consideration of the causes of war, its roots in social injustice and the power of a militaristic capitalism. There had existed since the late nineteenth century a Socialist Quaker Society, but it had few members and little influence. The war, however, led to a swing to the left in the Society, and broadly socialist ideas became widespread. The war also led some to join Friends precisely because of their pacifist stance; some of these had fought in the trenches and been converted to pacifism by the experience. These 'converts' to Friends, together with those who had suffered imprisonment, brought new experiences and insights into the Society, and would be its dominant figures in the following inter-war years. The modern image of the Society of Friends, identified primarily by its social concern and commitment to peace, is the product of this time.

Older and more conservative Friends were alarmed by all this, and felt their beloved Society had been captured by quasi-Bolsheviks. The letters pages of *The Friend* provide evidence of their discontent and distress, and the changes in the Society brought pain to many. But young Friends in the 1920s turned strongly away from the past. They were the ones who abhorred the very word 'missionary', and some even rejected their Christian heritage and called themselves 'Universalists', ready to find the Inner Light in any tradition. There was also a continuing debate about how to work together with sympathetic individuals and groups, without expecting any denominational commitment, and the term 'Wider Fellowship' occurs often in discussions at this time.

It is clear that this 'new-look' Quakerism 'spoke to Clifford's condition', as Friends would say, and in it he found his spiritual home for the rest of his life. At no point did he directly write about the nature or development of his faith, but a folder among his papers[15] with various notes from different periods allows us to see something of his changing beliefs. One is an undated 11-page address entitled 'The Manner and Method of Jesus' Teaching'; both from its content, and from the fact that it written out in full and in English, one can assume that it was a talk for his Bible class in Liverpool. Here he stresses the authority with which Jesus spoke, and his 'self-assertiveness', which must stem from his divine nature, and goes on, 'Those who reject the miraculous, and reject traditional theories and theologies about Jesus, but accept him as a teacher, have got to face this problem.' But some notes for Bible study classes dated in 1917 show a very different emphasis. Writing of Jesus' birth he notes that only two of the Gospels describe the Virgin Birth, that there are similar stories in other religious traditions, and that recent research suggests that the early Church had traditions of both a natural and supernatural birth. Notes on the death of Jesus also make no reference to the Resurrection. A talk on 'Jesus as Teacher' says that Jesus spoke from the standpoint of his contemporaries, using 'current conceptions of things as means to convey truth'. 'He formed no creed ... which would suit all times and nations, but gave principles which men must learn to work for themselves.' This suggests his faith was becoming more liberal.

Although the story of his 'conversion' remains unrecorded, from now on he describes himself as a 'Friend by convincement', and, to the alarm of his father-in-law, 'a pacifist and something of a socialist'.[16] One influence on him at this time must have been Henry Hodgkin. He had been very active in the peace movement during the war, and he was one of the founders, and the first chairman, of the Fellowship of Reconciliation, an interdenominational pacifist body which has proved one of the most enduring. He remained secretary of the FFMA, but had moved a long way from his evangelical roots. His elder brother Edward had moved even further. He was a successful businessman and chairman of sixteen companies, who must have 'seemed an unlikely social revolutionary'. Yet that was what he had become, as he chaired the War and Social Order Committee, the main vehicle for the spreading of socialist ideas within the Society of Friends. Was the Society, he asked rhetorically, to be merely a set of 'spiritual epicures, or is it realising that it has a message for the world, which must be given, come what may?' Described as the 'formidable Clerk of the [Darlington] Monthly Meeting',[17] he was Clifford's host for a week in March 1920 during the latter's deputation work in the north-east. This took Clifford not just to Friends' Mission Halls, but to adult schools, a girls' school at Polam Hall, and meetings of miners.[18] Another man who became a close friend of Clifford at this time was Peter Scott, who had turned to pacifism and Friends as a result of his experiences in the trenches of the Western Front. In the 1920s he would be responsible for the 'Home Mission' work of the Society.

From then on Clifford was unquestionably a Quaker, although he did not need to be accepted as such by any local Meeting in England. He was already a member of the Sichuan YM and that was sufficient.[19] But becoming a Quaker meant for him acquiring new insights and emphases, rather than renouncing earlier beliefs and practices. 'The Lord's Supper' had been important to him; he refers in a letter of 1927[20] to attending communion while on board ship, and he probably did so on other occasions as well. And one important part of his evangelical heritage remained – his devotion to the person of Jesus, as one young Friend found to her surprise when she met Clifford during his second furlough in 1927: 'Most of the young Friends of that day (myself among them) were very chary of describing themselves as Christians. We stressed the Universality of the Inward Light, we claimed that all religions were much the same; we would accept Jesus as leader but certainly not as Lord. To find a man, only a little older than ourselves, of proved intellectual ability, to whom Christ was a living and central reality and whose life was so obviously dedicated to his service, was a disturbing and challenging experience to us.'[21] The centrality of Jesus to Clifford's spiritual life must have been an important factor in helping him retain the trust of missionary colleagues in China, when he diverged from them in many other matters, political and religious.

Clifford and Margaret had originally intended to leave England in March 1920; that had been postponed to June, and then it was decided that the University Board of Governors would hold its only ever meeting in England in July, at the Queen's Hotel in Upper Norwood. It was clearly important for Clifford to be present to report from the front-line, so to speak – but this meant a further delay in their departure, and their time in New Zealand would be much shorter than they had hoped. The Board received reports on the growth of the University: most of the roads and paths across the campus were now complete, and trees and shrubs planted. Two colleges were now complete. Vandeman College (Baptist) had opened in October 1919, and Hart College, built by the Canadians, in April 1920. This was intended to house the science departments as well as being a student dormitory. Clifford's chemistry laboratory would now be more spacious, but there would still be no supply of gas, electricity or water.[22]

An important question for the Board was the future of the Education Department and the Normal School. These were Harry Silcock's main responsibility; it was also an essential element in building up a competent Christian education system throughout Sichuan, and had been notably successful. Two of its first four graduates in 1919 would go on to become presidents of the University, Zhang Lingao (Lincoln Chang) and Fang Shuxuan. Yet Silcock was now on furlough; the Canadian Secretary of the Education Union, E.W. Wallace, was also at home on leave, and another teacher was due to go home the following January. The future of the whole Department was uncertain. And now the FFMA had asked Silcock to take over from Henry Hodgkin as its General Secretary in London; after 10 years Hodgkin was about to resign and return to China. This shows how fragile the university enterprise still was, and how dependent on a small number of people. Even more, it shows the weakness of the FFMA. Silcock was still a Congregationalist, and would not join Friends until 1922. RJD, unaware of how much things had changed among Friends at home, was appalled: 'Just think of the situation – that the Society of Friends cannot find a man to be secretary of the FFMA, and has to go to a Congregationalist like yourself to fill the gap. Is it not lamentable?'[23]

Silcock was a major loss to Huaxi in many ways. His departure not only deprived Clifford of a close friend and colleague, and almost halved Friends' contribution to the University, but in him the University lost a man whose personal qualities made him especially indispensible. Clifford made this point in a letter to Silcock sympathising with his ultimate decision to remain in London rather than return to Chengdu, but which also shows a growing dissatisfaction with the spiritual atmosphere at Huaxi. He was missed 'not in general as a missionary or a teacher but from the point of view of your contribution as a personality to the University and the whole Christian church out here ... I am far from satisfied with the type of Christian influence and spirit in the University. Others have said to me repeatedly that you were giving something almost unique – a *type* of Christianity very much needed to complement the University. You had won a remarkable place too in the eyes of the students.'[24]

Once the meeting of the Board was over, the Stubbs set out for New Zealand via the Panama Canal, on a ship full of Australian soldiers and war brides, taking fifty-three days to reach Wellington. They spent less than three weeks there, crossing the country from Auckland to Dunedin, visiting old friends and places, talking to students, hoping to find support and recruits. But Friends were very thin on the ground: the only Friends' Meeting House was in Auckland. Friends were also few in Australia, where Clifford visited Sydney, Melbourne and Brisbane, but had to miss out on Adelaide and Hobart. They did find a doctor and his wife who were interested in coming to Sichuan, and there would be others; but the FFMA had no money and eventually they had to offer their services to other missions.

Then it was Hong Kong, arriving in mid-October for a brief meeting with Clifford's sister Winifred; then on to Shanghai and upriver to Sichuan, taking a steamer through the Gorges for the first time.

6

1921–1926, Chengdu

The Stubbs family returned to Chengdu in the middle of December 1920, having travelled safely through a Sichuan more troubled by bandits than for many years. This was far from the only change they would notice. Clifford had acquired a new way of looking at the world during his time in England, and returned a convinced Quaker; but the change in attitudes that had taken place in China during those eighteen months, especially among the young, was far greater, and a building up of intense nationalist feeling had made Christian universities like Huaxi, and the missionary movement as a whole, a target of fierce hostility.

The presence of missionaries in China was a result of treaties concluded in the previous century between China and various foreign powers, notably Britain. These treaties had been forced on China by a series of military defeats, and would come to be referred to by Chinese as the 'Unequal Treaties'. It was the Treaty of Tianjin in 1858, during the Second Opium War, which gave missionaries the right to travel and settle throughout the Chinese Empire, and some Chinese will still say today that Christianity came to China sitting astride a cannon ball. Under the treaties, foreign citizens in China enjoyed 'extraterritorial' rights, which meant that they were under the authority of their own consuls, and not subject to the Chinese legal system. The Chinese Customs Service, and later the Salt Tax administration, were put under the control of foreign officials, although they were answerable to the Chinese government rather than their own. And to protect their citizens, foreign powers sent gunboats up Chinese rivers, primarily the Yangzi. Major warships, cruisers for example, could get as far as Hankou in central China; only much smaller river boats could get through the Yangzi Gorges, but by 1900 the first British gunboats were patrolling as far inland as Chongqing, 1500 miles from the sea. They would be followed by French, American, Japanese and, until the First World War, German boats.

During his first tour of duty Clifford seems not to have concerned himself much with the rights and wrongs of this. He was, after all, fully occupied with learning the language, setting up a chemistry department, and becoming a husband and father, and before 1919 it did not seem a major issue. In the 1920s it became one, as the Chinese rebelled against the injustice and humiliation of their treatment by foreign powers, and this conflict was one in which missionaries were deeply implicated by the privileges they enjoyed. Quakers, and Clifford in particular, became ever more concerned to find ways in which they could show their sympathy with the Chinese, and detach themselves from these privileges; but they had little support from many of their fellow missionaries, who felt they had a higher calling than mere politics, and this absolved them from considering the matter.

The symbolic moment which marked the birth of Chinese patriotism, the birth of 'New China' itself, took place on 4th May 1919, when several thousand students demonstrated in protest outside the Tiananmen Gate of the Forbidden City in Peking. The Versailles conference had just agreed that German concessions seized by Japan in 1914, notably the eastern port city of Qingdao, should remain under Japanese control instead of being returned to China. This decision was the result of secret agreements made in 1918 between Japan and the nominal Chinese government in Peking, of which even the Chinese delegates at Versailles had been unaware. Angry Chinese students in Paris blockaded the delegates in their hotel, preventing them from signing the treaty. The same anger provoked the Tiananmen demonstration, which was followed by the burning of the home of the minister responsible, and sparked off similar protests throughout the country. May 4th 1919 has come to be seen as a key date in the history of modern China, initiating a process that would lead eventually to the establishment of communist rule in 1949. To this day, May 4th is celebrated as 'Youth Day'.

The patriotism of young Chinese was further enhanced by the effects of the Great War. Apart from the presence on the Western Front of Chinese labour battalions, who built roads, dug trenches, buried bodies, and carried out other low-level manual tasks, China had not been directly engaged in the war, but its impact on Chinese attitudes towards the West was nevertheless significant. From the late nineteenth century onwards many Chinese had recognised the superiority of the West in the fields of science and technology, and as the Chinese Empire moved towards its collapse they felt that it might indeed be in some ways a higher civilisation than their own. Missionaries had been only too ready to encourage this, and in particular sought to persuade the Chinese that Western science was somehow the consequence of Christianity. But any belief in the moral superiority of Western civilisation died in the trenches of the Western Front. The images of industrial slaughter brought to China by the new medium of the cinema showed that Western technology, uncontrolled by humane feeling and moral principle, was a terrible thing. The contradiction between the formal teachings of Christianity and the behaviour of the Christian nations was glaring. In 1915 Sichuan's Governor Hu Jingyi said to a Quaker missionary: 'Jesus said, "Whosoever smite thee on thy right cheek, turn to him the other also." How about the followers of Jesus in Europe now?'[1] It was not easy to find an answer.

The 1920s would see a ferment of ideas and debate among China's intellectuals, a debate in which Christianity would appear not so much untrue as irrelevant, and in which most missionaries were incapable of engaging. May 4th 1919 gave political force to ideas associated with the 'New Thought Movement', sometimes called the 'Chinese Renaissance', whose origins can be traced to the founding of a journal called *New Youth* in 1915. The writers, many of them teachers at Peking University who had studied overseas, rejected Confucianism entirely, looking for a new set of values that would help regenerate their country. 'Mr Confucius' would be replaced by 'Mr Science and Mr Democracy'. The emancipation and education of women was to become a reality. Classical Chinese, hitherto the medium for all serious literature, and all educational texts, was to be replaced by a written form of spoken

Chinese – Mandarin. In the 1920s many of these young scholars would turn to Marxism, but one of the best known, Hu Shi, remained committed to the liberalism he had learned while studying in Chicago under John Dewey, and would show some interest in the ideas of Quakerism. It was largely thanks to him that the most immediate impact of the New Thought Movement was on language: by 1920 the Ministry of Education had ordered that all school textbooks should be written in Mandarin. In the same year a group of students brought out the first Mandarin newspaper in Chengdu.[2] Just as the Protestant Reformers in Europe, by translating the Bible, had encouraged a massive expansion in literacy, so in China the benefits of education could now be spread far more widely than ever before. Robert Simkin in 1925 expresses the sense of liberation this gave. He had been reading some recent magazine articles in Chinese – 'full of new terms, educational, philosophical, sociological, but they are much easier to read than the old classical style because they are more nearly the style of everyday speech ... when one turns from the discouraging political conditions to these other facts one is filled with hope for the future. It has been refreshing to read in modern Chinese ideas one has for years been struggling to express.'[3]

Developments like this were welcomed by missionaries, but the movement also posed serious new challenges, as Christianity came under attack not from a traditionalist, Confucian point of view but in the name of modern nationalism and science. There should be no place for any superstition in New China, especially one so closely linked to the imperialist powers. In 1920 the mathematician and atheist philosopher Bertrand Russell came to China on a lecture tour. His works had been widely translated into Chinese and had provoked great interest. His assertion that the methods of science – empiricism and scepticism – were the best route to truth met with widespread approval; and he also made it very clear that Christianity was no longer the dominant force in the West that missionaries claimed it to be. This was reinforced by the experience of the growing number of Chinese who had studied in the West.

The early 1920s saw a series of anti-Christian movements led by young Chinese intellectuals, with mission schools and universities as their main target.[4] In 1922 the Anti-Christian Student Federation and the Great Federation of Anti-Religionists held a series of conferences, filled the newspapers with protests, and organised demonstrations and student strikes. While these movements were encouraged by socialists and communists, and the language used often had a Marxist flavour, they enjoyed the support of a wide spectrum of Chinese intellectuals including a liberal like Hu Shi. On his return Clifford noticed how anti-Christian propaganda had increased: 'Many articles appear in the numerous magazines which are read by the student class, attacking Christianity and all religion on professedly scientific and philosophical grounds. Another prominent aspect of the student mind is the intense but rather negative patriotism, mainly directed in violent hatred against Japan, though anti-foreign in general.'[5]

In the immediate aftermath of May 4th, after Clifford's departure on furlough, there had been trouble at Huaxi. Silcock reported to Beech (who was on furlough), 'We are having a little trouble with discipline but are gladly seizing the opportunity to put the screws on a little. I think we have won out without having to turn anyone away; the offenders have all given their word to behave properly and if they do not then they know quite well it will be instant dismissal. The young teachers were amazed to find that we were quite prepared to close the whole school rather than have any nonsense.' But he anticipated more trouble: if the question of Japan's occupation of Qingdao was not resolved, 'we shall not be able to do much with our students this coming year. Political conditions have cut them off from us a good deal this past year.' In September 'the situation among the students is quieter, but we do not feel like taking the slightest risks after last June.' His missionary colleagues meanwhile were increasingly discouraged: 'with most the iron is entering into their souls. Pray for us, we need it now if ever.'[6]

At the end of 1919 serious disturbances involving students took place in the city, described in a letter from Ernest Sawdon, Head of the Chongqing Friends' School. A recently formed Student Union, which brought together all the students in Chengdu, including those from Huaxi, organised a protest against shopkeepers selling Japanese goods. This ended with an attack on the Chamber of Commerce, in the course of which a student was killed. The students then took twenty-eight merchants as hostages. At first they were going to beat one of them to death in revenge, but decided instead to humiliate them by stripping them naked and leading them through the streets. Then, according to Sawdon, 'the Christian students prevailed upon the others to allow them to dress first. During the procession there were calls to loot and burn shops suspected of selling Japanese goods, and here again the Christian students showed of what spirit they were made by trying to prevent this and in many cases succeeding. The proctor of our Middle School dormitory [Fang Shuxuan] was very nearly beaten himself for his efforts to calm the anger of some of those from other schools, and I think one can be proud of the part our students took in preventing worse things happening.'[7] Sawdon was writing from Chongqing, his account is a second-hand one, and one can question to what extent he really understood the dynamics of what went on; after all, the Huaxi students were Chinese themselves and shared the universal indignation at Japanese encroachments and the shameful condition of their country. But the episode shows the genuine anger of the students as well as their volatility and incoherence. Over the following years these qualities, combined with their sense of helplessness in a Sichuan under warlord control, led to behaviour which could be infuriatingly irrational, and extremely violent in its rhetoric, though rarely in action.

Clifford encountered this new politics shortly after his return and was less than happy with it. 'We had hardly got back before our higher schools, following rather lamely it seemed in the wake of the Student Association mainly comprised of government school students in the city, struck for several weeks from attending classes as a political demonstration, originally anti-Japanese anti-government, but I am afraid also very much pro- the saving of students' face. (I need not explain the why and wherefore.) One result of course was that a month of the best study time was lost – and the remainder of our academic year was, to me at any rate, a frantic and unsuccessful attempt to overtake arrears.'[8] But as time went by he would come to sympathise more with the aspirations of young China. The older or more conservative missionaries tended to dismiss the whole nationalist movement as 'Bolshevism' – this was the view of both RJD and Leonard Wigham[9] – and could find few points of sympathy with it. Clifford, however, younger, always politically aware, and further sensitised to new political tendencies after his year at home, grew into the role of a mediator between old and new, between Chinese and foreigner.

In 1921–22 Henry Hodgkin returned to China for the first time since 1910, and forcefully brought the new more politically and socially oriented Quakerism to a wide audience. He and his wife Joy toured China from north to south, giving lectures and meeting a wide range of influential people. His experience of international affairs, his intellectual prestige and reputation as a pacifist, and his knowledge of China, guaranteed him an audience wider than most Christians could attract. The force of his personality, his vision of Christian pacifism strengthened by his wartime experience, and his international perspective, attracted large audiences as he tried to give them a new perception of what Christianity could be. In speaking to non-Christian groups he was able to draw a contrast between military and educational ideals which made sense to them. He preached the 'Christian Revolution' and its relevance to China's needs in education, and social and political reform. In Canton he had an audience with the Nationalist leader Sun Yatsen; in Peking he met and was impressed by Hu Shi. Hu had been put off Christianity by the fundamentalists he had met when studying in America – 'He told me once that he was an atheist, but that he thought much of Quakers. I believe he is a man who has a real religious experience but he does not know how to interpret it.'[10]

Hodgkin in his travels followed closely behind Bertrand Russell, sometimes addressing the same organisations. He was the first religious speaker to be invited to address the Hunan Educational Association, who had previously invited both Russell and John Dewey. (One of its members was a young teacher called Mao Zedong; one wonders if he was present.) Hodgkin had worked with Russell as a pacifist during the war, and welcomed his pacifist message in China; yet Russell was also fiercely attacking religion, and Christianity in particular. It was an uncomfortable irony to be closer in his pacifism to an unbeliever than to the majority of the missionary body, who seemed never to have thought about the subject. 'Is it not a grievous thing that the peace position has had to wait for the advent of an agnostic to be really well stated in China when the land is full of apostles of the Prince of Peace?'[11] Intelligent Chinese, he wrote, 'want to be convinced that Christ has a solution for the needs of the country, and I feel that the weakness of the missionary body is in constructive thinking as to how the Kingdom of God is to come in China.' In China society has always taken precedence over the individual, and if Christianity was to appeal to the Chinese it had to develop a social, and indeed a political gospel. Most missionaries, however, were politically ignorant, had no under-standing of the Christian pacifist tradition, and were incapable of exploiting the political situation that was developing. 'There is a lot of what is called Bolshevist thinking and writing. But much of this is really a preparation for our message if we had eyes to see it. To many missionaries I fear it seems to be nothing but a menace.'[12]

Hodgkin had begun his tour with three months in Sichuan, and provided a brief boost of energy and renewed self-confidence to a Friends' Mission badly in need of them. Short of funds and recruits, out of tune with the changes that had taken place in the Society of Friends at home, with some missionaries having taken up business posts, and others under pressure to do the same to save money, they felt mis-understood and neglected. Tiredness and overwork did not help. The war, though far away, had delayed furloughs, and caused tension and distress as people thought of loved ones at home in danger of death or imprisonment. Worse anxiety came from continuing conflict in Sichuan, as warlords fought for supremacy, and church members like everyone else suffered from exorbitant taxation to pay for it. In 1920 Chengdu had been besieged three times, as well as suffering a cholera outbreak which had closed the University for a while. Mary-Jane Davidson had died in 1918, and since then RJD seemed to have lost his zest for life. That Friends at home were turning away from the idea of missions altogether, and the loss of financial support that meant, made things worse, and the decision that Silcock would be taken away from them to become FFMA secretary in London was the final straw. 'We are struggling to hold the front line in these heathen lands,' RJD had written to Silcock in 1920 on hearing of his appointment, 'and it is most discouraging to us to feel that the folk at home draw from our small numbers to stir up their enthusiasm and organise their work. If this is needful, is there not something wrong at home?'[13]

Hodgkin's presence showed they were not forgotten, the vigour of his personality cheered them up, and he even found a new wife for RJD.[14] He first visited Chongqing, and was pleased by how well the boys at the Friends' High School responded to his talk on the need for mutual understanding between China and Japan. 'I dare say there is no other school in the city where my message, spoken straight out as it was, would have been received with patience. It means very much that our group of Chinese students are being so taught when feeling runs so high.'[15]

He spent over a month in Chengdu, a week of it with Clifford and Margaret. He gave lectures in schools and colleges, and met a wide variety of Chinese. Some of them had studied and been impressed by the Bible, but wanted no connection with any church and were wary of missionaries. This was a common position among educated Chinese, who could not feel at home in a church of the poor and uneducated, and would be aware of the limited educational attainments of many of the missionaries themselves. 'So much of the preaching of the gospel here has become conventional,' thought Hodgkin; what was needed was a Christian revolutionary point of view, and a group of young men who would help Chinese Christians to see 'the meaning of Christ in relation to social order'. One young man who responded was Clifford's colleague Shi Rucong. Inspired by Hodgkin, he and his brother founded a local branch of the Fellowship of Reconciliation, and started a newspaper to publicise its ideals.[16]

In February Hodgkin attended the annual meetings in Suining of the Sichuan Yearly Meeting and the Committee of Missionaries, and once more infused them with new confidence. By telling the YM of the work of Friends around the world, he made them realise they were part of something bigger than a small church in a single province. When he spoke of Friends' relief work in Germany he inspired those who had found it hard to love their enemies. And he cheered up the COM by insisting that they should have a 'stunt' evening when they entertained each other. He was shocked to hear they had not had one for four years (since the death of Mary-Jane Davidson, and perhaps this was no coincidence). Clifford was now in his element, leading a singsong with "Ninety-nine blue bottles", and "months and months and months etc". Then he and a colleague dressed up as Dr and Mrs Hodgkin and canoodled while someone sang a versified set of COM minutes. 'We all laughed till we ached. I think I shall laugh all this year when I recall the scene.'[17]

After his travels around China, Hodgkin arranged a conference in February 1922 between Japanese and Chinese Christian leaders in Hangzhou, then visited Japan and Korea, and before returning home in May he was present at a major conference in Shanghai of all the Protestant churches in China. This led to the creation of the National Christian Council of China, and in 1923 he was invited to return to become one of its national secretaries. He held this post for five years, providing a Quaker input at the heart of Protestant China, and finding himself at the centre of the ideological storms that would rage in the missionary world. Similar councils would be set up in provinces and cities around China, including Sichuan and Chengdu.

After his return Clifford emerges as a key figure in the Mission and the Yearly Meeting. The Central Executive of the YM had been set up in 1919, as a means of gradually devolving control of the mission work from foreigners to Chinese, and in February 1921, immediately after his return, he was chosen as its chairman despite the presence of RJD and other senior missionaries. He was recognised as the best fitted to help Chinese and foreigners work together in harmony. Its 1921 meeting was seen as especially successful, and dispersed the doubts that some had had over its creation. Silcock in London was enthusiastic: 'I find it difficult to write in a constrained way about the progress that has been made by the C[entral] E[xecutive]. The advance made in this direction is of unusual importance.'[18]

Over the next few years it became ever more clearly a Chinese institution. In 1922 Clifford passed on the chairmanship to Dr Luo

Binsan, the first Chinese Quaker doctor, sent by the FFMA to study in Peking and now working at the Friends' Hospital in Tongchuan. Luo had also been one of the three Chinese delegates to the All-Friends Conference in London in 1920.[19] Clifford became the YM Executive's 'English Secretary'. In 1923 he noted on the English minutes that they were merely a free translation of the Chinese minutes, which were authoritative. The same year the YM asked for the Annual University Report to be published in Chinese as well as English, and formally asked Clifford to present this request to the Senate.[20] (It is a comment on the university authorities that this request needed to be made.) It was also proposed, with Clifford in favour but many colleagues not, that the whole executive should be elected by the YM, with no places reserved for missionaries, and in 1925 this was done for the first time.

The University was now having an impact on Christian institutions in Sichuan, by creating an educated Christian elite which was ready, and indeed keen, to exercise leadership within the church. This brought with it a new problem – the social gulf between the educated class, and the often illiterate country people who made up the majority of Chinese Friends. They resented being patronised by the scholars, treated as 'country cousins'; and a gap opened between the Monthly Meetings in Chengdu and Chongqing, and those in the smaller, more rural centres of Tongchuan, Suining and Tongliang. There was also the problem of funding. Clifford had hoped that devolution of power to the executive would lead to greater self-support: 'As you know, I am much against an injudicious subsidising of the work out here, and think every encouragement should be given to the church to shoulder responsibility.'[21] The snag was, and would remain, that nearly all the leading Chinese Friends were working for, and paid by, the Mission, and there were few other sources of funds. Membership of YM had stabilised at around 500, and it would grow no further, while the Central Executive Minutes for 1923 give a list of thirty-one paid workers, and another seven just dismissed, presumably for financial reasons.[22] This was a very long way from Friends' ideal of an unpaid ministry, and raised the question of how far the YM could ever be 'independent' while it was so reliant on overseas funding.

Clifford did much to enable Chinese and foreigners to work together in the Meeting; relations between them in the University were an altogether bigger problem. In the early 1920s most missionaries in China remained strikingly unaware of how anti-Christian and anti-foreign feelings were growing, and how their bullish talk of turning China into a Christian nation was making things worse. In 1922 a book was published with the insensitive title of 'The Christian Occupation of China', which could have been calculated to provoke nationalist anger.[23] Upcountry missionaries can be forgiven for their unawareness of the anti-Christian movements, which were an urban phenomenon, but those in the cities and the universities were just as blind. The official reports from the Huaxi Senate to the Board of Governors give a rosy picture of harmony between staff and students.[24] In 1920 it was noted that political unrest affected the students but 'with few exceptions their conduct has been all that a person could require. We have not, as have several other institutions, been forced to close down temporarily and the great majority have been decidedly loyal to the institution.' For several years students' loyalty to the University is a keynote of the reports. In 1922, despite a background of student riots in the city, of 'ultra-nationalism', Huaxi had experienced no outstanding difficulties, and there was 'a recognised *entente cordiale* between students and faculty'. 1923 saw 'a year of constant progress'. Relations between teachers and students had never been more cordial, and students had shown courage in 'resisting intimidation of the Student Unions'. Certainly the University was popular: student numbers at university level went up from 69 in 1920 to 146 in 1923.

Of course it was necessary in the reports to give a positive impression to supporters back at home, and the president, Joseph Beech, was nothing if not a salesman. And it is true that Huaxi, in the remote west, suffered much less than Christian colleges in East China from student hostility. But they also indicate a degree of complacency among the staff, and ignorance of their students' true feelings. Hodgkin on his visit had felt that something was not right in the University he had helped to found. At a Senate meeting, 'I had a sense of the inadequacy of the discussion, the emphasising of smaller issues and a failure to get to the bottom of the matter. I don't know quite what is wrong, but I cannot help feeling that all is not as it should be, and that perhaps the men out there are suffering from too many committees and the overloading of the organisational side of things.' Too much concentration on day-to-day business perhaps led to inertia over broader issues, and in turn to complacency. Hodgkin cited as an example the reaction of the Senate to the student strike referred to above. It had persuaded the students to return to work, and break their ties with the Students' Union in the city, but had no 'strong policy to suggest whereby what was right and truly Christian in this movement could have found expression.' Once the immediate problem was solved the matter was dropped and no further thought given to it.[25]

It was an upcountry missionary on a visit, Henry Davidson from Suining, RJD's younger brother, who had a better sense of what was really happening. In 1920 he had written that 'even in the Union University and the Middle School there are strong anti-Christian influences at work, these influences are often not seen by missionaries, but Chinese whose true Christian character none of us would doubt do see and regret them.'[26] This could well be a reference to Yang Shao-quan; whoever it was, it suggests that Davidson was more trusted by Chinese at Huaxi than many of the staff were. The following year he wrote in stronger terms. 'There is a pretty strong anti-Christian element in the University, and the Christian element is not strong enough to combat it, and the completeness of the Gospel of Christ has not taken sufficient hold of its professors among students and graduates.' He had been especially shocked to hear from Clifford that a Christian graduate had addressed the student body on the occasion of Confucius' birthday, saying that Confucius was a greater teacher than Jesus, 'for he told men to do what they were able to do, but Christ taught what it was impossible for man to do.'[27]

In the same letter he suggests a reason for this – 'the apparent gulf between Chinese and foreigners'. There was little contact between teachers and students outside the classroom; once teaching was over the staff returned to their fine houses in 'Canadian Crescent' or 'Baptist Row', which Chinese, apart from servants, would rarely enter. 'I felt,'

Davidson continued, 'the great danger there is in the establishing of a great foreign institution in the midst of a great Chinese population, where the foreigners are the overlords, and where they live a life largely different and separated from those whom they are there to teach.'

A recent development had made things worse. The Language School, where new missionaries spent two years studying the language, had been relocated from the city to the campus, and thirty young recruits, almost all from North America, were living and studying there. That this was felt to have damaged relations between foreigners and Chinese on campus says something about the calibre of these new recruits. Silcock commented cautiously that he hoped the spirit of the University was strong enough to cope with the problem, and that these young people needed to be helped to a right view of the relations between foreigners and Chinese.[28]

These failings were far from unique to Huaxi. A Chinese historian, Jerome Ch'en, has noted, 'Few of them [missionaries] made true friends among the Chinese; fewer still treated the Chinese as their equals. In spite of advice against it, racial prejudice undeniably existed among the ambassadors of God.' Ch'en quotes D. Willard Lyon, who had founded the Chinese Y.M.C.A. in 1895, as saying in 1932, 'I don't know that I ever heard of a missionary who invited one of his Chinese co-workers to come to eat with him on a par.' Pearl Buck recalled '. . . the small white clean Presbyterian American world and the big loving merry not-too-clean Chinese world, and there was no communication between them.'[29] These features were less likely to have been true of isolated missionaries in smaller places, like the Jacksons in Tongliang, who must have been socially very dependent on their Chinese friends; but they were common wherever there were a large number of missionaries in a single place, whose social needs could be satisfied without reaching out to their Chinese neighbours and colleagues. This would also have affected their command of Chinese: their language might be adequate for the classroom or the pulpit, or for dealing with servants, but they would be much less at home in the language of everyday conversation.

Some teachers at Huaxi were actively reluctant to mix with the Chinese socially. During the 1920s the number of Chinese teachers increased, and when in 1925 a staff tennis club was formed, some questioned whether Chinese should be allowed to join. A clear majority voted that they should, and set a membership fee that they could afford. But there were those who voted against, who were reluctant to treat Chinese colleagues as equals. Somewhat later there were objections to Chinese attending the weekly staff prayer meeting – one wonders what the objectors thought they were in China for. Their problem was probably rooted in language – a Chinese presence would entail conducting the meeting in Chinese, and this was still too alien a language for their devotions. Once more the objectors were firmly outvoted. These were some of the issues on which the few Friends at Huaxi had to take a stand. John Rodwell, who attended Senate meetings as the FFMA representative, reported that 'Stubbs and Simkin have both made some weighty and convincing pleading for better relations with our Chinese colleagues. My heart swells with pride when I listen to them.'[30]

This social distance must have had a damaging effect on missionaries' understanding of the world around them. They were unlikely to pick up the nuances of courtesy and social behaviour, and offence might often, if unintentionally, be caused. One aspect of Chinese good manners is that when a visitor calls you should put aside whatever you are doing, however urgent it might be. It is unlikely that busy missionaries were always ready to do this. A young Friend, William Hope Gill, who spent a year on the campus in the early 1920s, recounted at a Memorial Service for Clifford in 1930 an illuminating incident. 'I was once calling after a missionary, who was riding along on his bicycle, but he didn't stop and didn't even look round. Some time afterwards when I saw him I asked him why he didn't stop when I called him, and he said, "Oh, was it you? I thought it was a Chinese." Clifford would have got off his bicycle and gone back to meet me . . . Whenever a student or other Chinese came he was shown in straight away – he was made to feel at home and Clifford would, no matter what he was doing, I have seen him leave his meals and often gone without any in order not to disappoint and not turn away a Chinese who came to him.'[31]

Henry Davidson wrote in similar terms in an obituary in *The Friend*.[32]

'Many are willing to give assistance in large and important matters, but become impatient at trivial calls upon their time. But Clifford Stubbs went further than this, he willingly left what he was doing to attend to the needs of an individual no matter how trivial those needs were ... His meals, his sleep and all personal things ceased for the moment to exist when a student or anyone else claimed his attention.' This was his evangelism; although he preached and held Bible study classes, in the end he knew that these were peripheral. 'To help [students] to find the centre of their lives in God, and following Christ to lose themselves in the cause of human love, is not easy. To counteract the forces of indifference to and prejudice against Christianity, the most vital influence is that of a personal life ...'[33]

A few years later a colleague wrote of Clifford's skill in dealing with Chinese officials: 'You ... can do things the Chinese way, *rang* gracefully and yet get forward.'[34] '*Rang*' means to yield, make space for the other person, give way. Clifford understood how to negotiate in China, avoiding confrontation yet moving towards agreement. It is significant that the writer uses a Chinese word for a form of social behaviour that has no real equivalent in English. Clifford was able to approach the Chinese with a combination of intelligence and empathy which overcame cultural difference; William Sewell reported in 1926, 'A Chinese said to me the other day about Dr Stubbs that he was a Chinese man and not a foreigner ... I don't see that he could have a higher compliment paid.'[35]

In 1923 the Stubbs embarked on a new venture which brought Clifford into touch with a quite different class of Chinese, to whose needs he would be just as attentive. In the summer, like most foreigners, they would go to one of the mountain resorts to enjoy the cool air during the vacation. Large communities gathered there, in Bailudin or Mount Emei (there were over 40 missionary bungalows on the lower slopes of Mount Emei alone[36]), playing tennis and socialising, largely happy with each other's company. It is likely that the Stubbs found this atmosphere narrow and increasingly unsympathetic, and in 1923 they rented a bungalow in the mountains west of Guanxian, near a village called

Nanyumiao, where they could relax in a wholly Chinese setting. The following year they built their own bungalow there. Nanyumiao was a 'little Switzerland' (memories of 1913! – once more they named their bungalow 'Marécottes') among the Tibetan foothills: 'the most delightful little valley – cool air, clear-running and tumbling streams, fir-clad slopes,'[37] accessible along bamboo suspension bridges across steep ravines. But solitude was not their aim. Colleagues and friends, foreign and Chinese, without distinction, were welcome and frequent guests; they could select their own missionary company, and the very simple conditions, and the informality of life there, made it a good place for forging deeper friendships than was possible in the busy world of Chengdu.

It is telling and characteristic that the Stubbs had no qualms about taking their children to such a remote spot, despite the violence affecting so much of the country. Political antipathy to foreigners meant nothing up in the hills. They trusted the Chinese, and very quickly made themselves loved there. Initially this was because all foreigners were believed to have medical skills, and every morning saw a crowd of *bing ren* (sick people) seeking treatment. They did what they could with ointments, santonin, quinine and advice. This, together with their friendliness – Clifford would never pass a man on the road without engaging him in conversation – made them well-known throughout the district, as a later visitor records. 'We began hearing of Stubbs' fame when we were yet many miles from his house ... He has a great reputation, not as a Doctor of Science but as a Doctor of Medicine. His cures are known far and wide, and his reputation as a destroyer of worms and other digestive troubles is secure ... It was a treat to see the way in which everyone who passed his house called on him, and how he made everyone welcome and listened to their troubles ... his deftness in administering castor oil to babies shows long practice.'[38]

But they did not forget they were missionaries, singing hymns in their porch before dinner and holding occasional meetings for the villagers in the local temple. On treks with friends in the hills they might have an impromptu meeting for worship, and the carriers would sit quietly around and listen. In 1925 a Chinese teacher at the Friends' Primary

School was a guest, and 'spent hours telling Bible stories round the fire to a breathless group of listeners. I hear him now holding forth about Moses. Eight carriers from Nanyumiao are up here with us; they are good fellows, simple peasants, and they and I are on very friendly terms; they are always willing to help, and seem to have a real regard for me.'[39]

By summer 1924 their bungalow was finished, but Clifford would be the only one to go there. In 1921 their only son John Stubbs had been born; he was a sickly child from the outset, and for a while they feared for his life. 'John is far from robust yet and had a setback last month and is recovering very slowly. Perhaps we shall not keep him, but we have by no means given up hope yet,' Clifford wrote in 1923. A year later John was having serious digestive problems, and they were advised to take him back to England for specialist treatment.[40] So in April 1924 Margaret and the children left for England, and Clifford remained on his own for the next two years. This was a common experience for missionary families, as health or the education of children enforced long periods of separation. Clifford put a characteristically brave face on it: 'It [separation] is quite an adventure for us, isn't it?' But it was very hard when the moment of separation came, as he saw them on to the boat in Chongqing. 'I said this morning we shouldn't weep much when the time came to part, didn't I? I had to swallow pretty hard and bite my tongue when I said goodbye to the two girlies at their supper, and as the launch left, your figures growing less and less distinct ... it was probably good that the last moments were so brief.'[41]

Two new colleagues enter Clifford's life at about this time, whose sympathetic presence helped to ease the pain of separation. One was John Rodwell, who moved into Qinlonggai with his wife Dorothy and their children, after nearly fifteen years spent in rural mission work. Of all the missionary (as opposed to academic) Friends he was the closest to Clifford in temperament and beliefs. He had become increasingly critical of traditional missionary work, and the structures it had created. When he moved to Tongchuan in 1920 he found a meeting that was an entirely parasitic organisation, dependent on foreign money, which would collapse at once if those funds were withdrawn. All depended on a paid ministry, which was quite alien to the spirit and tradition of Friends. He himself spent most of his time, he wrote, pottering at this and that, living in a fine house and garden, better off than many people at home. 'Would Christ occupy this position?'[42]

At this point he had nearly resigned, but colleagues both foreign and Chinese urged him to stay on. Like Clifford he understood and sympathised with the forces of Chinese nationalism, and was a strong supporter of devolving power and responsibility to the Chinese. He also shared Clifford's sense of fun – it was he and Clifford who had dressed up as the Hodgkins to entertain at the 1921 COM – and had even trained as a chemist as a young man. With the Rodwells, Clifford could enjoy family life in the absence of his own, and he often stayed over at Qinlonggai before the Sunday services. Soon a custom developed of playing bridge on Saturday evenings – this was breaking the strict missionary taboo on cards because of their association with gambling. Irene Hutchinson was shocked when she found out and Margaret back at home was clearly anxious. Clifford explained somewhat awkwardly: 'I forget now exactly what finally decided me to play cards. I think perhaps I feel that the Chinese anyhow are realising we don't play for money, and that is the thing we want to give our witness against. Then I found out how much John and Dorothy enjoyed it, and being in a similar position myself, did not see why if there were no good reason we should not get the recreation and relaxation of an occasional game.'[43]

The other new colleague was even more significant, as he was a qualified chemist who had been appointed to join Clifford in the Chemistry Department. William and Hilda Sewell were graduates of Leeds University, where William had stayed on as a lecturer. The Vice-Chancellor, Sir Michael Sadler, was deeply interested in China and was a member of the West China Union University Board of Governors; he suggested that the Sewells might find it worthwhile to spend a year or two in Chengdu. They were also typical of the post-war generation of Young Friends, and made it clear that they did not see themselves as missionaries; they would accept appointment solely to the University (i.e. not to the Mission), although they would be members of the Yearly Meeting. They would go to China to learn as well as teach. Despite this, Harry Silcock in London felt 'their personality will tell in other spheres, and they will be a strength to the COM'. He had never felt more positive about a candidature.[44] William Sewell would be Clifford's colleague, friend and successor, and would stay in China for nearly 30 years. They arrived shortly before Christmas in 1924, and took up residence in the Stubbs house on the campus; Clifford remained with them, a guest for the time being in his own home. This situation might have been difficult had they not got on so well. 'The Sewells have fairly taken hold of things at home,' he told Margaret after a couple of weeks. 'I can tell you the corners get dusted out, and the silver cleaned, and the verandah swept, in a way unknown for months. He is quiet, and dry; she vivacious, and fairly keeps us in order. A very nice couple, real sports and often rag each other gently.' And they enjoyed a game of bridge.

Since Clifford's return at the end of 1920 student numbers had grown, and even in 1921 Henry Davidson thought he was seriously over-worked: 'He has a tremendous lot to do in the way of teaching, far too much to my thinking, and he has not time to give to the social life of the dormitories.'[45] The number of students taking science had grown from three in 1919 to fourteen in 1920, to twenty-four in 1921 and thirty-five in 1922. The growth of the Medical School – a response to local Chinese demand – placed extra pressure on chemistry as an essential pre-med subject. The Chinese Medical Association was refusing to recognise the Medical School because of its understaffing. Like the other science subjects chemistry was essentially a one-man department, and the Senate Report in 1923 had asked the Board for four extra chemistry teachers.[46] Clifford had been relying ever more on Chinese assistants – two senior students Wu Xuanxi and Gao Changjiang, but most importantly Shi Rucong, who was increasingly experienced and useful, 'of very great service in teaching and management, without him I could hardly have carried on'.[47]

Equipment and supplies were a continual problem, the greater as

114

transport to Sichuan was increasingly interrupted by war and banditry. Most chemical supplies were ordered from Merck of Darmstadt in Germany, and letters from Silcock, who dealt with the orders in London, show the problems. The quantities were too small for Merck to bother with, but larger quantities could not be afforded. Consignments never arrived, and no one was interested in tracking them down. Chemistry books were out of print. Equipment was broken en route, and the insurers required this to be confirmed by their agents in Shanghai. 'Getting these German firms to insure the goods seems so complicated ... they have apparently no idea of the immense distance between Shanghai and Chengdu.'[48]

But work continued, students were taught, and Clifford found plenty to be positive about. 'In my own department one achievement of interest has been our design of an alcohol still (I always have to explain it is for scientific not human consumption) which has reduced the cost of alcohol to half of what we were paying. My friends have rather worried about my beery smell! We have since been working on the problem of sugar refining.'[49] In his official report to the FFMA for 1923 he makes only the briefest reference to his teaching: 'At the chemistry laboratory, the installation of a gas plant has taken considerable time, but added much to efficiency. One is still preparing new courses, and much time has been given to preparation of a short textbook in Organic Chemistry, the terminology of which, it may be mentioned in passing, has been radically revised and let us hope finally settled by a government commission.'[50] A standardised terminology, however, would have to wait until the 1930s.

In 1924 the Senate asked all heads of department to write an account of their work for the Annual Report to the Board of Governors,[51] and here for the first time Clifford describes his work and the principles which underlay it, in some detail. The May 4th generation of Chinese were very keen on science, seeing in it the salvation of their country, yet their prevailing idea of it was positivist and materialistic. Clifford tried to give them a different vision. 'The primary aim of teaching Chemistry in the West China Union University is the task of enlightenment and spiritual emancipation of the Chinese people ... Narrow, often superstitious views of the world and its order have long prevailed, and still prevail to a surprising extent even in circles supposedly cultured. To overcome this, mere instruction and facts are insufficient – the mind must be led into a grander conception of the plan and beauty of the Universe. I have been struck by the emphasis laid on this aspect of chemical teaching by a Chinese friend, a teacher in our secondary school. Again, even when the facts of scientific discovery are known, the prevailing tendency is for them to be regarded from a merely utilitarian and mechanistic point of view. Hence it is a first duty to inculcate through our teaching the true spirit of science, of patient research, of wonder, of valuing truth for its own sake. To present science as part of the wider evangel of Christianity is especially necessary in a land where materialism is so strong and where science is often supposed to be the enemy of faith.'

The practical aims of the Department were to train Middle School science teachers, prepare medical students, and help in the economic development of the country. He noted that China was 'a country rich in resources, almost untouched by the chemical industry'. The aim in all the teaching was to relate theory to practical application. Two or three graduates had gone into industry, and some study had been made of methods used in local sugar and soap industries.

Most teaching was done in the junior division: there were forty-eight students taking preparatory chemistry, thirty-four taking inorganic chemistry and twenty pre-meds taking organic chemistry. Teaching was at an elementary level, but these were key classes for the Department and needed his best thought and energy. 'Individual lab work under good guidance is essential', and only Clifford could provide this. He also took the seniors for lab work. A Chinese assistant taught some junior classes. By now, he had at last proper laboratories in the newly opened science building – the Atherton Building. There was a large laboratory for sixty students to do individual work, and a smaller one for the seniors, together with lecture, preparation and store rooms, and a private laboratory for the staff. The gas generating plant which he had bought in 1919 had now been operating for two years, but generally, he concluded this section, the equipment was still inadequate.

1 *(above)*: The Stubbs family in 1902.
From left: Clifford, Winifred, Eric, Frederick and Emma.

2 *(below):* 1913: Clifford and the Lees family in Switzerland.
From left: Gordon, Margaret, Antony, Rose.

3: Clifford Stubbs 'swanking' in his Doctoral robes, 1913.

4 *(above)*: Missionaries on houseboat. Clifford in cap.

5 *(below)*: Chengdu, Qinlonggai: Friends' Mission Residence.

6 *(above)*: June 2nd 1915, wedding of Clifford and Margaret. Back row from left: Margaret Silcock, Harry Silcock, Robin Davidson, ? Wilkinson (best man), RJD, Kathleen Davidson, Mary-Jane Davidson.

7 *(below)*: The Stubbs' house under construction.

8: Henry Hodgkin.

9 *(left)*: Yang Shaoquan being awarded an Honorary Degree in 1934. He is wearing his 1911 Revolution medal.

10 *(below)*: 1919: the first graduates of the Education Department, including two future Presidents of the University – Zhang Lingao (2nd left) and Fang Shuxuan (far right).

華西協合大學校正科畢業攝

11 *(above left)*: Clifford and Shi Rucong at Nanyumiao.

12 *(above right)*: Margaret Stubbs.

13 *(left)*: 1917: Harry Silcock with trainee teachers. (Students wore uniform for ceremonial occasions).

14 *(above)*: Administration Building designed by Frederick Rowntree.

15 *(below)*: The Stubbs household in 1923. On the left, Leng Jiaxin with family; on the right, Pen Si (cook) with family.

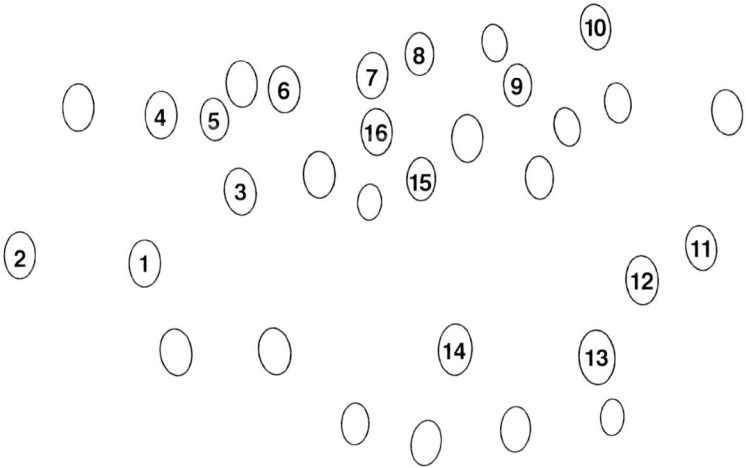

16 *(above)*: Group of Quaker missionaries in 1916.

17 *(below)*: Key: those mentioned in the book are numbered as follows:
1. Ernest Sawdon 2. Harry Silcock 3. Mira Cumber 4. Robin Davidson
5. Mary-Jane Davidson 6. RJD 7. Leonard Wigham 8. Robert Simkin
9. Irene Hutchinson 10. John Rodwell 11. Henry Davidson
12. Margaret Stubbs 13. Clifford Stubbs 14. Laura Davidson
15. Kathleen Davidson 16. Margaret Silcock

18 *(above)*: Chemistry laboratory.

19 *(below)*: 1924: the first women students at Huaxi, with their warden, Alice Brethorst (in hat).

20: William Sewell

21: Cheng Zhixuan

22 *(above left)*: Yang Guoping.

23 *(above right)*: Clifford Stubbs on furlough in England, 1927.

24 *(above)*: The Friends' College in 1926.
25 *(below)*: The Baby Austin.

26: 1927: the Stubbs in England. Margaret, Ruth and John on left, Clifford and Jean on right, Antony, Rose and Gordon Lees in centre, and other family members.

27 *(above)*: The Library prepared for Clifford's funeral.

28 *(below)*: Plaque on the Clifford Stubbs Memorial Building; picture taken in 2000.

Another major deficiency was the total absence of any research. 'This is a reproach to the University, while its being carried on would be a big contribution to the scientific spirit we are seeking to inculcate.' It is notable that Clifford is the only person in the report to make any reference to research. Huaxi was still far from being a university as he understood the term. But he ended on an optimistic note: 'Increased facilities in our new laboratories, the hope of a colleague from abroad, the increasingly efficient Chinese assistants, and the assurance of continued support in equipment from the home lands, all contribute to a hopeful outlook for the future.'

The workload sounds incredible – in 1924 he was teaching twenty-two hours per week – and this does not include his other responsibilities, to University and Mission. He took services and study groups at Qinlonggai, went on YMCA retreats, he was the FFMA official representative in Chengdu on various union committees, and he was Treasurer of the Chengdu Meeting. In 1922 he took over from Simkin as Principal of the Friends' College, and in 1923 he became Dean of the Science Faculty. 'There are lots of jobs,' he commented wryly.[52]

The cottage at Nanyumiao provided a welcome retreat, and he spent short periods there at Christmas and Easter as well as during the summer. Although his family had gone he was rarely there alone. At the end of July there were ten adult guests and three children (and six servants) staying, and he had to put up tents to accommodate them all. He set up beehives there, as he had on the campus, and got a supply of good local honey. But nature had its unfriendly side too – in the evenings there were 'vicious mosquitoes' and invasions of flying ants, and one day Leng Jiaxin found and killed a five-foot snake in the kitchen. 'If you weren't my matey Margaret, but some other kind of wife, I wouldn't tell you this, for fear you have a nightmare!'

The more energetic guests were taken on treks into the mountains; one of these was a week's hike to a Tibetan area further west, where they visited a lamasery. 'We had been told the lamas were not very friendly, but we got on very cordially with them. One of the head men was a very courteous and instructive guide, and we asked hundreds of questions! To become a regular lama a man must have studied eleven years in Lhasa, which from here involves a journey of several months. The apprentice usually makes the journey when he is 25 to 30, and on his return is entitled to wear the red lama's robe. The system is very deeply rooted among the people: almost every family has at least one son a lama. ... The religion seems very much sheer superstition – turning of prayer-wheels and reciting of the Buddhist classics. A few of the men seemed to have kindliness and nobility, but most seemed dirty, ignorant and lazy. The sacrifices the people make for this religion must be very great.'[53]

Work was not ignored even in Nanyumiao. Clifford used the time there to prepare textbooks in Chinese, and was normally helped by one of his Chinese assistants. Each new book required new terminology, and a Chinese input was essential. In 1923 Gao Changjiang helped him with the elementary class textbook; the following year Shi Rucong came, and they worked together on the more demanding second year course. Staying at Nanyumiao was a new experience for these urban Chinese, and Shi got the first cold bath of his life when Clifford lured him to bathe in the stream. It must have taken him aback, to plunge into the icy cold meltwater from the snows of Tibet. But he thoroughly enjoyed it: 'He wants me to photograph him bathing in the pool. He has been very good in helping, has quite entered into the spirit of things, and I think is enjoying himself very much.' Part of the time the two of them were alone in the cottage, and they took walks and a bathe every day as a relaxation from their work. 'It has been good to have this time with Shi, and I have got to know him better. He often speaks of himself as a Christian. I think it would help him however if he more definitely associated himself with the Church. If our meeting at Qinlonggai becomes more definitely a Friends Meeting, I hope he will join in with us more. He and I often talk about matters of the spirit.'[54]

The University remained a little enclave of peace in the war-torn province. In 1923 Chengdu had been besieged three times; another siege in February 1924 brought to power there, for a while, the most vivid personality among the Sichuan warlords, General Yang Sen. Notionally a supporter of the government in Peking, he was an enthusiastic moderniser, and almost his first action on arrival was to visit the University and express his support for all it was doing. He was especially interested in watching a dissection class in the Anatomy Department, and later gave them four cadavers (of unknown origin). In April he performed the opening ceremony for the new Biology Building and in May gave a speech on the University's fourteenth birthday. The more he saw of the University the more he approved of it (this was already his fourth visit), but his main thought was of shame that the Chinese had not yet built a university of their own. The next year he welcomed the participants to the West China Missionary Conference with a speech in the city's Public Park: 'I hope Christianity can aid me in my work. I wish, though a militarist, to develop with all my power such things as education, industry, etc. The present activities of Christianity are of course admirable in this regard.'[55]

Clifford was rather taken with Yang. 'I like Yang in many ways. There is something straightforward about him ... I should like some time to ask him for a weekend – at home or at Nanyumiao – just to have a quiet friendly time, not a lot of show and swarms of guests. He must get very sick of that sort of thing.' Yang soon set about building a new road to Guanxian, and by January 1925 Clifford was able to cycle there in a single morning, and get up to Nanyumiao before nightfall. He even considered getting a motorbike and sidecar. But it was only an earth road, and by the end of the year peasants were planting turnips on it.[56]

Within the city, however, Yang's improvements were more lasting. To widen the streets wayside shrines were torn down, and property owners forced to surrender a slice of their land; new roads and pavements were then laid down in concrete. The Friends' compound in Qinlonggai lost a strip of its frontage, and the Meeting House now opened directly on to the street instead of a courtyard. The changes in the city were celebrated by Margaret Simkin: 'I was astounded to ride all the way from the North Gate to the South Bridge ... along wide smooth streets. I felt as one does landing in New York City from the country! I felt I should not be surprised to see a trolley-car come around the corner; I could imagine I was in Shanghai! Of course one might not be so thrilled if just out from home, but to one who has become Chinese-ized it is truly marvellous ... Moreover the city gates are left open all night now and some of the streets are lighted with electricity!'[57] There were now three public parks (Manchu city park, Central Park, Lanmu Park) public libraries, two moving picture houses and a theatre.[58] Almost immediately sedan chairs were replaced by rickshaws and even the occasional motor vehicle could be seen.

Yang was genuinely interested in sport and encouraged football and tennis in the cities he controlled, and he himself could sometimes be seen on a bicycle. 'Yang Sen was leaving just behind us, on a bicycle! He pedalled up quite a bit of a hill, and away at a good pace, with his bodyguard pelting after him. How they would perspire! I hear Mrs Yang, or one of them, rides too, on a woman's cycle.' The number of Yang's wives was uncertain, and usually grew in the telling. He was certainly prepared to use them for publicity purposes regardless of their feelings. To show his support for women's emancipation, including the ability to swim, he ordered one of his wives to enter the river before a large crowd. She was reluctant, so he dressed her up in peasant clothes to shame her, and threw her in.[59]

Now he had another idea. In the autumn of 1924 the University had admitted its first eight women students, and to show his support Yang proposed sending one of his wives to join them. This required a very tactful response. Educating women together with men was a controversial notion anyway, and for a Christian university to accept a concubine was unthinkable. On the other hand it would be unwise to offend Yang. But once things were gently explained to him he proved reasonable, and a compromise was reached whereby the concubine would sit the entrance exam and fail. She was not told this, of course.

Women's education was a move that had been debated to and fro between the mission boards for several years, with arguments for progress and caution fully aired on both sides. To start with, the eight young women had to be chaperoned everywhere ('almost over-jealously' thought Clifford) and were never allowed to be alone with male students, but these rules did not last very long. The admission of women students was a key event at this point in the University's history, and a marked success; it is also worth noting that most of the first eight were so academically advanced that they went straight into the second year. By 1927 there would be thirty women students, and fifty-seven by 1929, and a Women's College would be set up, on a par with the already existing denominational colleges. Joseph Beech claimed that 'it has placed [the University] in advance of anything hitherto thought of,' and hoped that now Huaxi had shown the way, other colleges in Chengdu would feel able to follow suit. The Government Training College almost immediately did. The enthusiasm of young women for education was illustrated by a Middle School girl who wrote in an essay that her aims in life were to see God, and go to the West China Union University.[60]

Clifford's hope of getting Yang Sen up to Nanyumiao was never realistic, though not quite as absurd as it might seem as Yang's athletic interests included mountaineering. But he did come to dinner with Clifford and the Sewells in April 1925, together with ten armed bodyguards who took up positions on the verandah and around the garden. Sewell demonstrated a few experiments in dyeing, and they showed him a range of pictures – the only ones that interested him were of soldiers and hunting. In the course of the evening Clifford 'told him how the way of "might is right" seemed utterly wrong; and he became suddenly thoughtful, perhaps displeased'. Clifford recalled this after Yang's fall in August that year, when two of his generals were bribed to desert: he was driven out of Chengdu and seemed 'down and out'. Down he may have been, but not out, and he continued to be a player in the lethal contests of Sichuan warlords for several years.[61]

As the 1920s progressed, relations with Chinese colleagues and students became an increasingly important issue at Huaxi. Chinese teachers and alumni wanted a greater say in how the University was run, and this was not easy to reconcile with the already cumbersome structure of senate, mission boards and board of governors. In 1922 President Beech wrote that 'we have made a great step forward in the history of the University by bringing three of our Chinese into the Senate.' There were actually three members and two 'alternates', and it is worth noting that two of the five were Friends – Yang Shaoquan as a full member and Fang Shuxuan as alternate.[62] Friends' contribution in terms of finance and foreign staff might have been small and decreasing, but they compensated with the calibre of their Chinese members. Fang had studied in England for two years after graduating in 1919; on his return he had become Principal of the Normal School, thus taking over Harry Silcock's responsibility for teacher-training – an essential aspect of a mission university intended to provide teachers for mission schools.

But a mere three members of Senate were hardly enough to satisfy the growing nationalist sentiment in China, and the Senate and the Board of Governors were forced to recognise that there needed to be a greater Chinese input in the University. The Senate proposed creating a body of distinguished local Chinese 'advisers and patrons', to get their opinions on the University's policies, and thus make it 'less exotic and more in intimate union with best Chinese life'. It was also hoped that these moves would encourage wealthy local Chinese to make donations to the University, which would do more than anything to give the Chinese a sense of ownership.[63] In 1923 the Board also co-opted its first Chinese member, Guo Pingwen [P.W. Kuo], the founder of Nanjing University, Vice-Chairman of the World Education Congress, and a Presbyterian.

In 1924 the Board, prodded perhaps by its new Chinese member, told the participating Missions that urgent attention should be given to making work 'more Chinese'. 'No policy can prove efficient in China today unless it satisfies nationalist aspirations, and no activity appeals to the Chinese as Christian if it seems to counter the great Christian principle of racial equality upon which at the moment all their thought is concentrated.' It asked the Missions to appoint more Chinese to the staff, and increase the number of Chinese on the Senate. The University should participate in national and provincial education associations, and develop Chinese financial support. They should even consider whether religious education should remain compulsory, 'so that all liberty may be accorded consistent with loyalty to the spirit of Christ'.[64]

This was in part at least a response to the latest campaign against Christian education in China, the 'Educational Rights Movement' of

1924, which enjoyed even wider support than its predecessors. Like them it involved student demonstrations and strikes, but also drew up a series of specific aims. The more extreme wanted the Chinese government to take over all Christian schools and expel the foreign teachers; but most wanted them to submit to government regulation through a process of registration. Ironically, the Christian colleges were engaged at the same time in discussing more coordination of their work, strengthening their efficiency and raising their standards through uniform curricula, graduation requirements, etc. 'Now is the hour of opportunity,' they proclaimed, 'so to strengthen the Christian schools of China that from them shall come the men and the women who will make China a Christian nation.'[65] They do not seem to have realised that these words would be read by Chinese, who would see in them an even greater threat to their identity and nationhood.

1924 saw far less disorder in Chengdu than in eastern China – perhaps Yang Sen kept too firm a grip – but the question of registration could not be avoided. Two of the main requirements were that religious worship and education should become optional; and that colleges should appoint more Chinese staff, and have a Chinese president or at least vice-president. Removing the requirement for religious education would be controversial both among missionaries and even more in the home countries, where a sharp drop in donations could be expected if the colleges were no longer trying to make their students into Christians. A Senate discussion in 1926, reported by Rodwell, reveals these concerns, and how hard it was for many to see things from the Chinese angle: 'It seemed to me that most of the speakers for the compulsory course were thinking too much of the foreign constituency on the field and at home, and too little of the vast Chinese constituency out here. I know of no Chinese leader who is in favour of compulsory religious education. I spoke to the above effect.'[66] But the demands of the government could not be ignored if Christian colleges were to survive; correspondence and discussion, between mission boards and missionaries, between colleges and government authorities, went on for years. There might also be other advantages in registration: the Sichuan Education Commissioner advised Beech that if the University was registered students might be eligible for local government scholarships.[67] The tumultuous political changes in China in the late 1920s delayed the process, they brought new governments to power with new requirements, and after much expenditure of time and paper Huaxi would only complete the process of registration in 1933.

Finding more Chinese teachers, let alone one to take over as president or vice-president, would not be easy, however desirable. There were not many qualified Chinese graduates in West China, and Sichuan was seen as so remote, backward and dangerous – known as 'The Devil's Cave' – that no one from the coastal provinces would want to move there. In 1923, of sixty-one faculty members in total, only eleven were Chinese, although many of the foreigners were part-time, spending much of their time in mission work. As for a president/vice-president, there were hardly any Christian Chinese in Chengdu of suitable calibre. Yang Shaoquan might have seemed an obvious choice – mature, experienced and with the prestige of his revolutionary past. But fatally he was not a graduate: for over a millennium educated Chinese had achieved status through passing examinations, and this attitude carried on into the new world of Western-style universities. It was clear that Yang would not be acceptable to the alumni. Fang Shuxuan was a possibility but was still too young.[68]

The appointment of Chinese staff also created a new cause of resentment and division. Understandably they felt that they should be paid the same as their foreign colleagues for doing the same work, and provided with similar houses, yet there was no way in which university funds could meet this demand. Foreign teachers were paid by their missions, not by the University, and these were in any case reducing their grants. Clifford, we know, felt he was paid too much, and didn't need such a large house; but American missionaries received salaries twice those of the British, and their houses were correspondingly grander. When Robert Simkin placed himself under the American Friends' Board of Foreign Missions they built him a finer house than he would ever have had with the FFMA. Clifford was very struck by it: 'a most wonderful place, one wanders through a whole maze of rooms, cupboards, bathrooms, etc, etc. all very convenient and palatial.'[69] The

University could not build such houses for Chinese teachers, but nor did it want them to live in the city and cease to be part of the community. The 1922 Senate Report[70] had already described housing as a 'burning question', and debated a number of alternatives. Eventually it was decided to create a 'model village' near the University for both Chinese and foreigners, rent houses out, or offer loans to Chinese teachers to build their own houses there. The loans could be repaid as their salary permitted. This found some support from Chinese staff, and over the following years progress was made as funds permitted; but the different scale of their houses was a daily visible sign of discrimination, and a good deal of ill-feeling remained.

One area in which the Chinese were unquestionably playing a greater part was the church. In January 1925 the third West China Christian Conference was held in Chengdu, bringing together members of all the Protestant churches in Sichuan. The previous one had been held in 1908, when Chinese attendance had been limited to five 'visitors'. The 1925 Conference was attended by 287 Chinese Christians, and 157 missionaries. There were a number of women present who were ready to stand up and take part. The leading speaker was Chinese – Cheng Jingyi of the National Christian Council of China. 'He gave us day-by-day devotional talks that took us to the heart of things,' Clifford reported. 'I am glad that his contribution, probably the deepest one of the Conference, was a Chinese one ... In this conference the Chinese enthusiastically and independently took the leading place.' It was interesting to note that, when the perennial question of 'ancestor-worship' came up, the Chinese 'were unanimous in believing that many of the old customs, including bowing before the tablet of one's ancestors, etc., should be tolerated, if not retained within the Christian Church.'[71] A distinctive Chinese Christian viewpoint was beginning to emerge, a 'Christianity with Chinese characteristics', against compulsory religious teaching and comfortable with honouring the ancestors. Missionaries would have to adjust to this and it would not be easy.

At least the Conference was a fairly amicable occasion. This was quite an achievement, since hostility between fundamentalist and 'modernist' or liberal missionaries had been increasing since the start of the decade. Fundamentalist preachers had come from America to fight heresy in the missionary community, and one of their main targets had been Henry Hodgkin. In 1924 they had tried to prevent him speaking at a missionary conference in East China, and in 1926 the controversy led to the China Inland Mission withdrawing from the National Christian Council altogether. As early as 1919 the Church Missionary Society had stopped sending its Chinese evangelists to the annual Summer Bible School at Huaxi 'in view of the very advanced critical views on the Scripture held by some of the teachers of the University staff [these would have included Robert Simkin]. Our workers are not men of highly trained minds, capable of thought and discrimination ...' Some years before 'a highly respected senior missionary' had boasted publicly of throwing every communication from the University into the waste paper basket unread. Clifford and the Sewells were anxious about hosting a pair of CIM people for the Conference, but they turned out to be 'nice folks, and we are enjoying having them, dwelling on the things we have in common rather than our differences in theology.'[72]

Clifford's sympathy with Chinese aspirations, and his ability to get on well with people like Yang Sen, led to his being elected University Vice-President in March 1925. His modest amazement is doubtless genuine. 'I had a terrible shock this afternoon when I heard my name proposed as Vice-President ... I feel my qualifications for the job are in many ways inadequate, in fact I hardly know whether I ought to tackle it. On the other hand it may be a call to some opportunity of useful service ... The work will involve mainly more committees etc. though there may be some entertaining etc. I shall have to try to get more Chinese teaching assistance next term.' There were indeed 'lots of jobs', and here was one more.[73]

By the summer he felt it was 'pretty well a sinecure. I go to two cabinet meetings a week, where Joe Beech discourses at great length about all the current news, and that is about all. However, I am hoping next term to have more time to give especially to the social side, getting in touch with people etc.' His letters to Margaret make some brief references to new people he has met in the city, but his modesty conceals how important this work was. A more emphatic account of his achievement comes from John Rodwell on the occasion of Clifford's return home the following year. 'We have been extremely thankful that Clifford was the Vice-President of the University during the last year, he has won hosts of friends among the Chinese and has undoubtedly contributed a great deal to the maintenance of a friendly feeling between foreigners and Chinese up here.'[74]

Rodwell's praise is deeply significant, since only a month after Clifford's appointment had come the 'May 30th Incident' in Shanghai, the killing of unarmed Chinese students by the British Police force. As one of the students was from Sichuan this caused particular anger in the province. This was greatest as usual in Chongqing, where the presence of British gunboats on the river was a continual provocation. The British Consul there ordered all foreign women to go downriver, and the men took refuge in one of the merchant compounds on the river bank, under gunboat protection. Chengdu was more peaceful: there were fiery speeches, parades and demonstrations, but little personal hostility. Yang Sen made it clear that no foreigners were to be harmed. He even sent some soldiers to guard the Stubbs home, and they grazed their horses on the lawn. He also attended in person the rather muted graduation ceremony on 23rd June. 'He addressed the gathering, making it clear that he had only friendship for an institution which though founded by foreigners was only seeking China's good.' The Senate also issued a cautious statement which 'while not prejudging the case, expressed our sympathy and sorrow'.[75]

However, disturbances in Chongqing, which included the bayoneting of some Chinese by Royal Marines, further inflamed feelings in the whole province. The Chengdu Chamber of Commerce announced a boycott of British goods. The whole student body of Chengdu turned against Yang Sen because of his pro-foreign attitude, and organised a strike of servants at Huaxi. The British Consul advised all foreigners to leave, but most of them, unperturbed by politics, had already gone to the hills and ignored him. The servant strike had little effect as there were few foreigners in residence to serve.[76]

Margaret was anxious as she read alarming accounts in the British newspapers, and Frederick Stubbs terrified his granddaughters with tales of the horrors of China. Clifford's letters are mainly concerned to reassure her: 'Things often seem worse when dished up at the English end ... I hope thou won't listen to scary people like my Pater who will talk about that awful China and about women and children having no business to go there.' The Consul in Chongqing had panicked needlessly, he wrote; missionaries in Chengdu felt secure enough to go to the mountains for the summer as usual, and the consul there was happy with this. In Nanyumiao itself no one had even heard of the Shanghai Incident.[77] Nationalism was very much confined to the cities; country people were more concerned with mere survival. China was full of paradoxes, and violent anti-foreign demonstrations were only part of the picture. When foreigners travelled by water they still took care to display their national flags for protection, and Chinese would often join them because it was safer. 'And all this after the recent anti-foreign agitation!' exclaimed Margaret Simkin. 'It would be laughable if it were not so pitiable. Think of it, a Chinese does not dare travel in his own country without the protection of the despised foreigner!'[78]

That summer Clifford writes not of hostility and fear, but of an atmosphere of friendliness and calm: 'It is really remarkable how quiet and often friendly the people are – particularly of course the people we know, who seem to have taken pains to show their friendliness to us.' His own students were 'out for order' and seemed ashamed of the destruction caused by riots in other parts of China. 'I have been impressed, despite the wild talk, with the civilisation and restraint shown the last few weeks. They are a great civilised people, not Balkan hotheads ... The friendly spirit shown at the present time is very striking. I wonder whether in "Christian England" – as at the beginning of the war, when tales of German atrocities were in circulation – would such friendliness be shown to aliens?' At the same time the events made him think more deeply about the underlying causes of antagonism. 'I hope it will lead to some international action to lessen the causes of friction between China and foreign nations. Why should we retain extraterritoriality, and gun-boats on the Yangzi etc.?'[79]

He realised that it was a turning point in relations between Britain and China, and that nothing would be the same again. But many other missionaries did not, and John Rodwell reported much 'bitter anti-Chinese talk'.[80] Chinese Christians, who shared the anger of their compatriots at the killings in Shanghai, appealed to them to dissociate themselves from the shootings and make some statement of support. The Chengdu Monthly Meeting wrote to Silcock in London about 'the badly killing of the unarmed Chinese students who struggled unselfishly and nobly for humane treatment towards Chinese labourers ... The light of Truth of our Lord seems greatly overshadowed by the dark clouds of the militarism, imperialism and capitalism.' Their position was very vulnerable, as Yang Guoping pointed out. 'It is just as difficult for the Chinese to work for the Christian church and school as our English friends. In some cases we are facing more difficulty and dangerous condition. Letters and notices often come to us with the threats that if we do not leave our work at once we will be treated with force or put to death.'[81]

Yet despite pleas like this most missionaries, according to a press cutting, refused to make any comment on the shootings, and took refuge in protocol. The gist of replies 'was that the May 30th affair in Shanghai was now a subject for judicial enquiry and since missionaries in their work in China had no connection with any government the question was not legitimate. Missionaries do not engage in politics but are here purely for spreading the gospel.' Some had been against making any response to the appeals at all. In Guanxian Clifford and Rodwell had done what they could to modify the reply from missionaries holidaying there; the result was 'not as pro-China as some of us wished, but it does definitely express sympathy. Our Chinese friends seem pleased with it.'[82]

In November the local group of the Fellowship of Reconciliation invited all those interested to a meeting at Clifford's house, to discuss relations between China and the Western powers. About thirty people came, Chinese and foreign. Yang Guoping opened the discussion, 'very outspoken about the Chinese mistrust of foreigners etc., putting anti-foreign feeling down largely to political treaties etc. We felt we only got to the beginning of things ... a number are evidently very interested and keen to get somewhere.' Clifford read out a statement he had prepared, addressed to 'Chinese Friends'. It starts with asserting that missionaries were in no sense agents of their governments (this was widely believed to be the case), then went on to say that 'the political status of foreigners in China, founded on treaties of many years ago, which were largely imposed by force of arms, we feel to be on a wrong basis, and a root cause of national suspicion and ill-feeling. Our desire is to give up the basing of our status and rights on such treaties, and live and work here only by the goodwill of the Chinese people … As regards the presence of foreign forces in China, we regret and repudiate this, and will not willingly avail ourselves of their protection, and desire to use our utmost influence for their withdrawal.'[83] He knew that this went beyond what many of his colleagues felt. 'Foreign friends are not all of one mind on this question here, any more than at Home, and some would be very unwilling to relinquish foreign rights in China. We do not want to offend or seem to sit in judgment on them – fine devoted people often – but I feel that to be silent for fear of giving offence may also be wrong.'[84] This statement sets out the political concerns which were to play a large part in Clifford's life over the next few years. He felt that he should only be in China if this was the wish of the Chinese, and as he was preparing to set off home in January 1926 he was especially delighted – in his words 'bowled over' – by praise and good wishes from Yang Guoping at the Chengdu Monthly Meeting, and pleased most of all by the assurance that they wanted him to return.[85]

One man in the city whom Clifford had befriended was Cheng Zhixuan, a noted Confucian scholar-official, and a former head of the Sichuan Provincial Education Bureau. In the autumn of 1925 he agreed to come to Huaxi as its full-time Chinese Executive Officer, with responsibilities for administration, and strengthening links with city authorities and educationists, thus making Huaxi 'more Chinese'. He was 'a well-to-do man, but lives extremely simply. His domestic staff consists only of an old woman. His place is quiet, with trees and bamboos.' He might have taken some persuading to come, but it probably took even more to persuade colleagues at Huaxi to invite him, for Cheng was not a Christian and had no interest in becoming one. He was a Buddhist and a vegetarian, whose intention was to end his days in a monastery. But leading Chinese Christians like Fang Shuxuan approved, and Clifford felt him to be 'in sympathy with our aims'. He was one of those Chinese for whom Quakerism had a special appeal, and soon he came to live in the Friends' College. He would stay there for 10 years until his retirement in 1937, when he left to become a monk on the Buddhist sacred mountain of Wutaishan. He regularly attended the daily Meeting for Worship, and was a much respected adviser to the students. Clifford and he exchanged views on matters of the spirit, and Clifford recounts a long talk with him about transmigration, over boiled eggs and toasted currant buns. The following year a Chinese Department was set up with Cheng as its head; this was also located in the Friends' College.[86]

A further example of 'inter-faith dialogue' took place that autumn when two Buddhist priests, one of whom had the title 'Ta Yung Fa Sz (the illustrious one)', gave a lecture to a Christian audience at the YMCA. John Rodwell then invited them to Qinlonggai to meet a small group of Chinese Christians, together with Clifford and two American Methodists. Rodwell found it 'a stimulating and thought-provoking occasion'. The two Buddhists 'had a deep spiritual understanding of what was involved in the teaching of Jesus.' They were 'very intelligent … our Christians did not have things all their own way by any means. There was a very friendly spirit throughout the meeting; we met, as the Ta Yung Fa Sz put it, on the basis of a common search for Truth.'[87]

A long-awaited event took place at the beginning of January 1926, when the Friends' College was finally completed, and its students would no longer have to live in temporary accommodation. It had been planned for almost as long as Clifford had been in China. Materials had been bought before the war but had deteriorated over time, and this, together with the financial effects of the war and fluctuating exchange rates, had greatly multiplied the final cost. But now the building, designed and supervised by Harry Silcock's architect brother Arnold, was complete. It was an important moment for the University as a whole, as it stood at the end of the northward vista across the campus, and completed the overall design. 'Because of its location on the central axis and its exquisite fine style of architecture, it constitutes one of the outstanding and most beautiful features in our array of buildings.' While comparatively small, its proportions and its harmonious combination of Western and Chinese styles made it one of the most beautiful buildings on the campus. No longer were Friends shamed before the other missions, who had built their colleges years before. It had rooms for thirty to forty students on the upper floor, while the lower floor accommodated the Faculty of Education, closely associated with Friends since its establishment by Harry Silcock, and now run by Fang Shuxuan. The opening of the college, just before his departure on furlough, was a happy conclusion to Clifford's second tour of duty.[88]

7

1926–1927, England

Clifford returned to England in March 1926 convinced that Quakerism had a special appeal to the Chinese, and hoping that the Society at home would be able to respond to this. In 1923 he had written to C.E. Jacob, a leading member of the FFMA: 'I feel strongly that Friends' conceptions of Christian truth and life have a great opening here in China. Many earnest young Chinese who, partly through a superficial view no doubt are repelled by and opposed to a ceremonial and ecclesiastical type of religion, are peculiarly open to being reached by Friends. Quite a number – some of them members of other branches of the Church – have said this to me. I am sure that in the University etc. the influence of Friends is quite out of all proportion to their numbers. I mention this, not from any narrow denominational point of view, for which I don't care twopence, but because I feel this is really the religious outlook (under whatever name) that China needs and that in many ways she seems ready to respond to.'[1]

One of these 'members of other churches' was Song Chengzhi, a convert of the Church Missionary Society. 'He is worried by the ranks and orders of the Anglican Church. He is really by all his convictions and tendencies a Friend. He is much concerned for the growth of an indigenous, self-supporting church.' Song told him of a group of Christians in Peking who had dispensed with a professional ministry – 'they think every member of the Church should earn his living in one of the ordinary occupations.'[2] Another Anglican with doubts about the 'church system' was C.W. Hsiung, 'a disciple of Hodgkin' and a Chinese scholar of some standing, who in 1926 resigned from the Anglican

Church to work with Friends at Qinlonggai, where he became head-master of the primary school.[3]

These men had never made a choice of Anglicanism in preference to other denominations. In 1898 the first West China Missionary Con-ference had divided up the province of Sichuan between the various denominational societies, agreeing not to encroach on each other's territory.[4] This meant that the brand of Christianity a convert adopted depended on where he lived. Then the Chinese tradition of loyalty to one's teacher made it hard to move into another denomination. Good relations between missionaries also depended on refraining from 'poaching' converts, especially able ones like Song and Hsiung. Clifford had taken care to discuss Hsiung's move several months before with Bishop Howard Mowll, who was understanding about the situation but naturally disappointed at losing him. Everyone recognised that Song Chengzhi would remain with the Anglicans: he was already seen as one of the outstanding Christian leaders in Sichuan and, despite his doubts about ranks and orders, would soon be consecrated as the first Chinese Bishop in Sichuan.

Later on another young Anglican, out of sympathy with the 'church system', and drawn to Friends, approached Clifford for advice, but fearful of the misunderstanding that might ensue if he joined them. Clifford advised him to discuss his doubts with Bishop Mowll.[5] Anglicanism, with its hierarchies and rituals more marked than in other Protestant churches, seems to have posed a particular problem for the Chinese, and suggests why they found Friends appealing. So much of Christian practice was alien to the religious traditions of China. The Chinese followed the 'three teachings' of Confucianism, Daoism and Buddhism, without any need to identify themselves specifically with one rather than another (except in the case of 'religious professionals' like Buddhist monks). As missionaries would solemnly repeat, 'denomi-nationalism does not interest the Chinese mind'. The Chinese had no dogmas or creeds, no sacraments, no salaried ministry, no regular Sunday morning communal rituals, no sermons ... So Friends, who also had none of these things (except Sunday Meeting), had a natural appeal which the other denominations lacked. It may also be that the

Quaker way of doing business, trying to ascertain the 'spirit of the meeting' and being prepared to delay decisions rather than closing matters off with a vote, was appealing to the Chinese preference for harmony over open confrontation.

Then Friends had a social and political awareness which was less evident in other Christian groups. There were too many followers of the Prince of Peace, as Hodgkin had noted in 1921, who had nothing of consequence to say about the Peace that China so desperately needed. 'In China our preaching had force, because we believed in driving away all war,' Ernest Sawdon told the London Yearly Meeting in 1926.[6] There were of course many individual missionaries of other societies who were concerned with the political situation, who were critical of the 'unequal treaties' under whose provisions they lived in China, and who were sympathetic to Chinese nationalism. But Friends perhaps more clearly than most related their faith to questions of peace and international relations, and were supported in this by Friends at home.

The Quaker practice of silent worship was also attractive, at least to educated Chinese. Meetings 'after the manner of Friends' had rarely been held in the early days of the Friends' Mission, as they were hardly a suitable medium for evangelism; but by the 1920s they were held each Sunday at Qinlonggai in addition to a programmed meeting. Hodgkin noted in 1924 that the Chinese were not only interested in the practical side of religion – good works, etc. – as most missionaries thought, but had a capacity for mysticism, and appreciated silence. The silence in Meeting, he wrote, was usually broken by missionaries.[7] In the autumn of 1926 Hodgkin accompanied the influential American Quaker mystic Rufus Jones and a small group of Chinese and foreign Christians to a retreat on the Confucian holy mountain of Taishan in Shandong province. There they became acquainted with silent meditation according to the principles of Zen Buddhism. 'The worshipper gathers into the silence, withdraws from the world, and concentrates upon the eternal ground of truth and life,' Jones explained in *The Friend*. Like Hodgkin, he concluded that China was more open to a mystical type of religion than many other countries.[8]

Clifford also liked going up mountains. China is dotted with holy mountains, and they play an important part in Chinese spiritual life. 'The benevolent man loves mountains', Confucius said,[9] and mountains are a key element in Chinese landscape painting. An enlightened Bishop of Hong Kong in the mid-twentieth century advised missionaries to look at Chinese painting rather than scripture if they wanted to understand the spiritual life of the Chinese. Pictures often depict a scholar standing alone on a mountain side, gazing into the void, seeking to apprehend the *Dao*, the underlying harmony of nature. Clifford never mentions Daoism, but it is one of the formative influences on the Chinese sensibility, and Clifford's love of climbing mountains might well have appealed to his Chinese friends, even if he would usually be carrying, not a scholar's staff, but a barometer to measure the mountain's height.

During his furlough Clifford wrote articles and addressed a wide range of audiences about his work, and we can see him performing a difficult balancing act. He has to reconcile his earlier evangelicalism – the person of Christ, we know, remained central to his own spiritual life – to the new insights of Quakerism, and persuade younger Friends, hostile to the whole idea of missions, that there was value in the work being done in China. A letter in *The Friend* from a Gerald Whichelo in October 1926 expressed the feelings he had to counter. What was the point of missions, Whichelo asked? Would we not resent the presence of Chinese missionaries in England? Sharing ideas was fine, but why make a business of it? Why go off and found a church? A couple of weeks later Clifford wrote an article in reply – 'Is our World Service Fundamentally Right?' It was important for Quakers to be open to the presence of the divine Spirit in other religious traditions, but also to 'share with the whole human family that vision of Truth and inflow of life in Christ ... not in the spirit of imposing a religion or culture of our own, but of pointing men to the One who can speak alike to their condition and ours. In the response of different races to universal truth we shall meet with diversity of expression, and we shall seek and expect to receive enrichment ourselves from their spiritual experience.'[10]

To the objection, forcefully put by many post-war Friends, that the behaviour of 'so-called Christian civilisation' deprived Christians of the right to preach their faith to others, he replied that this made it the more important to show the Chinese 'our best, since the worst is already at work in their midst'. We should seek to improve our own society, but self-improvement should not exclude the claims of a wider service. He also had to counter the objection to full-time salaried missionaries, something alien to Friends' traditions. 'It is difficult to exaggerate the value of the service of those who live the Christian life in business relations at home or abroad. But in principle and in its fruit the service is justified also of some who in no professional or mercenary spirit give their lives in ways which are made possible only with the support of others. It would surprise some who fear overmuch dependence on "words" to know how little comparatively of the service of Friends is given through preaching, how much in friendly intercourse, through education of the mind and healing of the body, or through interpreting and reconciling between those of different races.' A Chinese friend had told Rodwell, 'I tell you you are doing a great work, you are getting the Chinese to love the foreigners, this is much better than preaching at them, after all, friendship has religion in it.' What gave Clifford's concern such urgency was knowing how much Friends' institutions in China, 'educating the mind and healing the body' – schools, hospitals, the University – relied on financial and personal support from Friends at home.[11]

Clifford had returned to England on the Trans-Siberian Railway and spent a few days in Moscow, which had now been under Communist rule for eight years. He found there an 'impression of contentment and of good government', although the 'iron hand of authority' was evident. The churches were full on saints' days, and a noticeable number of men were present.[12] Perhaps the Bolshevism that so many foreigners in China feared would not be so bad after all. In England he found Friends' overseas work in a state of crisis that overshadowed any abstract debate about the rights and wrongs of missions, in desperate need of funds and recruits. The FFMA was almost bankrupt: in 1926 it had an income of £26,554 and a deficit for the year of £11,365. Up to then the annual deficits had been met largely from a reserve fund, but that had now declined from about £20,000 in 1920 to £1000. The Council for International Service (CIS.), which had been founded after the war to continue with relief work and the encouragement of peace and reconciliation, was in equally dire straits. So in September 1926 an 'Adjourned Yearly Meeting' was held in London to address the problem. It attracted a surprisingly large number of Young Friends, but to very little effect. The historian of Friends' overseas work, Ormerod Greenwood, is scathing about it.[13] It was 'extraordinarily ill-prepared', did not face the facts, and produced little but platitudes. The FFMA and the CIS were left to sort out their own problems, and by the end of 1927 they had united under the title of the Friends' Service Council (FSC), a name, as Greenwood says, that gives no indication of the work it did.

The words 'Foreign Missions' were dropped, although some evangelical Friends fought hard to retain them. They reflected that attitude of cultural superiority, of bringing light to the benighted heathen, which so damaged the reputation of Christianity among the Chinese. Clifford would have been happy with this, but his contribution to the debate, as recorded in *The Friend*, reveals an irritation at the way the discussion was going, and perhaps a recognition that the work in China was not going to get the support it so desperately needed. It was not a question of how much money should be spent 'but whether the Society was behind the movement'. 'He believed the nations of the world ... were hungering and in need of that way of life and truth which we had in Christ ... Was our attitude to be that we would let them hunger while we were discussing and differing amongst one another as to what kind of vessel we should take food in or about the different values in the food?' For him, as a 'Friend by convincement', it was 'one of the glories of the Society that we could agree to respect each other's point of view and believe in each other's sincerity'. Then he went on to outline his view of the role that Friends should play in the China of the 1920s. 'Some felt that we should not make it a part of our message to deal with social and industrial questions, but we felt we could not refrain, for we were agreed that our Christianity was a matter of the whole life. People in China were asking about the Treaties, which were won from an unwilling nation at the point of the sword. When we went back we could not be silent.'[14]

It was important to let the Chinese know that missionaries sympathised with their political aspirations for a genuinely independent and peaceful China. But during his furlough Clifford found that it was just as important to let the British know about the injustice of the Treaties, the reasons behind the turmoil in China – to be a missionary for China as well as to it. China was very much in the news at this time: the May 30th killings in Shanghai had been followed by the killing by British and French troops of fifty-two demonstrators in Canton in June 1925. This added fuel to the rage against Britain, and led to a boycott of British goods and businesses throughout China and a sixteen-month dock strike in Hong Kong. British businesses were hurting, and called on the government to do something, to send in troops, even to take over China in the name of the Empire.

Responding to this, the Society of Friends as a whole began to take a serious interest in China. They were concerned about the dangers of widening conflict, and tried in various ways to influence public and political opinion in favour of reconciliation, and a revision of the Treaties that governed the position of foreigners in China. Henry Hodgkin, who was in England on leave in 1925, was intensely active in the cause, addressing over 200 meetings around the country, seeing the Foreign Secretary and the Archbishop of Canterbury, leaders of the three political parties, and using the new medium of the radio to explain the complexities of the situation in China and urge modification of the Treaties, and the treatment of China as an equal sovereign power. The Foreign Secretary, Sir Austen Chamberlain, had just been awarded the Nobel Peace Prize for negotiating the Treaty of Locarno, and had also signed the Kellogg-Briand Pact outlawing war as an instrument of policy, so it is understandable that the government adopted a fairly moderate and conciliatory attitude towards China; it had accepted that the Treaties needed to be revised, if only there were a Chinese government with sufficient authority to negotiate with. On the other side was the British business community in Shanghai, and its vociferous and powerful allies in parliament and the press, calling for armed intervention. There was also a widespread feeling that a time of such uncertainty and danger was not one in which to give up the protection that the treaties offered.[15]

An important Quaker initiative at this time was the creation of the Universities' China Committee, whose aims included bringing distinguished Chinese speakers to give a series of lectures in British universities, and offering friendship and help to Chinese students. Although Friends were the initiators, and Silcock was its secretary, it was felt that an openly religious body would not win Chinese approval, while the word 'universities' would prove attractive. It quickly gained high-powered support. The Committee included the vice-chancellors of all the universities in Britain, a visit to Oxford brought on board the Master of Balliol and the Warden of All Souls, and a key supporter was Sir Charles Addis, Chairman of the Hongkong and Shanghai Bank. It was finally set up in the summer of 1926, with a Royal Charter and £200,000 from the Boxer Indemnity Fund.

Its first invited speaker, already in Britain in late 1926, was Hu Shi, a key figure among the May 4th generation of scholars, who had impressed Hodgkin in 1921, and, according to Silcock, was 'the most famous man in China'.[16] After staying for a week with the Silcocks in Hampstead he devoted the month of November to a very successful speaking tour of British universities, charming his audiences with his intelligence and humour – 'he certainly gets down to realities and talks great good sense to Chinese and Britishers alike.'[17] 'He does not call himself a Christian,' wrote Silcock, 'yet I feel there is a great deal in common between his attitude and ours over religious things. I was charmed to find how simple, unassuming and young he was, and when a man is known as "the Father of the Renaissance" and a famous poet and scholar, one is all the more pleased to find him approachable and friendly.' The previous day Silcock had met the Bengali poet Rabindranath Tagore, who like Hu had a very positive attitude towards Quakers. These meetings confirmed Clifford's belief that Quakerism had a particular appeal to people from the East. 'One thing almost frightened me,' wrote Silcock, 'was the very high estimation both these men have for the Society of Friends. If only we could live up to what people in other countries expect of us!'[18] Unfortunately they could not. For all Clifford's efforts to interest Young Friends in China, over the next ten years there would only be one recruit from Britain to the Mission in Sichuan.

Young Friends' lack of interest in China was matched by Young China's suspicion of Christianity. Hu Shi's tour had been 'such an outstanding success that for several months the Committee was unwilling to undertake anything else for fear they would not be able to keep the high standard.'[19] When they suggested inviting a distinguished Christian Chinese academic Timothy Liu Tingfang, who was a colleague of Hu Shi at Peking University, Hu advised against it: he liked Liu as a friend, but felt that, as a Christian, he would not be seen in China as a genuine representative of the country.[20]

By the middle of 1926 the situation in China had grown more acute, as Chinese nationalism organised itself, politically and militarily, to take the country back from the warlords and the imperialists. The veteran nationalist leader Sun Yatsen, after several years in obscurity, had based himself in Canton in 1923, and called on the Russians for advice. Their revolution had been successful, and Sun wanted to learn their secret. So the Communist International (Comintern) in Moscow sent the experienced revolutionary Mikhail Borodin to Canton, to advise and collaborate with Sun. The Nationalist Party, the Guomindang, was refounded along Leninist lines, with stronger organisation and discipline. Sun proclaimed his 'Three Principles' – Nationalism, Democracy, Socialism. To create a competent military force an officers' training academy was founded at Whampoa just south of Canton. Finally, a formal alliance was agreed with the fledgling Communist Party, which had only 300 members, but was already influential in labour unions.

In March 1925 Sun Yatsen died, leaving a testament that was very pro-Soviet in tone. The effective leadership of the Guomindang now passed to the commandant of the Whampoa Academy, General Chiang Kaishek. The alliance with the Communists went through a difficult phase, as Chiang and most of the Whampoa officers, who came from a landlord background, were deeply suspicious of them; but Moscow ordered the Communist Party to maintain the alliance, and told the Chinese they were not yet ready for a Communist revolution. By July

1926 the Nationalists had the men and the resources to embark on a campaign against the warlords – the 'Northern Expedition'. The warlords to their rear, in the south-western provinces of Guangxi and Yunnan, seeing how the wind was blowing, offered Chiang their support. It was a hybrid army, with nationalist, communist and warlord loyalties, but initially it was very successful in taking over Hunan province to the north and reaching the Yangzi river by August. There they encountered the troops of Wu Peifu, one of the most powerful warlords, and fighting along the middle Yangzi was fierce. They took Hankou at the beginning of October, and set up a government there; Chiang then continued eastwards into Jiangxi Province which, after more heavy fighting, he took over by mid-November. While in Jiangxi he gave an interview to a Western journalist which must have caused extreme alarm in the British business community. He said it was his intention to set up a government like that in the Soviet Union; mere revision of the treaties with foreign powers would not be enough, all the foreign concessions must be surrendered, and foreigners serving in the Chinese customs service would be dismissed. All this would be done immediately, not over a period of years. Missionaries, however, would be welcome to remain: 'I have no quarrel with Christianity ... The elimination of missions from China is not part of our programme, and they may function in this country without interference as always.'[21]

Despite Chiang's words, many church buildings were looted and destroyed as the Northern Expedition passed through southern China; perhaps this shows the limits of his authority over the armies he led. The British authorities ordered the evacuation of all missionaries from South and Central China; forced now to recognise the importance of politics, they left for Shanghai or home, many exceedingly bitter at Chinese 'ingratitude'. Missionaries in Sichuan were also told to leave, but since this would mean leaving their comparative security to travel through the war zone on the middle Yangzi they mostly stayed put.

But then an incident in Sichuan itself altered their situation very much for the worse. It took place on 6th September in the Yangzi city of Wanxian, downriver from Chongqing, where the resident warlord was Clifford's old acquaintance Yang Sen. He believed that some of his soldiers had been drowned by the wash of a British steamer – what had actually happened is uncertain – and to extract compensation he seized two passenger steamers with their British officers. Over the following week three British gunboats moved to Wanxian, and tried to seize back the steamers and rescue the imprisoned officers. In the ensuing chaos one of the kidnapped officers was drowned, and seven British seamen were killed. The city was bombarded and many of its wooden houses caught fire. The number of Chinese killed was estimated as anything from 100 to 5000.

The 'Wanxian Incident' provoked fierce anti-British riots and demonstrations in Chongqing. All foreigners had to move for several weeks into a merchant compound on the riverbank, where gunboats could protect them. Communist influence was particularly strong among unionised workers in Chongqing, and its warlord Liu Xiang soon declared his loyalty to the Guomindang. The Friends' High School was invaded by a local militia and the headmaster Yang Fangling beaten up, illustrating the dangers faced by Chinese Christians. In Chengdu over 10,000 students demonstrated against Britain, but there the violence was confined to words. Student demonstrations always had something of the theatrical about them. According to a report in the *Shanghai Times*, almost certainly by a missionary, 'To witness one of these demonstrations, and listen to the wild denunciations one would naturally feel that the nationals against whom this venom was directed were anathema ... [yet] a few hours later those agitators could be seen hobnobbing with these dreadful imperialists in a most friendly manner.' Rodwell also commented, 'all this slanging and flinging of mud does not mean half to the Chinese what it would mean to a member of the white races'. The British Consul advised all women and children to leave for the coast, but privately thought the trouble would not be too bad as the Guomindang hated Yang Sen and were glad to see him attacked.[22]

Things did get worse in Huaxi, as the Chengdu Students' Union intimidated foreigners' servants into going on strike, and the gatekeeper at Qinlonggai was paraded through the streets in sackcloth and ashes, forced to repeat 'I am a foreign slave'.[23] After two weeks a settlement of the strike was negotiated by Yang Shaoquan, and things calmed down. Then at the beginning of January events downriver, when Chinese crowds stormed into the British concessions in Hankou and Jiujiang and took them over, led the British Consul once more to order all British citizens to leave, and this time he meant it. The Sewells, the Rodwells and others left for Shanghai, and by the end of January only twenty foreigners, Americans and Canadians, were left in Chengdu. The University was now almost entirely run by its Chinese staff, as were most Christian churches in China. The sudden evacuation was – in the event wrongly – understood to mean that the British government intended armed intervention in China. A large number of troops and warships had arrived in Shanghai, and it was assumed that the British authorities wanted their citizens out of the way before starting an invasion. An anguished cable was received in London from the Sichuan Yearly Meeting: 'Urge Government Conciliation. Force useless.'[24]

In November Clifford joined a Quaker delegation to the Foreign Office, and was relieved to find that feeling in the government, unlike that in parliament and the press, was very much in favour of conciliation. 'I am delighted by the attitude taken up by men like this in official position,' Silcock wrote to Hodgkin after the meeting. 'We need to secure a public opinion which can adequately back up the officials.'[25] In this, Clifford, as the most articulate and politically committed of the missionaries now in England, came to play an important part, addressing meetings up and down the country and contributing letters and articles to newspapers. In October 1926 he wrote 'A Plain Guide to the Chinese Puzzle' for the *Sunday Express*. In November he wrote a long and impassioned letter to the *Manchester Guardian* calling for Britain to take the initiative to remove the causes of injustice and humiliation that so embittered the Chinese. It was essential to revise the Treaties, and to give up any rights not freely granted by the Chinese. While this might take time, and was especially difficult when there was no effective central government in China, one action that could be taken immediately was to withdraw all foreign armed forces. 'Imagine the feelings of a young Chinese patriot arriving, as I have done, from the interior of Sichuan at the port of Chongqing on the Yangzi, 1500 miles from its mouth. And there, with their menacing armaments, lie the sinister grey forms of British, American, Japanese and French gunboats. What, to the Chinese view, is their purpose there? Would we tolerate alien war vessels dominating the Manchester Ship Canal? I believe in the fundamental reasonableness and responsiveness of the Chinese, and that generous action would result in a new atmosphere being created.'[26]

In January he wrote again on the significance of events in Hankou, where Chinese had taken over the British concession, the British troops had been withdrawn, and the British authorities had invited the Chinese police to maintain order. This was indeed a key turning-point in Anglo–Chinese relations, and Clifford hoped that 'the principles of what has taken place in Hankou will be extended to British policy generally, including those war vessels in Chinese inland waters, whose provocative effect on Chinese national feeling is without doubt'. Later in 1927 he was stung by the report of an American businessman's crudely prejudiced speech on China to write again in support of Chinese Nationalism: 'Leaders in intellectual life, in social service, in medicine, in the Christian Church, all are behind this movement.'[27]

The meetings he addressed around the country were mostly arranged by local Friends or the League of Nations Union, and often drew a large attendance. In October he was at the Lancashire and Cheshire (Friends') Quarterly Meeting, and in mid-November he spoke to the League of Nations Union in Warrington, after which 'leading townspeople testified to the fair and frank approach of the lecturer'. This was followed by 'the most successful meeting organised by Friends' in Liverpool, where he spoke on 'What is happening in China'. In Wrexham in December his address was on 'China and its People'.[28] After Christmas he was off to Yorkshire and the north-east, addressing meetings in Ilkley, Leeds, Bishop Auckland, and Sunderland. This last was 'one of the largest I have had, mayor in the chair with his gilded paraphernalia, and backed by the League of Nations Union. Everywhere one naturally finds great interest in China.' In Newcastle he spoke at the Quarterly Meeting, to Young Friends and a mothers' group, and engaged in a discussion on 'how to promote the International Mind among children especially. [The organiser] spoke of a questionnaire in which 80% of the children had expressed aversion to live in China, based sometimes on a dislike of rice pudding, but often on serious misconceptions due to the cinema.'[29]

Early in 1927 he visited Sidcot and Saffron Walden Friends' Schools, and in April spoke at a debate on China attended by well over 500 people in Hoxton Friends' Mission, sharing the platform with Labour and Tory MPs. One of those present has left an account of the extraordinary impact that Clifford made. 'After we had got 650 people in the Hall, we closed the doors, and there was a large crowd left outside. It was pretty obvious there was a rowdy element in the meeting. After one or two had spoken, Clifford Stubbs got up to speak. As long as I live I shall remember the great silence that gathered over the meeting while he was speaking. There was absolutely no discord. Many who were there and other speakers afterwards said it was a most extraordinary meeting.'[30]

Earlier in the month he had been to Weston-super-Mare. 'Last night's meeting was a thriller. Despite downpour the hall was packed ... They said there were 700 there, many smoking, a truly proletarian audience.' Later in the year he visited Barry in South Wales, and the Rhondda Valley where, after a 180 mile drive from London, he went straight to a meeting in 'a crowded hall, smoke-laden atmosphere: I let myself go and had a pretty good time, though I might have made better use of it. I think it was appreciated.'[31] It is notable that so many working class people, despite their own troubles in the aftermath of the General Strike, took a deep interest in what was happening in China. They at least were developing the International Mind.

At the end of April he and Margaret went to Ireland and spoke at the Munster Quarterly Meeting in Cork, followed by the Dublin Yearly Meeting in May. Friends' Quarterly Meetings throughout the British Isles discussed the Chinese situation that spring, and Clifford must have made many other unrecorded visits and speeches. The highest-profile occasion, however, had been on 16th February 1927, when he addressed the Parliamentary Committee of the National Council for the Prevention of War at the House of Commons. There was a large audience of MPs from all three parties, and some outsiders including the Chinese Chargé d'Affaires. A vote of thanks was proposed by the former Labour Party leader J.R. Clynes, and seconded by the Tory Lady Astor.[32] This was reported in the press in Britain and in China. 'Striking Survey by Dr. C.M. Stubbs' was the sub-heading in the *Manchester Guardian*. After a brief account of events since the 1911 Revolution, he made the point that China was a naturally united country, without the divisions of culture or religion that existed in, for example, Ireland. The Nationalist movement enjoyed widespread support, not just among students, but increasingly among merchants and workmen. It was not merely the effect of Russian influence: Nationalism was as strong in West China as elsewhere, yet Russian influence had hardly penetrated there. A war psychology was developing in China, with Britain seen as the enemy. But, he pointed out, not a single life had been taken in retaliation for the killing of Chinese. The Nationalists did not aim at killing or even expelling the foreigner, provided he renounced the privileges granted him by the Treaties. He ended by warning of a new danger, of a new kind of militarism: 'The student class had always looked down on the profession of war, but there were now hundreds of students who had left universities to undertake military training. The view was now being heard in China that the Western nations would listen to nothing but force, just as people in England were fond of saying the Chinese will listen to nothing but force.'[33]

A lengthy report also appeared on 10th March in the *North China Daily News*, where it was accompanied by a vitriolic editorial headed 'A Knife in the Back'. This was written by the acting editor Rodney Gilbert.[34] The British Community, he wrote, was accustomed to 'the misrepresentations of the ignorant and self important, like Mr H.G. Wells, ... but when our own people, those who have lived in China and ought to be able "to tell a hawk from a handsaw", speak in the same strain, we justly feel aggrieved.' It seemed that Clifford wanted to present a picture 'of a downtrodden people, groaning under the heel of the brutal British,' but had nothing to say of Britain's 'extraordinary patience under a campaign of slander and violence ... or her forbearance in the face of the boycott ...' Clifford had complained that the Chinese had no voice in the government of Shanghai, but this was a

147

'city which does not belong to them, which they have done nothing whatever to develop, and which they are obviously incapable of administrating.' Finally, 'Dr Stubbs confessed his limitations of experience of the whole of China. One hardly knows whether to be sorry or thankful for these limitations, which in truth are obvious enough. Had he known more, he might have said less; but from what he has said we fear that further experience would only have presented to one of his peculiar mentality greater opportunity for vilifying his fellow-countrymen in the Far East.'

By March 1927 there were over 20,000 foreign troops in Shanghai, and forty-two warships in or near the port. The threat these forces seemed to pose served to increase anti-British and anti-foreign feeling. Yet, as Clifford pointed out, one of the most remarkable features of this period is that not a single British person in China was killed, despite the shooting of Chinese in Shanghai, Canton and Wanxian. Throughout the country there were isolated groups of missionaries far from any foreign gunboat, yet none was harmed, though in some places churches were attacked or destroyed. The remarkable restraint of the Chinese that Clifford had praised the previous year seemed to be continuing. But an episode at the beginning of March changed things, and bore out Clifford's warning of a new kind of militarism. When the Nationalist troops reached Nanjing a section of the army, probably linked with extreme left-wingers seeking to provoke trouble, looted missionary compounds and foreign consulates, and deliberately killed several foreigners. This led to the evacuation of all foreigners while British and American warships laid down a covering bombardment.

This event naturally caused both outrage and panic in the foreign community in Shanghai, including many missionaries evacuated from inland. The Nationalist armies were approaching from the west and south, and armed militias of the communist-led unions in the city rose against the troops of the warlord Sun Chuanfang. People recalled the Boxer Rising of 1900, when hundreds of missionaries had been killed; a repetition seemed possible. They were all, Quakers included, extremely glad of the presence of the army and navy protecting the International Settlement, barricaded off from the rest of the city by barbed wire. In

April conflict became ferocious throughout the Chinese section of the city. The fighting was more complex than foreigners realised: it was a three-sided battle, between warlord soldiers, Nationalists, and communist militias, for this was the moment that Chiang Kaishek chose to turn on his communist allies. He was helped by a Shanghai gangster organisation, the Green Gang, who ruthlessly killed all those they could track down. Several thousand communist supporters were slaughtered over a few days.

These events made Friends' demands that foreign troops should be withdrawn seem dangerously naive. Clifford's speech at the House of Commons in February now appeared to be out of touch with current realities in China. William Sewell from Shanghai made the point gently, 'that it was just the sort of address that any of them might have given a year ago – but Clifford was certainly not alive on the subject of Russian influence and propaganda in China. I think it is really since he got home that the subject has become so great and very apparent.'[35] A much fiercer response came from the veteran Quaker missionary Isaac Mason, who had been in Shanghai for over 10 years seconded to the Christian Literature Society. He had clearly acquired something of the 'Shanghai Mind', and was in full agreement with the *North China Daily News*: the Chinese were wholly responsible for the present situation, foreigners were without blame. 'Nobody is oppressing China now; she is at present her own worst enemy, unless it be the Bolshevists; and those who profess to speak for her should state the facts, and not be always trying to lay the blame elsewhere. The present generation of foreigners in China is here lawfully ... it is only reasonable that the property of those engaged in lawful occupations should receive protection ... "Christ's gospel of goodwill" has been shown and unfortunately it has not yet been responded to. The fair and generous attitude of Great Britain is scarcely mentioned ... and even prominent Christians are still agitating as though no offers of treaty revision had been made.' As for Clifford, 'he hopelessly mistakes the present conditions, of which he has not "actual knowledge"; and if he held his peace it would be accounted unto him for wisdom.'[36]

This letter provoked a number of replies. Clifford (hoping that a gentle answer would turn away wrath?) admitted that much of what Mason wrote about the Chinese was true, and that 'Nanjing has come to many as a shock to their faith'. But even there things could have been so much worse, and writing as he was from Ireland, where he was at the Dublin Yearly Meeting, he made comparisons with the reaction there 'of national feeling against alien domination and unequal privileges'. Henry Davidson wrote more bluntly: 'As far as we can see, Isaac Mason accounts the security of human life and property as of so great importance that he is willing that in the last resort any and every means should be employed to preserve them.' Clifford's friend Peter Scott, writing from the viewpoint of a man who had served in the trenches, was blunter still: 'The lives of every one of the foreigners could have been saved by their withdrawal. I gather that the Chinese would have made no attempt to stop them going; rather that this was what they wanted, and the trouble has arisen because they would not go. The argument resolves itself therefore into this, that Isaac Mason claims the right to have the Chinese shot down to save the material possessions of the foreigners in China. This, though perhaps it sounds brutal, is the only thing it can mean. I do not suppose that anyone would venture to say that we had the right to shoot down the Chinese so that our missionaries might remain there to teach them the doctrines of peace.'[37]

Others joined in the correspondence as the year went on, including some representatives of the 'War Friends' of 1914, and others who resented the way the Society seemed to have been taken over by Bolsheviks who they said were packing the meetings to get their way. Their attack was mainly directed at the Meeting for Sufferings, and an appeal it had made in February for the withdrawal of foreign troops and naval ships from China. The correspondence eventually grew so acrimonious that in November the editor of *The Friend* felt obliged to terminate it, and correspondents were rebuked for their offences against 'the tradition of Quaker courtesy'.[38] It remained the most difficult of questions, to determine how pacifist principles should be put into practice.

Hu Shi's visit was not only important in informing people about China, and creating a more sympathetic attitude towards his country, but it also made him realise that there was a large body of opinion in Britain friendly to his country, something that was not very evident from the press. Clifford and Silcock kept closely in touch with Chinese students in Britain, especially members of their Christian Union, assuring them of their sympathy and understanding. Silcock was delighted to find that several of their leaders were 'out-and-out pacifists'. Few of the other Missionary Societies shared this attitude, especially after the Nanjing Incident had raised tensions. When Silcock attended the regular meetings of Missionary Society Secretaries, 'I always feel I am a hopeless radical … and I generally come away finding it hard work to keep smiling.' Other societies did not feel a campaign of information about China was necessary, and they refused even to reply to an appeal from the London Chinese Students' Christian Union for a public statement of sympathy. One Anglican said vehemently that it would be an act of disloyalty to the government. Silcock found it ironic that Foreign Office officials, with whom he was in regular contact, were more sympathetic, and committed to a conciliatory policy in China, than some of the Missionary Societies.[39]

Clifford did not spend all his time in Britain involved in Chinese affairs. It was a time for renewal of family life after a two-year gap, and getting to know his children once more. He bought a Baby Austin, just big enough to hold them all, and in the summers they had memorable expeditions and picnics and explored the North Yorkshire Moors. The car was also useful for getting around the country to attend meetings, in sun, rain or snow, and he soon became master of its inner workings. He gave lifts to men on the road, often seeking for work and unable to afford a bike to get on. He didn't just think about China, but also about the dire social conditions in Britain, especially in the mining areas. 'I should just like to say,' wrote Silcock, 'how greatly CMS is appreciated … particularly because of his readiness to throw himself into any aspect of the life and service of Friends. The fact that a missionary suggested going down to one of the distressed areas came almost as a shock to a number of Friends who evidently thought that missionaries had no interest outside their special concern.'[40]

In July 1927 he spent a week in the mining villages of Somerset with three other Friends, including Peter Scott. This followed a visit to the Forest of Dean coalfield earlier in the year, where they had helped to establish a Friends' Meeting.[41] The aim was partly to learn about conditions in mining districts in the aftermath of the strike and to show solidarity with the miners. 'We were having a very interesting talk with the miners' agent this morning about the conditions. 1000 out of 6000 are unemployed: seams very narrow, the hauling sometimes done by men more or less on all fours. The owners have victimised some men, and still have not made an agreement with them, being unwilling to recognise their agent.' 'It is a nice place we are staying at, and nice people. After the first night we had a bed each, but I fancy the host and hostess sleep on the floor. He is an ex-miner.'

But the visit was also an exercise in Quaker evangelism, to offer miners who had come through terrible times a source of spiritual strength and comfort that the traditional churches did not give. Virtually all the meetings were held out of doors, in the streets or market squares, and included periods of worship. 'And how the people listened!' wrote Peter Scott. 'In Radstock, which is not a large place, about 200 people stood for some two hours ... at Midsomer Norton, about the same number. At many of the smaller places there were close on a hundred, who were so interested that at the end they crowded round for questions and discussion.' One man who turned up after the meeting complained, 'We've got two chapels and one church in this village; we don't want another,' but was answered by someone who had been present, 'You've not heard what has been said; this is something quite different.'[42]

What was said was that 'the good news of Jesus had nothing to do with any scheme of salvation from future punishment, with the different doctrines concerning his death which have grown up through the ages and which have so often been insisted on as essential to Christianity. But rather that we actually *know* God instead of only knowing *about* him ... the idea that the living indwelling Christ is our authority, not the external one of a book or a church ... To so many of these people who have passed through a time of stress and suffering both mental and physical which we little realise, this message has come with a wonderful sense of liberation.' Clifford added in a letter to Margaret,

'Our message was no doubt appreciated: we were told some of the young men never entered a place of worship. We spoke a good deal about religion for the whole life – peace, industrial relations, as well as personally.'[43]

The week led to the creation of a regular group meeting in Midsomer Norton, and in November a larger group of Friends went back to repeat the exercise, still in the open air despite the cold, rain and falling darkness, still drawing large, intensely engaged crowds. Whatever the effect on the people of Somerset, it was a profoundly moving experience for the four Friends. 'We were drawn together in a deep sense of fellowship in the Presence which showed its results in the meetings … At times the sense of power almost made us hold our breath. Clifford Stubbs perhaps best expressed it when he said that we felt as if we were being caught up in a stream of life.'[44]

Clifford did not return to Somerset in November; by then he was back in China. In July, encouraged by letters from colleagues who were still there, he started to think about his return, if conditions and consuls permitted. Only seven foreigners were still at Huaxi; twenty-one colleagues were in Shanghai waiting until they could go back upriver. Reports from Chengdu suggested that all was peaceful in the University, and feelings in the city were positive. The Chinese teachers were keeping things going, but were increasingly anxious about the University's future unless some foreigners could return. But Chongqing was still very dangerous, and the British authorities would not allow any of their nationals to go upriver beyond Hankou. It was unlikely that permission would be given for another six months. As a group the staff in Shanghai wanted Clifford to be ready to go as soon as permission was granted. Sewell wrote that 'People out here feel that Clifford should be amongst the first to go back because of his proved ability for friendship with the Chinese.' Moreover, 'all letters from Chengdu urge the need of the science teaching and the feeling that the work can hardly go on without more additions to the teaching staff.'[45]

There was to be a meeting of the University Board of Governors in Toronto in October. Clifford and Silcock were both due to attend, and Clifford floated the idea that he might continue from Canada directly to

Shanghai – if he could not go any further he could still occupy his time there usefully in language study. At the end of August the China Committee endorsed this plan. But even if he could go on to Chengdu, there would be no question of women and children going. So this would mean a further period of family separation. There was also the question of the children's education; now that his daughters were approaching their teens, could they get a decent schooling in Chengdu? The Rodwells had just resigned from the Mission for this very reason; duty to family and the call to work in China could no longer be reconciled.

Clifford, ever optimistic, still hoped they could. 'God has entrusted our children to us, they need our care, especially during these years of their lives, and we cannot feel it right that we should be separated from them for years together – we believe God does not give us conflicting duties. Nor does one parent remaining in England seem a satisfactory solution; for our children need their father and M. and I are very dependent on one another, also for our service as well as our happiness.' There might be a temporary separation of a year or so, and then they could be together again. Before the evacuation the Canadians had run a school which educated up to matric level, so Ruth and Jean could stay until they were 16 or 17. But all would depend on what happened in China.[46]

8

1927–1930, Chengdu

His final furlough, with its intense political activity and contact with socialist politicians interested in China, had strengthened Clifford's political awareness, and this is apparent in an early letter to Margaret written on the voyage to Canada with Silcock. They were travelling third class, but on Sunday they attended the church service in the first-class saloon. 'A very "bourgeois" congregation it seemed, and it struck me how in the service itself, with much adoration, self-humbling, prayer for King etc., there seemed no recognition of the Christ to be found in the common man, and the "underdog". But how Jesus identified himself with these!' He also noted how few third-class passengers bothered to attend. There is a sharpness that was not there before when he describes encounters with crass imperialism, for example with a 'learned professor of Semitic languages, who thinks it is Britain's duty to keep the world in order by blowing up those who don't behave themselves'.[1]

During the voyage Clifford drafted a 'Statement on the Relation of the Society of Friends in China to the question of Defence by Armed Forces of the British Government.'[2] Now he was returning to China, the question of how pacifist principles should be put into practice was of immediate importance. What should be his and his colleagues' attitude towards the British military presence in China? He began by noting that many Chinese saw missionaries as 'advance agents of imperialism'. Even those Chinese closely associated with missions felt 'that in the last resort the latter are depending for their presence and safety in China, not on the good will of the people but on the armed forces of their nation'. Missionaries were loyal British subjects with the obligations that status implied, but for Friends any association with armed force was at variance with their principles and message. How to deal with this contradiction?

He accepted the British government's assurance that British forces in China had no aggressive intent, and that they were there for 'police' reasons. But Quakers still believed that it was wrong to keep armed forces in a foreign country, on the basis of treaties imposed on the Chinese by force. So he proposed that the Society should make a public statement that Quaker missionaries renounced any claim to be protected by British armed forces in China, and that they should not be required (i.e. by consuls) to place themselves under such protection. They themselves would take responsibility for any 'mischance' that might occur as a result of this, and would refuse any compensation exacted by threatened or actual force. 'While some may feel that our attitude endangers others,' he concluded, 'we express our conviction that such refusal to depend on armed force is in the long run the securest defence of the community; and our earnest desire so to apply our principles that if any suffer it may be those alone who accept them and are prepared to pay the price.'

When this document came before the China Committee there was formal agreement with its views, but also considerable unease. Missionary mothers in particular were concerned about the danger to their children. It was felt unwise to publish, and it was referred to a sub-committee for revision.[3]

At the end of September Clifford and Silcock reached Toronto, and met a group of Huaxi colleagues, before the formal meeting of the Board of Governors. Back in Chengdu the Senate, currently largely Chinese with only seven foreigners present, had made what were felt to be questionable decisions; for example, to continue the Medical School with only two foreign staff, 'involving dependence in part on some very poorly qualified Chinese ... [this] raised stormy feelings on the part of efficiency advocates. Also, would there be a welcome to foreigners to return, involving pushing some of these Chinese out? ... I was disappointed to find Beech has swung considerably over to the "conservative" side, distrustful of Chinese leadership.' The key question to be resolved by the Board, at which ten members of the faculty were in attendance, was whether registration with the Chinese government, and the appointment of a Chinese president, should go ahead. In practical terms it was a question of whether the Board could trust the Senate to make the final decision, after presenting its own views; Silcock and Clifford argued for this, as did most of the Canadians. Beech was against, as were Bishop Mowll of the Church Missionary Society, and the Chairman of the Board Sir Joseph Flavelle, a wealthy Canadian businessman and philanthropist. The sense of the meeting, according to Clifford, was in favour of registration, but a decision was postponed for three weeks – 'this deferring of action is quite "Quakerly", though I regret that we could not have unitedly agreed to the policy of trust in Chinese leadership.'[4]

Clifford would not be present at the next meeting, nor would he have been very happy with the outcome, as registration was approved, but with two conditions – (a) that registration should not interfere with the distinctive Christian character of the University; and (b) that the property should remain vested in the Board of Trustees according to the University's constitution. Silcock voted against the conditions, but was in the minority.[5] Clifford had decided to leave for China when he heard that three Canadian colleagues had left Shanghai for Chengdu, and an American colleague had already reached Chongqing. If they had gone, perhaps he could follow, and it seemed worthwhile to risk the journey. So he left Toronto for Vancouver, and embarked on the SS *Empress of Asia* for China.

When Clifford reached China at the end of October 1927 he would need all his reserves of optimism to deal with what he found both in China and in the missionary community. The divisions among for-eigners between the imperialistic majority, and the small number that could be called pro-Chinese, were very marked. The conciliatory atti-tude the British government had shown over the past year found no reflection here. He stopped off in Yokohama and found some evac-uated missionaries, especially the women, full of a bitter and resentful attitude towards the 'ingratitude' of the Chinese. In Shanghai there were still some British gunboats and soldiers, but most had left, confirming that Britain had no aggressive intentions. The troops moreover had behaved well. The Chinese consequently were feeling less hostile towards the British, but foreign attitudes towards the Chinese, even among missionaries, remained largely ones of superiority and contempt.

The Hodgkins met him at the quayside and he stayed with them for the weekend, going to a concert on the first evening – a reminder that Shanghai had more to it than politics and violence. But mostly he was catching up on the current political situation in China. Chiang Kaishek's elimination of the Shanghai Communists in April had not resulted in greater stability. The provisional Nationalist government in Hankou, which consisted mainly of left-wing Nationalists and Communists, had expelled Chiang from the Guomindang, and he had set up a counter-government in Nanjing. But by July the Hankou government had imploded, the Communists had been driven out and the Russian advisers sent home. Hankou was now in the hands of an opportunist general from Hunan, Tang Shengzhi, who had allied himself to the Communists the previous year. Meanwhile the northern warlords had launched counterattacks against the Nationalists in the Yangzi valley, and a Communist uprising had seized the capital city of Jiangxi province, though only for a week before they were driven out with much loss of life. Everywhere under Nationalist control suspected communists were killed and their bodies left lying in the streets as a warning. Nationalist politicians and generals quarrelled and plotted, and in August Chiang Kaishek had resigned, though this was to prove a mere tactical retreat, and he would be back by January.

It was difficult to find much cause for hope in this confused situation, where the Nationalists seemed no different from the warlords, except for being even more brutal. In March Hodgkin had described the Nationalist movement as 'an unstable combination of 5 groups: right, centre, left, left of left, communists', and felt that the most hopeful groups were the right and centre, loyal to the ideas of Sun Yatsen. But they too lacked any stability, breadth of outlook or honesty. By September he had come round to regretting the expulsion of the Communists. Sun had allied himself with them because of their enthusiasm and ability – would the nationalist movement have these qualities without the communists? Expelling them had been like cutting out the heart to save the life.[6]

This is a remarkable statement from a Secretary of the National Christian Council. It is not surprising that Hodgkin was demonised by the Shanghai press with the enthusiastic support of Christian fundamentalists. The Shanghai English-language newspapers, mainly the *North China Daily News*, followed a diehard imperialist line, and 1927 saw them at their 'most virulent'.[7] Any expression of sympathy with Chinese nationalism was clear evidence of crypto-Communism. Fundamentalist missionaries had published a pamphlet[8] denouncing the NCC as the 'Bolshevik Aid Society', and all liberal Christians as 'camouflaged Red propagandists'. 'Modernism is only a polite name for religious Bolshevism.' Curiously, their opposition to Bolshevism concentrated more on its threat to property than to religion. Reports in the Shanghai press were often copied uncritically by English newspapers, and this included the attacks on Hodgkin, and distortions of his views. For example in April the Catholic journal *The Tablet* had quoted Hodgkin as saying that the first duty of Christian missionaries in China was to give the people a group of nationalist leaders of the Lenin type.[9] The NCC, according to *The Times*, 'openly condoned anti-Christian atrocities, professing to see therein a Divine purpose for the purification of the Church.'[10] Silcock did his best to correct these impressions, and sent his sympathy. It was bad enough for him, he wrote, reading *The Times* or the *Morning Post*, 'but to be right in Shanghai must be almost torture to one's spirit very often.'[11] All this had taken its toll on Hodgkin, and might have been a factor in his decision to leave China for good the following year.

The Shanghai press also reported that Quaker missionaries intended to renounce British citizenship, to 'denationalise' themselves, in order to work in China. There was some substance in this, as back in 1921 Hodgkin had raised it as a possibility,[12] and Clifford had reconsidered it as an option in 1927, but it had never been seriously followed up. To show his love for mankind, God had come to earth and become a man; should he not do the same, and to show his love for the Chinese, become one of them and renounce the privileges of British citizenship? But further thought suggested that it would not have much effect. 'We must take our share of the responsibility we have inherited as members of human society, and rather seek to Christianise the relations between nations by working from within than get rid of our responsibility by withdrawal. As a practical consideration, it also seemed doubtful whether denationalisation would in fact convince others of one's *bona fides*';[13] he would still be visibly a foreigner, and treated as such.

In his reports home Clifford tried to keep a sense of balance when he considered the state of Chinese Nationalism. A Chongqing-based Quaker businessman, and a good friend of the Mission, B.M. Barry, was utterly disillusioned and bitter. 'From what he had suffered he had, or said he had, absolutely no faith or enthusiasm left for the Chinese, that he had never met one Chinese who was really honest: a man he respected and long believed to be so had swindled him of seventy thousand taels.' Clifford felt it was important that Friends at home should not allow their hostility to British militarism to prevent them seeing how much China's condition was caused by internal failings as well as foreign intervention: 'I think we ought not to let a sentimental idealisation blind us to the very real evils and moral failure which work widespread harm in individual and social life. Through just this moral weakness ... the Nationalist movement has met such a large degree of political failure. But while saying this, I am sure our attitude should not be one of Pharisaic condemnation, but looking first at our own faults and degree of responsibility for China's ills, endeavour to put the relations from our own side on the right basis. I would urge my friends not to abandon faith in Chinese Nationalism – which must be distinguished from the merely political movement ... The ideals of value which have underlain the best side of the movement still remain, ideals of freedom, justice, national self-respect, uplift of the masses, the rule of the people, the refounding of social and intellectual life...'[14]

It was cheering, though, to be greeted by a message from Huaxi sent by the students of the Science Society, welcoming his return: 'Oh Dr Stubbs! you can hardly know how released we did feel since we heard of your return to China and it really cheered us up. Besides the telegram we write you just a few lines simply to express our joy and to show you our hearts, welcome to your immediate return to the Union University.'[15] Other news from Chengdu suggested that the city was fairly peaceful, but the same was not true of Chongqing, through which he would have to pass. Here British gunboats had just returned, generating more hostility by their very presence.

Meanwhile he had an extremely busy and social few days, seeing West China friends, and senior figures of the National Christian Council, renewing his acquaintance with Hu Shi, visiting local colleges, dealing with banks, stocking up for home and laboratory, buying a bicycle for Fang Shuxuan, a lawnmower for the Friends' College, and a host of other things he had been asked to get for colleagues still in Chengdu. He had his first Chinese feast, and promptly vomited it up in the street, a humiliating reminder of how his digestive system could not adjust to local food.[16]

One interesting meeting was with a wealthy financier and rising Nationalist star, Kong Xiangxi (H.H. Kung), brother-in-law of Chiang Kaishek, a Christian and a future prime minister. Discussing relations between their two countries, Kong said that the main problem was not the unequal treaties, extraterritoriality, or gunboats, but 'the overbearing and contemptuous attitude of many Britishers, expressed also in some of our official dealings,' which poisoned everyday relationships. On practical matters nothing had been done to grant Chinese representation on the Shanghai Municipal Council, and foreign Shanghai 'has not visibly budged from its die-hard attitude'.[17]

Missionaries were not that different. After a couple of days with the Hodgkins, Clifford moved to the Missionary Home, and there too he found a 'spirit of resentment and lack of sympathy with the Chinese – the "aloof" attitude of the injured critic – directed largely against the Nationalists'. On Sunday he attended the large Union Church – unfortunately it was Remembrance Day. 'The whole tenor of the service seemed to condone or exalt war ... no confession of the evil of war, of our own national sin – a special hymn making enlistment synonymous with dedication to Christ – death a Calvary; it was horrible! But as my heart burned I felt that here too we must seek to understand and share the good and truth underlying what others saw as a right expression, however admixed with wrong we cannot deny. The only reference to the Chinese in the service was a phrase in the prayer "for the great native population that they may understand, and see, and know and love"... Does the world need Friends' message, Christ's message?' Few in Shanghai were prepared to listen to it. That afternoon he went to a Friends' Meeting, attended by only eight people. Usually, he was told, there were more; he found it a 'quiet, strengthening time', but the contrast with the crowded, imperialistic service in the morning was stark.[18]

Over the coming weeks he wrote a fuller account of his experiences than for any other period of his life: not only are there regular letters to Margaret, but two articles for the *Manchester Guardian* describing conditions in the Yangzi Valley, and circular letters for Friends at home[19] about conditions in China and the state of the University, and Friends' Meetings in Sichuan, which had continued without a foreign presence for nearly a year. On 7th November he left for Hankou with a Canadian colleague called Harold Robertson, still unsure whether he would be able to go further upriver. They travelled on a British steamer, on which only nine of the thirty-eight berths were occupied. The number of steamers on the river showed life was beginning to return to normal, but few foreigners were prepared to risk travelling. Most of the ships were British or Japanese; Chinese ones had been commandeered by the army. A British cruiser was anchored off Nanjing, but there were few foreigners there to protect. 'Even in its capital the Government disappoints by its lack of power or will to secure the return of premises occupied by the military – houses, schools or consulate.'

Two days later they reached Jiujiang, where the foreign concession had been returned to Chinese rule, but a gunboat was still on station. It was 11th November, and the crew were celebrating Armistice Day 'in a hilarious way, with an excess of "glorious beer".' There were only fifteen foreigners living there, where eighty or so had been before. An acquaintance told him that there was no danger to life, but little security for business, and trade was more or less at a standstill. 'My general impression was that acute unfriendliness was past; that the chief trouble was due to unruly military, the foreigner now having to share to some extent what the Chinese suffer from this cause.'

They moved on into a war zone: Nanjing troops were on the point of driving Tang Shengzhi out of Hankou, and were taking the city over as they arrived. Tang had just fled by steamer downriver together with his senior officers, and the silver deposits from the Hankou banks. They left their army to fend for itself – which it did by turning to banditry, setting part of the city alight first. Clifford's steamer was met by this conflagration. 'As we watched the soaring flames . . . one man said, "It's only in the Chinese city; that's nothing." I thought of the terror and loss of perhaps hundreds of Chinese, but to the foreigner – "That's nothing." The British Vice-Consul came on board, and referring to the unsettled conditions of the day, said: "We were hoping there would be rioting, so that we could land troops, but . . ." (an expressive shrug of disappointment). That is how the British policy of conciliation is being interpreted by one of His Majesty's representatives.'

Hankou itself was tense but quiet, with martial law in force, barricades and barbed wire across the streets, and occasional firing to be heard. But the next day Clifford found he could move about freely, and no one paid much attention to him. Everywhere were signs of political as well as military conflict: 'The walls fairly shout slogans from all manner of posters, down with this, that, and the other, from imperialism to (the newest posters) Tang Shengzhi and the ruiners of the revolution . . . in the ex-Concessions the telegraph poles bear watchwords from the Nationalist programme – "Support peasants' and workers' organisations"; "Down with sex inequality"; "Reduce rent in the years of bad harvest"; and of course "Abrogate the unequal treaties". I don't think I noticed any offensive ones to which one could offer much objection.' The old British Concession was now under Chinese control, and outwardly there seemed to be little change from the past. The streets were clean, the water-carts were at work and the street lighting effective. A smart-looking lot of Chinese police had replaced the Sikh policemen employed by the British, and seemed to be doing their job well. The Chinese could now sit on the benches in the

163

river-front park, which were no longer reserved for foreigners. But behind the scenes the administration was still chaotic, there were continuous problems of political interference, and no real spirit of collaboration between British and Chinese.

Clifford was surprised to find how many missionaries had stayed in Hankou throughout the troubles. His colleague Lucy Harris was working in the London Mission Hospital, eager to return to her own hospital in Tongchuan, but forbidden by the Foreign Office, like all women, from going upriver. He particularly welcomed a talk with the American Methodist Bishop Logan Roots, who had lived through the troubles in Hankou without it shaking his faith in what was good in Chinese Nationalism. The summer had seen foreign-inspired communist terror, he told Clifford, but most of all he blamed Tang Shengzhi for this, and for the splits and failures of the Nationalist movement. Roots was a strong supporter of the National Christian Council, and would be called the 'Red Bishop of Hankou' for his contacts with left-wingers in the 1930s. 'I showed him the leaflet issued by Friends' Meeting for Sufferings – "Christianity and the Chinese Crisis", and he expressed entire unity with it.' But not all missionaries had responded to political change. 'I gather at the hospitals they have some difficulties over mutual relationships. I was told at one how in the course of months the Chinese doctor had not once been invited to tea with the foreign matron, and that other Chinese were treated with the same aloofness. Christian service can't be carried on in this attitude, which seems amazing at this time of day.'

The British Consul had no objection to Clifford and Robertson going on upriver, but 'at our own risk and discretion'. So they booked places on a British-owned steamer, the *Changwo*, leaving the next day, and set off. Seventeen miles upstream they met a boat returning: it had been fired on from the shore and one man had been killed. The *Changwo* turned back as well, and the captain announced he would only continue if escorted by a gunboat. Clifford's principles were now put to the test, and he decided to leave the ship. 'One question we have to face,' he had written before leaving Shanghai, 'is whether we should travel by a steamer escorted by a British gunboat through the bandit-infested area. My own feeling is clear, that I do not feel free to put myself under such protection, even if it means delay or travelling by an inferior boat. It might be said with justice that the escort is of a "police" nature, and were it a Chinese gunboat I would not feel so strongly; but to accept British armed protection is to give tacit assent to a "gunboat" policy which I believe to be wrong.'

Talking with the captain of his previous ship had confirmed his belief that the gunboat policy was not only wrong but ineffectual. 'Our captain does not value highly the presence of the Navy here. Now and again they make some reprisal against the soldiers who fire on passing steamers, but he thinks they are of little value as a patrol force. He and others on board take the usual contemptuous attitude towards the Chinese, and one can understand how under the provocation of existing conditions, they would like to hit back and "give it to the blighters in the neck". The impotence of the gunboat policy seems to me very evident. By the use of a many times larger force, and by ruthless action, no doubt within a certain zone a kind of order could be maintained – but at what a price. The present policy seems to effect little but annoyance and ill-feeling, and gives occasion to the agitator.'

When he told the captain of the *Changwo* he would have to dis-embark, the latter tried to persuade him that the escort was 'only to defend against lawless attacks'. Robertson agreed, but this was no surprise. Robertson was, he had told Margaret, 'tremendously "patriotic", and rather hankers, I am afraid, after the big stick method of dealing with the Chinese. If it comes to the test of travelling with a gunboat, I think it possible we may part company for a time further along. We really get on very well together personally.'[20] Clifford held firm, and Robertson went on alone. 'The way of Christ is not consistent with the use of violence even to defend one's rights. There is of course the difficult "policeman" question, and also the fact that in a world where we are members of a community we have to some extent to share in the action of the community, even when we personally disagree with it. But in this case it seems to me that the gunboat is inextricably connected with that method of violence in our dealings with another people, which we call the "gunboat policy"; it causes international friction, and (as at Wanxian etc.) it is liable to deal out death to innocent and guilty alike. Moreover, it seemed to me that this was one of the occasions, like the question of bearing arms in war, where the individual should bear witness, even by dissent from the view of the community, to what he sees to be right.'[21] So he went ashore and stayed several more days in Hankou. His stand on principle, and readiness to forgo military protection, captured the imagination of Friends at home, who might well have thought the danger even greater than it was, and was recalled by many with admiration after his death.

Finding a boat to continue his journey might not be easy. Only British and Japanese steamers were venturing beyond Hankou, and the Japanese carried armed guards as a matter of course. Chinese ships had not gone for months for fear of being commandeered by some armed force or other. However within three days he found another British boat that was to sail without an armed escort, so he was not delayed long. It came under fire within hours of leaving but was not hit; at other dangerous spots the captain ordered his passengers to shelter behind armoured plates on the bridge, but the rest of the journey was uneventful if slow. Vessels with gunboat escort were attacked more frequently, and Robertson was in greater danger than Clifford. To pass the time on the journey he read Sun Yatsen's *Three Principles of the People (Sanminzhuyi)*, the Bible of the Nationalist Movement. 'It has the characteristics and the defects of a political treatise with an aim in view, the stirring up of the Chinese mind to carry through the Revolution to the new order. Much of it is shallow, misinformed, and untrue – will not bear intelligent criticism – like, to venture an analogy, Lloyd George's speeches, yet one must not because of these defects, fail to recognise that much *is* true and he is appealing to real facts and real longings among the Chinese.'[22]

He reached Yichang on 26th November. Here he had to switch to a smaller boat for the onward voyage through the Gorges to Chongqing, and once more faced the problem of finding an acceptable steamer. The only British steamer on the route always had an escort; the Japanese had their armed guards. As it was a very profitable route there were plenty of other ships, Chinese-owned, but sailing under various foreign flags. This did not always protect them from being taken over by the military. He found a French-flagged ship, and apart from the French captain he was the only foreigner on board. 'She is probably an opium-runner, and there are Chinese soldiers on board! It may seem another case of the Devil and the Deep Sea; but I feel that while one cannot avoid being mixed up with conditions as they exist in this country, yet one owes it to one's Chinese Christian friends to refuse to identify oneself with the policy of foreign arms in China.'[23] There were bullet-holes in his cabin walls and bedstead, and they came under fire the first morning out. He described the experience to Margaret: 'I took what cover I could behind a box of stores, but had a nasty feeling that even if the box could stop a bullet (doubtful), my posterior was in an exposed position! There was quite a burst of firing, returned by soldiers on board, but though one could hear the bullets whizzing and some hitting the ship, no one on board was hit. Probably the actual risk of being hit is small, but one had a nasty helpless feeling, and I shouldn't want thee and the children to have the experience.'[24] Despite the French captain it was clear that the soldiers were in charge, and they soon turned the saloon into an opium den. Clifford took his meals in his cabin. But no one showed any antagonism on learning he was English, not even when passing Wanxian. The rest of the journey passed peacefully and he arrived in Chongqing on 2nd December.

While in Yichang he had a short but friendly meeting with his old warlord acquaintance Yang Sen. Always an ambitious troublemaker, Yang had brought his army out of Sichuan into Hubei, and the Nationalists had ordered him back again. Clifford disapproved of missionaries who cultivated the friendship of the military, 'Yet somehow I have always felt drawn to Yang Sen – cruel and tyrannical no doubt, yet with some straightforward qualities, and some real desire to rule well and do something constructive.' He tried to persuade Yang that the British government was not unfriendly towards China, told him of his experiences in England, and translated what he had written in the *Manchester Guardian* about the Wanxian affair. 'He went to some length to give me his version, which I am afraid I did not fully follow. At the end of our talk, I urged General Yang to aim, not merely at military

167

power, but at the establishment of righteousness, without which the true revolution could not make progress in China. He did not seem to take amiss my plain words, and escorted me courteously out of the room.'[25]

The meeting had been fixed up by one of Clifford's old students – nominally at least a member of the Chengdu Monthly Meeting. Wu Shilong, now on Yang Sen's civilian staff, had been quite close to Clifford, and was overjoyed to see him. 'Life in connection with the army and politicians is tending to pull him down, I fear, yet one feels that he is good at heart, only too weak to stand firm against the fast life and the atmosphere of "squeeze". In his goodness of friendship he wanted to wangle a free passage for me on one of the boats commandeered by Yang Sen, but I wasn't having any. It is good to feel one's hands are clean of an evil system – the same applies to the gunboat escort question – even at the risk of being quixotic.'[26] 'Such is one of our Chinese Friends,' he added in his Circular Letter. 'We in England can hardly understand the terrible social pressure on men in his position; only the strongest-founded characters can stand, and I am afraid that Mr Wu, though seeking in his way to follow the light of Christ, has not had that experience of the surrender of self to God through which the life of the true self is found. He confessed to me how devoid of joy he found his life ...'[27]

Clifford spent a week in Chongqing, mainly taken up with the complex transactions always involved in the transport of goods – local customs duties, red tape, delays, overcharging that had to be challenged. Then there was an interview with the British Consul, A.P. Blunt, who was 'all for asserting consular authority, making conditions etc. No British women to return inland, though a few by special grace and favour to be allowed in Chongqing.' A steamship captain had just been kidnapped below Yichang 'which has created a bit of a flutter, especially in the consular bosom, and that is a threatened hold-up of our going on.'[28] Despite this, Blunt was 'kind and hospitable', arranged passports for further travel inland, and soon modified his instructions by allowing one wife to each mission in Chengdu, application to be made through a named representative. He made Clifford the Friends' representative

168

(there was no one else): 'It feels quite unusual being episcopal; I have already exercised my prerogative by asking Hilda Sewell if she will be my "wife". Up to date I have had no reply! But I hope they can come up before long.'[29] The Sewells had been teaching in Lingnan University in Canton, and Clifford was desperate to get them back to Huaxi as soon as he could.

Consul Blunt's hand had been forced by Bishop Mowll, who had brought his wife to Chongqing without permission and with every intention of going on to Chengdu. The bishop later gave his version to Clifford, that Blunt had telegraphed to stop Mrs Mowll coming and the message had 'providentially' missed them at several places. Clifford could not let this piece of sanctimoniousness pass: 'Then quoth your naughty husband,' he told Margaret, '"I'm glad you think that Mr Blunt and Providence sometimes take different views of the situation." There was rather a shocked and strained feeling for a few moments! Come back and help me not to put my foot in it.'[30]

He also met Chongqing Friends, to see how they had fared without foreign support, and in a ferociously anti-foreign atmosphere. He was pleased to find that a small group had continued to meet every Sunday 'after the manner of Friends ... evidence that there is a residue of real life in the Meeting, but I am afraid the spiritual vitality is low.' The Chongqing Meeting had always been divided and unstable, and this had not changed. 'I did not go to Chongqing as an inquisitor, but from what I heard, I am afraid there is no doubt that in many of the individual members' lives, and in the corporate activities of the church, there is much utterly opposed to the Christian standard.' The Boys' High School was flourishing under its very effective head, Yang Fangling, but it was outside the city, and Yang's hypercritical attitude towards the failings of Friends in the city did not help: 'he seemed to me to go to an extreme, and beyond the facts, in his criticism of others; for sympathy and construction, as well as faithful dealing with evils, are needed in the meeting.' Clifford gave several talks to the boys, and also one to the Chongqing Christian Council, on Christians and International Questions, 'feeling able to speak with directness and freedom'.[31]

The hospitality he received, and the amount of Chinese food he had to eat, had its too frequent effect. 'My old friend Tummy couldn't stand all the Chinese food and there have been ructions,'[32] and he was laid up for a couple of days. Consul Blunt and other foreigners offered to care for him, but he preferred to stay with 'our own folk', the Yangs, who fed him a 'thin diet of milk, rice water and eggs, on which I managed to gain my equilibrium.' For Clifford 'our own folk' were not his fellow-countrymen, but his fellow-Quakers – who happened to be Chinese.

He had now joined up again with Robertson, and they set off overland for Chengdu with a train of forty carriers; the hours of walking each day completed his recovery. He had hoped to visit all the Friends' centres en route, but bandit activity prevented them going to Tongliang, and they made straight for Suining. Here Henry Davidson's hospital, and the Meeting, had been in the care of Dr Chen Xubing, by universal consent one of the finest of Chinese Friends, 'gold all through'.[33] Through his good relations with local people and officials he had avoided any threats to mission property and activities.

At Suining they came across a new motor road to Chengdu being built, which would reduce a five-day journey to one day by car, or two by bicycle. It was only an earth road, and there would be problems in wet weather; but already buses with a dozen passengers were making daily trips on the completed section.[34] Despite political troubles some modernisation was continuing in Sichuan, and Clifford saw its potential for the Mission's work. 'I think a Friends' Mission motor-car would be a great institution,' he wrote, remembering the usefulness and pleasure he had had from his Baby Austin. They reached Chengdu on 19th December, to the warmest of welcomes from Chinese and foreign colleagues. Clifford went to stay with the Simkins, who 'made me one of their family, which means very special avuncular distinction, as little Dorothy Simkin is the only foreign child at the University.'[35] He must have been especially welcome, since the Simkins had been the only foreign Friends in Sichuan for nearly a year, and only seven foreigners had remained in the University. He was a good contrast to the solemn and long-winded Robert, and livened up the household considerably. 'I think it does them good to have a mad specimen to keep them lively,' he wrote, and Margaret Simkin confirmed this. 'He is a delightful person, and we count it a privilege to have him with us ... He plays the piano and is congenial in every way ... he is a tremendous help in entertaining guests and a happy person to have about all the time.'[36]

It had been nearly a year since the evacuation, and nearly two years since Clifford had left on furlough. Despite the intervening problems the campus looked in excellent condition. New buildings had gone up – medical and educational blocks, and a Women's College – the number of women enrolled had quadrupled. All this demonstrated the University's confidence in a time of trouble. He would not have been surprised to hear how well his Chinese colleagues had performed. 'Much as the little handful of foreign teachers ... have done for the continuance of the University, the fact that it was able to carry on, and the hopeful outlook today, are due yet more to the splendid work of the Chinese members.' Those he singles out for comment include Yang Shaoquan and Fang Shuxuan, especially the latter; his Buddhist friend Cheng Zhixuan had worked hard to maintain good relations with the local authorities; and Huaxi now had a Chinese vice-president in Zhang Lingao [Lincoln Chang] who had been the real leader during the past year. The Acting President in Joseph Beech's absence, a Canadian medic G.W. Sparling, had been in China for 20 years but had only recently come to Huaxi, and this must have helped Zhang feel more confident in establishing his authority. As for the Chemistry Department, Wu Xuanxi, a recent graduate, had kept teaching going since Sewell's departure, with the help of a temporary teacher in organic chemistry. Shi Rucong had provided technical help, the apparatus was in good condition, and even the accounts were in order. At one point the faithful but unreliable Shi had nearly been sacked for 'laxness', but had, as usual, 'bucked up considerably' afterwards.[37] Clifford had some difficulty keeping hold of Wu, since he was also an ordained Anglican, and his own mission wanted him back to work for them – presumably they had sponsored his studies. In later years he would become disillusioned with the church, and returned to chemistry and Huaxi, eventually taking over from Sewell as head of department. His end was a sad one: at the outbreak of the Cultural Revolution in 1966 he was subjected to severe 'criticism', and was later found drowned in a paddy-field – an illustration of the turbulent future that lay ahead of Clifford's students.[38]

Staff and students at Huaxi were friendly and loyal, but elsewhere in the city nationalism, fired by the local press, was still threatening. Lacking the provocation of gunboats and businessmen it was not as intense as in Chongqing, but it was more specifically directed at Christian institutions as the main representatives of the imperial powers. As Christmas approached rumours grew of attacks on churches planned for that day, 'crude and scurrilous' posters were plastered on walls, and 'the Chengdu Christian Council rather got the wind up, and urged foreigners to keep off the streets'. At the Council's request, and to Clifford's dismay, soldiers were sent to guard the university and some of the churches. 'I am sorry that the Christians here, to some degree even Friends, seem to depend too much on such protection.' On Christmas Day itself Yang Shaoquan and Fang Shuxuan persuaded him to stay on the campus, so he was unable to join in the celebrations at the Meeting in Qinlonggai. There was a large attendance at the Meeting, but a quiet one, and they avoided provoking people with public decorations.[39]

But anti-Christian sentiment was only one aspect of politics in Chengdu. Sichuan was, oddly, more peaceful than much of China, but there was little cause for rejoicing in that. It was still in the hands of six or seven warlords, whose overriding political aim was to preserve their own power.[40] This they did by squeezing the population dry through taxation to pay for their ever larger armies. The largest armies, those of Liu Xiang of Chongqing, and Liu Wenhui of western Sichuan, had over 100,000 soldiers each; Yang Sen, by now a waning force, had a mere 30,000. Their attitude towards the rest of China was to give formal allegiance to whichever group was dominant. In late 1926 this seemed to be the left-wingers, so Liu Xiang in Chongqing suppressed the right-wing Nationalists. But by spring 1927 Chiang Kaishek was the rising power, and Liu ruthlessly turned on the left-wingers. He infiltrated agents into a mass meeting of the Great Anti-British Alliance; as the meeting began they opened fire on the leaders on the platform, killing about forty people. Over 200 were trampled to death in the subsequent panic.

He and his fellow generals paid lip service to the Nationalist Guomindang, and organised ceremonies honouring the Nationalist founder Sun Yatsen and giving public readings of his *Testament*. In return their armies were 'incorporated' into the National Revolutionary Army, and designated with official numbers – Liu Xiang's army was the 21st, Liu Wenhui's the 24th, and so on. Later Chiang appointed Liu Wenhui Provincial Governor. But none of this meant anything, and both sides were well aware of it. At best it was a tacit agreement that neither side would interfere with the other. The Sichuan warlords competed with each other, sometimes violently, for control of territory and their subordinates' allegiance, but they were agreed on one thing: that any political activity, especially of a revolutionary nature, should be suppressed. The following year Russian agents estimated there were only 200 Communist Party members in Sichuan, fewer than in any other province. The warlords also prevented their supposed allies in the Guomindang from organising locally; by 1929 it had only seventy-seven members.[41]

In this situation the young, especially students, who shared their compatriots' desire for a better and more just society, were intensely angry and frustrated. In the colleges of Chengdu there was seething discontent, but any open display was likely to bring down brutal punishment. An episode at the end of February 1928 showed the capacity of both sides for extreme violence: 'Several score of boys in one of the middle schools, assisted probably by outside gangs, waylaid the Principal and strangled him to death, and then threw the body down a well ... He was a political appointee, and owing to opposition had been in the habit of going to the school with an armed guard! The deed is supposed to have been the work of political *dangs*, of which there are many, some of a "red" variety, among the students. Next day the military authorities arrested some hundred or so students, and some teachers, of a number of schools, and 14 have been shot ... This is some of the fruit of the wild propaganda, and the cheapened valuation of life due to the military and "red" influences. One boy of 12 or so wept and called on his mother when he was sentenced, and the judges let him off.'[42]

There seemed little choice between extreme and sometimes violent revolutionary politics, and the army. Even graduates might choose the army as a career, since in Sichuan it offered the only pathway to influence and prosperity. Few preferred to become underpaid teachers with few prospects. 'One extraordinary thing is the way people of all classes are mixed up with the military. Last week one of our own students left to go to a military school in Japan (his father is an officer of some kind). Another ex-student has just gone to teach in a military school. Society is simply honeycombed with this parasitic growth.'[43] The military presence was very noticeable on the Huaxi campus itself, where it had established itself while most of the foreigners were away. Most of its 110 acres were still open fields, and though there was a grand brick gate on the riverside near the Stubbs's house the campus had no wall around it to prevent anyone who wished to from coming in. Troops of soldiers, over a thousand strong, would parade on the fields, marching and countermarching, practising the goosestep, and carrying out manoeuvres. Soldiers wandered around the campus at other times too, coming into teaching buildings or the gardens of teachers' houses, harassing students and shouting insults at foreigners.[44]

Clifford does not say too much about this in his letters to Margaret for fear of alarming her, but William Sewell after his return in April gives more detail about the soldiers' extreme rudeness and insolence, of how they would commandeer a laboratory to eat their lunch while a class was in progress. 'They are insolent and annoying and one day in the heat a foreigner will lose his temper and then things will get exciting. Friends here take the Quaker method of turning playing fields into farmland' – Clifford's cook Pen Si had planted rapeseed over the Quaker section – but this could not be done all over the campus as students needed space for sport and relaxation. Dickenson, the teacher of physical education, took direct action against trespassers, to Clifford's alarm: 'I shall be relieved if Dick gets away without having a row with the soldiers! He is quite fearless, and when they stroll round and invade foreign compounds and pick flowers, etc, as some of them are liable to do, Dick sails in and ejects them by physical force, or lands them in the ditch etc! They respect his vigour, and perhaps 99 times it may do no harm, but there is always the hundredth chance of stirring up a row.' Clifford's own response was rather different. One day when a soldier shouted insults at him he turned to the soldier, removed his hat and gave a low bow. The soldier was so disconcerted he immediately returned the bow and kept silence.[45]

The departure of nearly all missionaries from the province for a year had changed the relations of missionary and Chinese permanently, as the Chinese had perforce found themselves managing churches, schools and hospitals on their own. It was now necessary for missionaries not just to treat the Chinese as equals, but to see themselves more as advisers than managers. Clifford noted that the missions who found this most difficult were the Anglicans, Canadian Methodists, and the China Inland Mission. Students were far more critical of the teaching and administration, and there were said to be lists circulating of those foreigners who were acceptable and those who were not.[46] The changed attitude was evident at Yearly Meeting in January 1928, where 'there was no trace of anything but a friendly and cordial attitude, but it was also clear that the old unquestioning acceptance of the foreigner has gone.' At one stage a wholly Chinese committee was set up (Clifford and Simkin were in any case the only foreigners present) to decide which missionaries should be invited to return, and to what duties. This was a completely new departure. Its report was 'critical and discriminating, and frank words were spoken of this missionary and that which paralleled the frank discussion of Chinese workers – words perhaps it was right we should hear, but not publish. I wonder what was said of us in the committee?'[47] Despite any reservations there may have been, all twenty-three missionaries on the books were invited to come back – this included the sixty-four-year-old RJD, who it was hoped would revitalise the Chongqing Meeting – but in the event financial constraints meant that only fourteen would come. RJD was not among them – he was teaching in a Friends' school in Lebanon, and in any case was probably too old to adjust to the new political atmosphere. The

Friends' Mission had declined since it reached its maximum complement of thirty-nine only a decade before.

Writing to Margaret, Clifford says more of the purely domestic aspects of his return, back into the world of Chinese social rituals, a whirl of welcome parties, soon followed by Christmas parties, some visitors staying too long – 'though some talks have lasted a hour or two, I feel that is what I am here for.' The two Friends' houses had been empty for a year; the verandas had been fenced in to keep out thieves, and their possessions stored in the attic were all safe, except that rats had got at some of his papers. He extracted some necessities, but would not move back before Margaret's return. The cook Pen Si and his family were living in the servants' quarters, and keeping pigs in the garden – 'you can imagine the untidiness'. Pen was also cooking for the Simkins, 'who like ourselves alternate between feeling his annoyances, and that they might go further and fare worse. He is a *wendang* [reliable] fellow.' Soon after his arrival Leng Jiaxin turned up – 'he seemed very glad to see me, as I was to see him' – and within a couple of weeks he was Clifford's personal servant once more.[48]

Once he had settled back, he found himself with plenty of jobs again. In January he replaced Simkin as Principal of the Friends' College, and soon moved there, to live in a pair of rooms next to the entrance door. This brought him closer to the students – thirteen in residence at this point – and to the Buddhist Cheng Zhixuan, whose vegetarian food he sometimes shared. Others visited him, notably C.W. Hsiung from Qinlonggai, who was finding it no easier to get along with Friends than he had done with the Anglicans – perhaps they resented him as an outsider. He was disorganised and unmethodical, and without Rodwell's guidance he was not managing the Primary School well. He often came to see Clifford in his room at the Friends' College, to pour out his troubles, and one evening they went on so late into the night that the City gates were closed; he spent the night on Clifford's bed while Clifford dossed down on the sofa.[49] But Hsiung was sincerely committed, and moreover was a distinguished scholar with literary skills that were invaluable for the Mission. Later that year he would translate a pamphlet by Clifford on Friends' Principles.

In February Clifford was chosen as Dean of Science, by a Faculty that now had a majority of Chinese staff.[50] In April he was nominated by the Senate to be vice-president of the University once more, a job he was far less confident in taking on. This time the vice-presidency was certainly no sinecure; Joseph Beech was abroad, and it was uncertain if he would even return. Clifford would be joint vice-president with Zhang Lingao, who had been in office since the end of 1926, had worked with the acting president Sparling through the very tense year of 1927 and had been widely praised. Zhang, a convert of the American Methodist Mission from a very humble background, had graduated from the Education Department in 1919 together with Fang Shuxuan. He then went to America and studied for his M.A. and B.D. at North-Western University in Evanston, Illinois, after which he served his church as a pastor in the town of Zizhong.[51] Clifford did wonder if there was any need for a foreign vice-president, but recognised that Zhang, despite his ability, was still very inexperienced. A foreigner would also be less open to intimidation from the military than a Chinese; the extraterritorial privileges that Clifford was so anxious to renounce did have their uses.

Fortunately Clifford liked Zhang and got on well with him; it was his foreign colleagues he was less sure of. He knew that his pro-Chinese views had made him unpopular with some. When his nomination was put to the Senate, to ensure there would be a full discussion and a contested vote he nominated the Canadian Dr Wilford. Wilford was generally popular and widely trusted by the Chinese. The two of them left the room while the Senate debated, and Clifford was chosen. 'I think the soldier problem was on a good many people's minds, and the need of a man with social contacts who would deal with them in the name of the University. I do not know how the voting was when the ballot was taken. Robert [Simkin] told me that Lincoln Zhang, Fang [Shuxuan], Yang [Shaoquan], and other Chinese wanted me for the job, and that some weighty foreign friends felt strongly the burden of the property consideration [Chinese-owned property was always at risk of being commandeered by the military]. I think very likely too some have not full confidence in me in other ways … The job may not be altogether easy, though I am going to have faith in the loyal backing of those who did not make me their first choice. It is a great thing to have the support of Zhang, and other Chinese friends ... This will be a different job from the old sinecure under Beech. But I think strength and great Fellowship will be given.'[52]

Fortunately the Sewells had just returned to Chengdu and Clifford could now hand over much of the chemistry teaching. He still taught seven hours a week, but otherwise it was 'many hours of committees of one kind and another, and it has been a particularly busy time lately, what with Estimates to be prepared, and Athletic Meet, and Senate. There are difficult and ticklish problems, most of all the personal ones. There are various people, foreign and Chinese, who get across, or misunderstand one another, and especially after the easing up of the situation of last year where a common danger helped all to pull together – and with people now a bit tired, and with foreigners returning, and a tendency to drift back a bit to the old ways. I think you overrate my ability to warm and reconcile, old girl, in fact it is only too easy for some folks to get across or misunderstand me. So far my relations with Zhang have been very happy, and I see no reason why they should not be increasingly so.'[53]

To try and solve the 'soldier problem' he and Zhang went to see the senior general Deng Xihou. Chengdu was nominally in his area of control, but he was closely allied with two neighbouring warlords, Liu Wenhui and Tian Songyao – they had been classmates at Military School – and the city was in practice under joint control. A Chinese writer summed them up scathingly: 'Liu Wenhui's oppression of the people is heavier than that of the other militarists. Deng Xihou is crafty and cowardly besides. Tian Songyao is base and decadent.'[54] Clifford had been to a dinner with Deng the month before and as usual tried to find something good in him. 'He is a man not without good qualities and interests ... I think we should be friendly with these military men as men – and there are certain obligations one owes to them as constituting about the only government there is – but I don't feel one should run after them, or hide one's views about the wrongness of this militaristic system.' Now, Deng responded 'pleasantly' to their request that the soldiers should be removed from the campus, and Clifford was hopeful; but it would be nearly a year before they disappeared, and that was because they had gone off to fight Yang Sen. It later emerged that they were, nominally at least, under the command of Liu Wenhui, and Deng Xihou's pleasant evasions were a way of not admitting his powerlessness; and indeed most soldiers were so undisciplined that they disregarded any authority.[55]

Relations with the local military and civil chiefs, and with local education bodies, were an important part of Clifford's duties as vice-president. But more time would be taken up by day-to-day administration, financial and academic, establishing a working relationship with Zhang, helping Chinese and foreign teachers to work together in harmony, and easing returning foreigners into the new situation that existed post-evacuation. Problems and crises of all kinds could suddenly arise. At the end of May a student was suspected of stealing valuable photographic equipment from the laboratory, leaving his fingerprints behind – Clifford must have especially hated an enquiry of this sort. More serious was a row between a foreigner and a Chinese that erupted in June. The foreigner was the formidable Miss Alice Brethorst, in charge of the women's dormitory – 'one who is inclined to "run" things, is critical of others, including Zhang, and has a sharp tongue.' She believed that her powers had been infringed, and 'being tired and overwrought at the time ... the stage was set for a first-class explosion, which descended personally on poor Fang Shuxuan, who happened to be in the office at the time, and was followed up by a very indignant and strongly worded letter to Zhang. Zhang was very angry, and a very fireworky correspondence ensued between the two of them. Zhang was going to resign right away, and I was unfortunately dragged in to try and get something done to avert disaster. As my advice was that Miss Brethorst should lay down her executive burdens which tend to bring her up against Zhang, you can imagine I have been to some folks the bad boy in the piece.'[56]

Reconciliation was sometimes beyond even Clifford's powers, and his siding with the Chinese cannot have helped him with some of the foreign staff. There were still foreign teachers, though a minority,

179

unreconciled to the idea of Chinese authority over mission institutions, who did not wish to have Chinese at staff prayer meetings, or were just insensitive to the political changes taking place. In October the Secretary of the Canadian Mission, Ernest Hibberd, who had just returned from Shanghai, gave a sermon which expressed just the attitude that foreigners needed to avoid: 'while rightly emphasising the supreme truth to be found in Christ, [he] seems to breathe the spirit of *our* superiority in religion etc., which we have often deplored as being the wrong attitude to take. I wonder if the Shanghai atmosphere is to blame, or is he not awake to the new and more Christian attitude which is demanded of us nowadays?' At the summer graduation ceremony a man from the British and Foreign Bible Society followed the tradition of giving a Bible to each graduate, and Sewell noticed the anger on some students' faces. It made them look as if they had to be Christians to get a degree. The donor then made things worse with a patronising address, talking to them 'as if they were Sunday School kids'.[57]

However, relations between Chinese and foreigners at Huaxi were on the whole good, given the intensely nationalistic feeling still prevalent, especially among the young. But there was a brittleness which meant that small events could easily blow up into something bigger. In October some Middle School boys provoked a conflict by refusing to make way for an American teacher as he walked along a path in the opposite direction; so he walked straight through the group, knocking one of them over. Immediately protests and threats of strike action ensued, and the issue was taken up by the radical press. 'You know the kind of fuss that is made of an incident of this kind ... as far as I can make out, the students were to blame in the first place, but I don't think that "direct action" of this kind is wise, especially out here.' Fortunately the university students did not support the protest, and the teacher wrote a letter 'not of apology, but showing his friendly attitude, and regretting that such misunderstandings should arise.' The Middle School boys then 'put a paragraph in the papers, saying the incident was closed'. Any dispute at Huaxi could quickly be seized on and politicised by outsiders, and a bit of teenage cheek become a pretext for protest and demonstrations.[58]

The varied and demanding duties of vice-president did not prevent other calls on Clifford's time. One of these required his specialist chemical expertise. The Sichuan warlords had each been minting their own coins, many of which were a random combination of silver and copper. These debased coins had driven out the genuine silver dollars, and put up prices, increasing both the suffering of the poor and the profits of the generals. By May a serious effort was being made to deal with the problem, and some officials from the Chengdu Mint came to Huaxi to ask Clifford if he could help them to separate the silver and copper in these coins. 'I put on a small experiment, which went off very nicely; but whether they could carry it out on a large scale I don't know.' He also tested a recently minted coin, and found that it contained almost 90% of silver; if that was typical, the problem was on the way to solving itself.[59]

As soon as the term was over his duties to the Friends' Mission took over. He was still the only FSC missionary in Sichuan, and he needed to see how things were in Tongchuan and Suining. After a two-day retreat with Chengdu Friends – 'a happy harmonious time, though not impressing one in a *special* way as having liberated the streams of life' – he set out for Tongchuan, with C.W. Hsiung and his servant Leng Jiaxin. The three-day journey was difficult – it was the hottest and driest summer he had known, famine was predicted and prices were rising. 'Phew! Old Matey, it *is* hot. One lies naked on the bed and pours out perspiration,' he told Margaret. Hsiung, disorganised as ever, had forgotten to bring a mosquito net and suffered in the inns. Unusually, Clifford used a sedan chair for most of the journey; he had come to dislike this mode of transport, as he explained to a student who asked him 'why he didn't want to sit in a sedan chair, which would be easy and comfortable. He replied, "Sitting in the sedan chair would be inhuman. I wouldn't like to treat the Chinese people like cattle, and would never sit in it unless I was too ill to walk." '[60]

In Tongchuan about eighty Friends had gathered, coming in from the towns and villages around – sometimes a two-day journey. It was the largest gathering for two years. 'I am impressed with the independent and vigorous way in which the work has been going on, though many have spoken too of the need for the return of the missionaries ... Among many members one comes across evidence of political propaganda, which has been vigorous in this district. There is certainly a new if crude political consciousness about.' (Tongchuan was the HQ of the warlord Tian Songyao, who had appropriated the Mission residence as his home. It would be some years before he could be levered out.) The time passed in quiet meetings – not as quiet as Clifford would have liked – study groups, and discussing of aspects of the work like the school and the hospital. There was no Bible study. Clifford gave an address on Friends' Principles – 'the first time I think I have given an address on that subject, and I felt power was present.'[61]

Then there was a two-day journey to Suining, partly by river. His stay there was much less happy: there had been a dispute between the primary school head and one of his teachers, which was having serious repercussions on the whole Meeting. It was felt that only Clifford could resolve it. 'I wish a Chinese could have gone, but apparently no one is feeling able to do so.' The foreigner sometimes remained irreplaceable as a neutral mediator. His visit 'was of help to them there; the difficulty has been at least partially solved, and I hope they can work on together for the present.' On the way back he had an unexpected treat. He ran into a party of missionaries returning to Chengdu with four motor cars, and was able to drive part of the way back in a Baby Austin.[62]

The heat made his annual stay at Nanyumiao all the more welcome. He had intended to go to Guanxian by bus – a new venture – but the heat had given way to heavy rain and the motor road had become 'a worse morass even than the old road'. He took his bicycle, but even cycling became impossible, so he put it on a wheelbarrow and travelled in another one himself. When he reached his cottage at Nanyumiao he found that some of the things – tent, chair covers, crockery – he had 'too trustingly' left in the attic had been taken; but the people were as friendly as ever, the beauty and freshness of the place just the same. As usual the summer saw a succession of guests, foreign and Chinese, and treks into the hills, bathing in the mountain pools, handing out medicine to the crowd of patients who came every morning. There were more than usual this year – anything from typhoid to malnutrition – and Clifford had to fence off part of the front garden for the sake of privacy and hygiene. Leng Jiaxin did the cooking, his brother looked after their big black cow which they had brought from Chengdu. How had they brought it? Perhaps by boat to Guanxian, but how had it negotiated those bamboo bridges in the mountains? Sadly Clifford does not say. But the fresh milk was invaluable for some of his patients. He relaxed, read some novels, and composed his pamphlet on Friends' Principles. The Fangs came to stay, and Mrs Fang proved 'quite a sport', joining in a walk to a mountain village, in 'record time for a Chinese woman on foot ... I think it is an interesting and happy experience for them. Fang is quite struck with the beauty of the valley, and with its simple people.'[63]

His last few days there, at the end of August, were spent alone with Zhang Lingao. It was a time of bonding, before they returned to preside over a new university year. On Sunday they went down to the village, where they 'had a nice little meeting with some of the folks; talked to them of health of body and spirit.' They also put final touches to the Vice-Presidents' Annual Report for the Board of Governors, most of which Zhang had written, Clifford merely adding a postscript. 'I think it will be of value for them, for the first time, to have a report through a Chinese mind.' The Board certainly seems to have been taken aback. They thanked Zhang and Clifford 'for their deeply interesting and illuminating account', printed it with the warning 'For Private Circulation only' and forwarded it to the various mission boards, with the cautious proviso that 'the Governors do not necessarily endorse all the opinions therein'.[64]

At first it is not easy to see what had alarmed the governors. Zhang was quite as upbeat as Beech had been, giving a positive account of the local political situation, the standing of Huaxi in the community, and the dedication and loyalty of the students. With the departure of so many foreign teachers, substitutes had to be found from the staff of other Chengdu colleges, and 'nearly all of them told us we have the best group of students in West China, both in studies and character'. But it is also clear how much power had shifted to the Chinese, and that this was unlikely to change with foreigners' return. The Senate, with at least a temporary Chinese majority, had reorganised the administrative structure, setting up new offices of Dean of Students (Fang Shuxuan) and Business Manager. In a paragraph on 'The Character and Aim of the University' Zhang states that the University 'must be more truly Chinese in aim and program ... We do not think it so important to increase the number of Chinese teachers, but we don't think it wise at present for the administrative and disciplinary side to be in the hands of foreign members.' He proposes employing good local teachers, 'no matter where they come from, so long as their teaching ability and character are good', but there is no suggestion that they need to be Christians. The University should have a vision that goes beyond 'simply training our own workers as teachers, priests and physicians'. Some members at least of the Board would understand current circumstances in China well enough to sympathise, but if this apparent dilution of Huaxi's Christian purpose should reach the ears of financial benefactors there might be problems.

Throughout the whole of this year what exercised Clifford personally, above all else, was the question of if and when Margaret would be able to rejoin him, and whether the children should come with her. The hurdles to be overcome were permission from the British Consul in Chongqing (there was no longer a consulate in Chengdu), who followed policy laid down by the Foreign Office in London; and also from the China Committee of the FSC, who felt a responsibility for the safety of their workers, and in any case would pay the costs of passage. The British authorities were reluctant to allow women and children to come to Sichuan at all, in view of the hostility to foreigners and the dangers of banditry and war. If they were allowed, they had to formally agree to obey consular instructions, and to travel only in British steamers, which would involve gunboat escort. Chongqing, with its gunboats, was also considered, probably wrongly, safer than Chengdu. With the pressures Clifford was under from his work he felt the need of Margaret's loving presence and support more than ever, and there were practical reasons too. As vice-president he was expected to offer hospitality to all kinds of people, to develop the social contacts essential for his work, yet he had no home to which to invite them – he boarded with the Simkins, or merely occupied rooms in the Friends' College. He could not run a household single-handed. In June he wrote to the consul making these points, pointing out that he and Margaret had been apart for almost three out of the previous four years; and that General Deng Xihou 'has assured me emphatically that it is perfectly all right for families to return'. He was especially irritated – 'I felt regularly on the warpath' – to hear that Irene Hutchinson, who had managed to get to Chongqing but was not allowed to proceed to Chengdu, had spoken with the consul and recommended giving a single woman missionary (herself?) priority over Margaret. He wrote to her with unusual sharpness: 'I do not think it is possible for any unmarried person to realise quite what it means for husband and wife to be separated – at any rate what it has meant to Margaret and me the last few years. While we have, I think, cheerfully and happily acquiesced in this so far as it has seemed necessary, and God's will for us, I think it is a very serious thing for friends, or any rule, to prolong this separation beyond what we ourselves feel to be right. Whom God has joined together let not man put asunder.'[65]

Heat and end-of-term exhaustion increased the stress of separation. Yet it was even worse for Margaret in England as the final decisions had to be hers – whether to return, whether to bring the children, who would care for them if they remained in England. The girls were approaching adolescence and a mother's presence was especially important. Letters could take up to two months, and any advice from Clifford might well be out of date by the time it arrived. For several weeks in early 1928 Yang Sen's activities in the Gorges prevented any letters getting through at all. 'It seems so impossible,' she wrote in May 1928, 'to get thy thoughts about a thing because when you get mine the position has changed, and again by the time I get your thoughts back . . . I can't see any way, one way or another, it is all hidden. I am always thinking about this problem, sometimes quietly, sometimes I feel torn in two. There must be a solution. *What* is it going to be? What do you want it to be, what do I want it to be? I see no way. O God open the way and guide us.'[66]

She was also affected by newspaper coverage of China, which emphasised the violence, disorder, and hostility to Westerners. 'Are there any remembrances of the May affair in Shanghai? What a lot has happened in three years, and how differently our own affairs are working out in consequence. Shall you be going to our Nanyumiao this summer? If we had all been with you, could we all have gone? How are conditions actually?' She must have been aware that Clifford would downplay the hazards of life in Chengdu, so as not to worry her. His temperament, too, was so naturally optimistic and trusting. In May she went to a meeting addressed by the National Secretary of the Chinese YMCA, David Yu. 'He spoke very enthusiastically about the Nationalist movement – "the most hopeful thing in China" – and said that every Chinese supported the Nationalist movement... He said he was optimistic, but when asked as he often was whether the situation was "settling down" he said he was sure it would get worse first. The revolution movement has not "touched bottom" – the country must suffer to the last point and beyond endurance, and then the progress to the new China could begin.' She managed to get a private word with him afterwards, and asked him about taking the children back to China; he avoided giving a direct reply.[67]

Accounts from William Sewell did not help. He had a less positive view of the situation, was a natural writer, and his journal was widely circulated among Friends at home. His tales of the soldiers on campus breaking into laboratories or bathing naked in the pools alarmed the China Committee – and Margaret. Clifford had not mentioned this in his letters. How much else might he be holding back? The contrast between Clifford's optimism and Sewell's more critical views can be seen in the latter's comment on the brutal way in which the local police would treat thieves, 'whom they never catch themselves. CS says it is their nervous temperament. That is a kind way of putting it – I am afraid I should put it much more strongly.'[68]

It would be two months before Clifford could reply to Margaret's letter, and another six weeks before she would get the reply. 'I do not fully understand the forces that are pulling thee,' he wrote. 'Face the problems, dear, don't inhibit or repress thy fears. But of turmoils and dangers I do not think you need be afraid. I can sense a kind of general fear of "something that may happen" in folks in England – a fear of the unknown. When you are among the concrete Wangs and Changs and bedbugs out here (I have slain three these last few nights), you won't feel the same ... It may be rash, but I am not sure that David Yu is a true prophet when he says things have yet to touch bottom and be worse in China before they are better ... The saying, often heard out here, is to my mind founded on doubtful premises, and partly is a trace of the Buddhist wheel of life doctrine ... Dearest, decisions – final ones – must be with thee. God will open the way.'[69]

It was the children, and especially the two girls, who posed the most painful problem. For the girls it was not only a question of safety, but of education. It was becoming clear that the Canadian school for missionaries' children would not reopen for a year or more. The girls were now settled into boarding school in Saffron Walden, and everyone thought it was the best place for them – Mr and Mrs Lees, their grandparents, certainly did. But it was hard for Margaret to accept – perhaps she could educate them herself, perhaps the situation on the campus was not so bad; she tries to read between the lines of Clifford's letter written six weeks before – what really was his view about the girls coming? 'O Cliff, I so long to bring them, and am so torn to know what is right.' Over John there was less doubt: six years old and still very fragile, he could not be separated from his mother. In May the medical advice was that it would be safe for him to go, and on 20th May the China Committee gave permission for Margaret and John to sail in the autumn.[70]

In September Clifford was back at Huaxi, with duties crowding in upon him. Sewell had taken over as Principal of the Friends' College as well as Head of the Chemistry Department but was distracted by having just become a father. Clifford taught just one class, of beginners, but it was the largest and the rawest. Enrolment for the University was encouraging – 238 by late September. 'What a fine group of young men and women we have. I expect there will be problems enough among them to meet too.' Early in October he describes for Margaret the activities of a single week in the life of a vice-president.

On Monday afternoon he was invited to a Government Middle School to give a talk on the aims and spirit of science. 'The school seemed very well managed and equipped, everything was very neat and orderly: so much more "Chinese" too than our own western-modelled building.' Then he dropped in at the Methodist Girls School in the city, and ended with a game of tennis with Zhang Lingao and two colleagues.

On Tuesday he and Zhang were invited to the opening of a new Confucian shrine. 'It was very interesting – a lot of the real old stand-by scholars were there, and were drawn up reverently in front of the platform. Offerings of a bullock, a goat, and a pig had been prepared, and were placed on frames before the tablet. Rather to my consternation I was unexpectedly called on to make a speech (I was the only foreigner present), and tried to express our sense of Confucius, and what he stood for.' With some skill he balanced courtesy to his hosts with his Christian commitment, and spoke of Truth being one and coming by many channels. He juxtaposed the two Golden Rules of Jesus and Confucius, about treating others as you would wish to be treated, and on the importance of putting them into practice, to solve the problems of international conflict, militarism, illiteracy, exploitation of the weak by the strong. In an age of change one should not forget what is of truth and value from the past.

Wednesday was National Day – the anniversary of the 1911 Revolution. In the morning there was a parade in the public park, and all the city's students marched past, flags flying. Clifford and Zhang represented the University, 'togged up in our Sunday best. The big military and Party leaders were there on a platform, where we too had a place.' Once more he was the only foreigner present. The ceremony expressed the token loyalty of Sichuan to the Nationalist government, with the reading of Sun Yatsen's will before his portrait. 'A kind of catechism was repeated enthusiastically by those on the platform. One of the most ardent was a woman, quite a suffragette kind, a new type to me in China. It was interesting, and exhilarating, feeling the real political fervour; the military men seemed more perfunctory about it.'

Afterwards there was a reception for the foreign community at which, there being no British Consul, he had to speak on behalf of Britain; this was followed by a banquet with rather badly-cooked 'foreign-style' food. However great Clifford's skill in social mixing, there was one line which he would not cross. Drinking has always been an important aspect of (male) Chinese social life; in an otherwise intensely formal world it took you out of yourself, lubricated relationships, and carried with it no association with disorder or violence. Getting decently drunk was not just acceptable, it was desirable. But alcohol was something no Protestant missionary, however liberal, would touch, and this was one side of Chinese culture for which Clifford had no sympathy or understanding. 'It was sickening to see the generals pressing the guests who took wine, Jap consul, French fathers etc., and quite a number were getting on the tipsy side before it was over,' he tutted.

Thursday must have been a relief. It was used for a 'Retreat', a time of self-questioning for a group of teachers and students to consider the spiritual condition of the University, and the effects of religious teaching and worship being voluntary. How many students were 'finding an integration of life in God?' 'How far were the lives of teachers oriented so as to touch the students, and to share with them in the utmost of our spiritual experience?' This was getting back to the heart of what Clifford had come to China for. Unmentioned in his account of the week, and fitted in somehow, was his teaching and the round of meetings and administration.[71]

One matter that rumbled on was registering the University with the government. It now had a Chinese vice-president, and religious education had been made optional. But the bureaucracy was time-consuming. The regulations from the Nationalist government in Nanjing had never reached them, so they applied according to the rules issued by the old government in Peking. Not surprisingly this was rejected. A new application had to be made under the far more demanding Nanjing rules, and this had to be made at once. Twenty copies of every form had to be returned, and they included lists of textbooks, the library catalogue, lists of laboratory equipment, lists of students' names, etc., etc. Fortunately it was clear by now that while the demands for information sounded peremptory, the follow-up was 'leisurely in practice'. At an equally leisurely pace work was continuing on a new Constitution that would reflect the changed circumstances. Previously the Aim of the University had been 'The advancement of the Kingdom of God, by means of higher education in West China under Christian auspices.' The new text was less explicit, and carefully designed to be understood in different ways. The Aim was now to 'cultivate the highest type of character, promoting higher learning and maintaining in all the spirit of love, sacrifice and service of the university's founders.'[72]

Government concern for the University was gradually extending beyond the requirements of registration. In December 1928 inspectors from the Board of Education came to examine the students in their knowledge of Sun Yatsen's *Three Principles of the People*. It was a friendly occasion, and Clifford was impressed by the questions the examiners asked. They were also treated to a volleyball match between students and staff, in which the latter were well-beaten.[73] Much more anxiety would be caused in 1929 by an instruction from the government that all universities would be required to introduce military training for their students, and pay an officer to be in charge of it. The Senate at this point decided to take no action, as government 'instructions' were often not followed up, especially in Sichuan, and at the end of the year Beech reported that there was no move so far to enforce it. Many of the staff were in favour of it, but it would be a very serious matter for Friends. Clifford's letter to Silcock on the question has not survived, but he was clearly searching desperately for some formula that would allow Friends to remain part of Huaxi. Silcock's reply gives an idea of the suggestions he had made. If the training were carried out by the government itself, Silcock thought Friends could 'acquiesce under duress', but not if the University itself had to do it. They could not remain a constituent part of such a body. If there were a conscience clause for those opposed, that might prevent immediate withdrawal but they could not remain permanently. Nor could they support the University materially while withdrawing from its management, as financial support from Friends at home would dry up. On the other hand they could not maintain a permanent veto in the face of opposition from the other missions.[74]

Towards the end of 1928 Clifford turned his attention again to the question of missionaries' status in China, and the rights and wrongs of relying on foreign military protection, by contributing an article 'Missionaries and Armed Defence' to a symposium on the subject in the *Chinese Recorder*, a major journal of missionary opinion. This can be taken as expressing his most developed views on a subject which had concerned him for several years. While accepting that the absolute pacifist position was not one that most Christians would adopt, he argued that 'the followers of Christ must seek more than taking part in a general progress of national and social ideals; they must stand for a way of life which is in advance of those ideals, and which may appear revolutionary and dangerous ... A special opportunity is before Christian missionaries in China today to commend the faith that dares to challenge current standards, and claim the whole of life for the Christian venture.' Some might be prepared to face danger themselves by renouncing armed protection, while hesitating to put their families at risk. 'But if parents see the way of non-violence to be right for themselves, is it not right for them, with open eyes, to accept the same way for the little ones for whom as yet they must decide?' One wonders what Margaret's view on this was. The best solution, he concluded, 'was to renounce, by agreement with one's government if possible, the employment of armed force in defence of us or our property. Should such agreement be impossible, we may when the event is upon us have to disobey our government and take the consequences. But at least we can, in no spirit of bravado and with all respect for those who differ from us, seek to make our own attitude clear.'[75]

It seemed important to express himself at this juncture, as he had recently been 'amazed' to hear from senior Chinese colleagues that over half the students at Huaxi 'suspect us of political connections or of being used for political purposes'.[76] That he was 'amazed' is significant. Of all the foreign teachers he was perhaps closest to the students yet he did not know they felt this way. No doubt traditional courtesy, and a desire not to offend, were the reason. Missionaries could be disturbingly unaware of what the Chinese around them really felt. Some in Chongqing in 1922 had been shocked to hear a Chinese Friend just returned from England telling an audience that only when he was there did he understand that missionaries were not government agents. The close contacts all missionaries had with their national consuls, and their obedience to consuls' orders over matters like evacuation in times of danger, reinforced Chinese views that they were under government control. It seemed that only very decisive gestures could remove this belief.

At the end of the year Margaret and John returned to China, and Clifford took time off to meet them in Chongqing. They were delayed for two weeks by an outbreak of fighting in the Gorges – Yang Sen taking on the other generals once more – which led to some steamers being fired on. With her return Clifford's letters cease, and we have little detail of his doings over the following year. Joseph Beech returned shortly afterwards, and Clifford hoped he could now give up the vice-presidency; but Beech had decided to take a much less hands-on role, to allow Zhang Lingao to be more prominent. The good working relationship Clifford had with Zhang was another important factor. So he did not give up the post until December 1929, when the Sewells' departure on furlough meant he had to be Head of Chemistry and Principal of the Friends' College once more.[77]

Margaret wrote every week to the girls at Saffron Walden, and although she naturally makes little reference to university matters we do get a few glimpses of Clifford. Within a few days of their return to Chengdu she writes, 'Daddy is very busy, he has lots of classes, committees and meetings. In a few days he has got to go on the road again to the Yearly Meeting that is at Suining. He is planning to go with one or two others by bicycle. It will take 3 days.' In fact it took four; it was extremely wet and cold, Clifford and Simkin fell off their bikes, and had to tramp through the mud, they were separated from their carriers so they had no hot food and had to sleep without their bedding.[78] Sichuan's modernisation was a slow process.

In April, 'Dad is dreadfully busy. I am going to meet him and get him home from a committee and home to bed.' In May, 'Dad is at a sort of Science Committee and I am alone at home.' But they also relaxed and had fun – there was a musical evening with 'a lovely Gramophone of the latest improvements, and we enjoyed songs, piano, organ, orchestra etc., besides some songs by a lady, and some by Dad. Dad's were funny ones – especially one that he made up verses (about 1 line each) about each of the guests.' A month later it was an event with students – 'One of the Socials the students are so fond of, with lots of speechifying and some stunts – Daddy did his squeaky arm, only instead of saying Caesar's oration he made a very foolish(!) speech about Chemistry making the students laugh at what he said and his squeaky arm.'[79]

At the end of June they went to Nanyumiao, and relaxed as far as the locals would allow them. On their first day after lunch they 'all rested with books and slept. I had had a wee snooze when I heard people approaching. I pretended to be asleep still, but they came up to the door, and asked me if I was asleep, so I had to wake up and talk. There was an old Chinese woman, and two or three young ones with 2 or so babies each, and a few other odd children. They sat round the door on benches and talked with me – sometimes we understood each other and sometimes we didn't! Dad was in the bedroom sleeping, and when he came out they had some more talk and asked for medicine for the babies – and a little girl about 11 kept asking for something I couldn't make out, and it turned out Dad had given a picture p.c. to a little patient this morning when she had taken her medicine, and these people had hoped to have some too – but they were only for sick children. They were very interested in looking about our room. At last we told them we were going out, and some men who had arrived went with us, down to the stream. On the way they wanted Dad to go in and see an ill woman, the mother of one of them, and Jack and I went on ahead. Then Jack paddled till Dad came. Dad had a bathe. There was quite a crowd of men and children and they were amused with Dad's antics. He dived in and then turned a somersault dive, and did some spluttering and joking.'[80]

This description makes clear how much their lives at Nanyumiao were lived in public, and it may have been to get away from this that a few weeks later Clifford and Margaret set out on a four-day trek into the mountains; some guests remained in the cottage and looked after John. They were accompanied by two bearers who carried bedding and tents, and also partly acted as guides. The bearers enjoyed the trip too – it took them to sights they had not seen before, and sleeping in a tent was an exciting novelty. Clifford and Margaret often followed a different, harder track from the bearers and so were entirely on their own in the wild. Like the Chinese they wore straw sandals – 'very good to walk in, light, and with a good grip, but they easily get muddy.' They cooled off with dips in the icy cold streams and pools. Margaret especially enjoyed the flowers – wild columbine, delphinium, purple orchis, willowherb, and bright blue gentians. In the evening they cooked eggs and potatoes on a camp fire – the bearers stuck with plain boiled rice – and sang a hymn before going to sleep. For two days they did not see another human being. Clifford was used to long walks in the mountains but this was special enough for him to write a detailed account of it.[81] They followed woodcutters' tracks, which had in places been carried away by landslides, and they had to cross the gap over precipices by clinging on to the roots of bamboos. In over a hundred places they had to cross streams or ravines along single tree trunks, some of which were at a sharp angle with steps cut into them. Few had handrails. They climbed up to well over 10,000 feet, to a watershed between two river systems, with magnificent views in all directions, to snow-covered mountains to the west and north. On the evening of the final day they missed their path – the bearers had taken another way – then found themselves blocked by fallen trees as night was falling. Eventually they found themselves in total darkness, and rain began to fall. They knew they were close to home, and pushed through undergrowth and thorns down a steep slope, emerging just by their bungalow to find everyone had gone to bed.

This journey reminds one how fearless Clifford was, unafraid of any danger either human or animal (snakes? tigers?). Margaret said of him that the keynotes of his character were adventure and trust,[82] but this trip shows how much the same could be said of her. It also says much for her physical stamina. Margaret has not appeared much in these pages, and it was the fate of missionary wives for their contribution to go largely unrecorded. Chinese social custom limited how much women could do – they could not preach, in chapel or market place, they could not socialise with officials. It was the husbands who wrote reports for head office and had achievements to describe. Wives were also much occupied with running a household, giving birth to and bringing up children. Margaret did some teaching of English at Huaxi, and also helped to run the Sunday school at Qinlonggai; but her contribution was crucial to their social life, to the open house they kept for Chinese colleagues and students, and we know how restricted Clifford felt in this way when she was absent. She was as ready as he to give time to establishing friendships with Chinese, and especially with women.

Although, compared with Clifford, she lacked formal education and probably knew nothing about chemistry she reveals an open, enquiring and intelligent attitude towards life. There can have been few missionary wives who, after saying goodbye to their husbands as she did in September 1927, would have gone to see an exhibition of modern art. It puzzled but intrigued her – 'extraordinary modern pictures – mostly figures, mostly unclothed, mostly distorted. We gasped and wondered at the horrid things for a while, wondering what was the key to the puzzle.' Then an assistant 'gave a little clue to a meaning – a revolt from sentimentality ... so leaving the copy of the actual, trying to embody the idea in form and colour, a blending and curving of line, and colour into a design which has meanings and ideas ... I can't say I like the effect.'[83] They may be 'horrid', but she wants to understand, not just reject.

The following February Clifford suggested she buy herself, as a birthday present, a new novel he had just seen favourably reviewed – *To The Lighthouse*. She not only found it interesting but also saw a connection with the modern pictures. 'A most extraordinary book it seems to me, like the modern pictures giving impressions in a quite different way from the old kind of picture or novel ... It is incoherent, like a person thinking, with all sorts of outside impressions and side thoughts coming in. Very clever, I should think, very interesting, and queer.' Margaret was no more afraid of Virginia Woolf than she was of the mountain gorges of Sichuan; she was indeed 'my matey Margaret, not some other kind of wife.' [84]

195

That autumn a temporary peace broke out in Sichuan, and brought soldiers back to the campus, 'though less bad than before in both numbers and insolence'.[85] The main trouble for Huaxi now came from nationalist feeling among students from other colleges in the city, especially the Silk School, which was not far from the Huaxi campus. This took place against a background of hostility stirred up by some local newspapers – the Chengdu tabloid press? – one of which was pursuing 'a campaign of vile innuendo' against staff and students. Students in groups of up to 200 would come on to the campus, and plaster the walls with slogans 'Down with Imperialism', 'Strike Down Christianity', and attacks on Zhang Lingao as a 'foreign slave'. Once they surrounded boys from the Middle School 'and tried to force them to kneel down and say "Down with Christianity". The boys replied that they could kill them but they would not comply.'[86]

They also pestered the women students. One day a boy took a snapshot of a girl from the Friends' Mission. She panicked – thinking her picture might be published 'along with imaginary filth' – and called on one of the male students for help. He grabbed the camera and removed the film, which was later developed and returned with the offending picture removed. This was enough to provoke mass parades with banners, and insulting posters and graffiti in the neighbourhood. Huaxi students remained calm, but one day a couple of them were reading one of the posters and commented on its illiteracy. This was overheard by a boy from the Silk School, which led to a furious argument. A quarrel is a common form of street entertainment in China: angry words and furious gestures are normal, but to be pro-voked into violence is to lose face. Unfortunately it was the Huaxi student who lost his self-control and struck his opponent.

This was a gift to the opposition. Huge processions were organised across the city, posters denouncing Huaxi were plastered everywhere, and students vowed not to rest until Huaxi was destroyed. The campus was invaded, a student was abducted, a foreign woman teacher was pushed off her bicycle, and senior members of staff insulted. But the Huaxi students kept their calm, and put their case to the city authorities; the press (with one exception) remained neutral. Heads of the other colleges put notices in the newspapers disassociating their institutions from the protests. The Commissioner for Education was known as a friend of Huaxi; but he was also principal of the Silk School. The honour of his school – and probably his lack of real control over its students – led him to propose a solution which put Huaxi entirely in the wrong. There seemed to be a stalemate.

This was resolved by the student who had struck the blow – incidentally a member of the Friends' College – who went to the Silk School, sought out his opponent and apologised. The apology was accepted, and the bubble of protest subsided as quickly as it had blown up. But the episode shows the febrile atmosphere in which foreigners could become scapegoats for all the discontents of the young – their shame at the condition of China, the inadequacies of their own institutions, and their own feelings of helplessness. It is also worth noting that despite the verbal violence, the irrational semi-hysteria of the protests which must have been very frightening to witness, the actual violence was minimal. It was an act of violence – under provocation – by a Huaxi student which had caused the trouble, and his readiness to lose face by apologising which resolved it. The leaders of Huaxi were rightly proud of their students, their self-control and their loyalty against intense opposition. For they were patriotic Chinese too.[87]

This was the background to Clifford and Margaret's major concern throughout 1929 – the possibility of Ruth and Jean joining them in China. For Margaret in particular the separation was painful, and the more so as first Ruth and then Jean fell seriously ill. In the summer Ruth went down with scarlet fever, and then an inflamed sinus which led to a major operation. Margaret thought of Ruth, dangerously ill, and herself unaware of what was happening. Even telegrams, thanks to the military, were delayed for over two weeks. 'You said you had just got my letter, the first one sympathising with you "over flu or something" and all through your illnesses you never had a word of sympathy from your Mum – but sometimes I was *specially* wanting to be with you, and I think these times were when you were specially wanting me, and somehow our spirits could feel each other. There is a wonderful way in which people who love one another can be in touch with one another even though bodies are far apart.'[88]

There was a seemingly irresolvable tension between their duty to their children, and their commitment to Huaxi and to China. Clifford had written to Silcock in 1928, 'You know how I feel about this question of separation from our children. God does not give us conflicting duties.' If Ruth and Jean could not come out, he would ask Friends to release them at the beginning of 1931, and would consider taking the whole family to New Zealand for several years. They hoped that the girls could come out in 1929, and that perhaps a 'Young Friend' could be found to come out with them in a 'governess' role, as a form of service. But Ruth's illness put paid to that, and medical advice was clear that she should not travel that summer. Silcock went to Birmingham to consult with their guardians – the girls' grandparents, and Henry Davidson's wife Laura. Armed with their support, and that of the China Committee, he knocked all Clifford and Margaret's hopes on the head one by one. 'There is of course the possibility that you may want the girls to come out later. If they wait till the winter ... it means delay coming upriver ... We think you would hardly bring them out in the Spring with the hot weather to follow so soon. By the autumn of 1930 the remaining time will only be two years at most and on educational grounds it would seem difficult to interfere so drastically with the girls' school life ... I may say it seems unlikely that any Young Friend would come out in the way you suggest.' The China Committee was responsible for the welfare of all missionaries and their families – and held the purse strings – but Silcock also understood what they were feeling: 'I cannot close without a message of deep sympathy with you both and with the children. I know a little from experience what these discussions mean to you and I want you to know how deeply many of us share with you.'[89]

Clifford did not give up – he wrote directly to the surgeon who had treated Ruth, describing the mild climatic conditions in Chengdu, 'not severe on Europeans', and on the skill of the staff in the Medical Faculty; but any effect this might have had was nullified when in the autumn Jean was rushed to hospital with appendicitis. But Clifford made it clear that, if the children could not come, 'we feel we should definitely plan to lay down our service here, at least for a number of years, in 1931, so that we can be with our children during their adolescent years.' But if the girls did come, then they would stay until 1932 or even 1933. This, it gradually became clear, was a powerful threat. The Sewells were due to leave on furlough, and if Clifford left early it would leave the Chemistry Department bereft of leadership. Both Huaxi, in the person of Joseph Beech, and the FSC were increasingly urgent that Clifford should stay until 1933.[90]

In October, Silcock wrote that the China Committee was now in favour of the girls going – but that was before Jean's appendicitis. The Lees were probably more reluctant, but by the spring seem to have accepted that the choice had to be that of the girls' parents, and in May they gave their permission. The question was now just the practical one, of who might escort them to China, first to Shanghai, and even more importantly, up the Yangzi. On 28th May Mrs Lees wrote to Margaret to tell her that a Mrs Taylor, who had previously lived in Chengdu, would be going out in the autumn and was ready to look after the girls on the voyage.[91]

By the time the letter arrived, Clifford was dead.

9

Afterwards

The University was stunned and appalled by Clifford's murder. 'In our dormitory there is no study,' wrote a teacher in the Women's College. 'They stand around in little groups just shocked. That it should be Dr Stubbs of all men is what I hear them saying . . . They are so ashamed that it should have taken place, and by their own people . . . I think for most of the girls this is one of the most soul-stirring experiences they have ever been through.' 'We have never known our students more deeply touched or more earnest in their expression of devotion,' wrote Margaret Simkin in *The Friend*. 'The students are stricken dumb, as we all are, but their spirit is beautiful.'[1]

It was the students who prepared the library for the funeral service with flowers and a hastily drawn portrait of Clifford. Margaret was struck with 'wonder and surprise' when she came in and saw how beautifully it had been done. Most of all it was their response that buoyed up her spirits during the ensuing days. When Clifford's sister Winifred heard the news in Hong Kong she said to her husband, 'It is horrible but she'll be as brave as brave.'[2] And so she was. Within two days of the funeral she was writing to Harry Silcock with a clear account of what had happened, to be circulated among Friends in England, in which she emphasises the love shown by Chinese friends and students.[3] 'His life, culminating in his death, is a triumph of love. On all sides are witnesses to his life's influence, and the love they bear him. The thought has been expressed many times these last few days that his sacrifice will bear fruit in other lives, in the Christian life of the University.' She was perhaps afraid that the news of Clifford's death would inflame hostility to China at home, and so negate everything Clifford had stood for. The response of the Chinese gave substance to the word VICTORY, which the students themselves had chosen to display at the funeral. It was the Victory of the Cross, of love over hatred.

It took courage for the students to display their grief and love as publicly as they had. While the Chengdu newspapers reported the news quite sympathetically, students from other colleges strolled around the campus as usual, openly scornful of all this grief for an imperialist foreigner. And while the military officials in Chengdu expressed their sorrow and promised to do all they could to find the murderers, further afield the response was different. The Mayor of Chongqing, when told that a foreigner had been killed, merely replied, 'It would have been better if there had been more of them.'[4] There was little liking for foreigners, especially for the British, and Clifford's life and work has to be seen against this background.

The shock-waves spread far beyond Chengdu. Letters of sympathy poured in, from Chinese and missionaries around the Province, friends in other parts of China – relatives, too: not only was Margaret's sister-in-law Winifred in China, but her brother Alec was with the Baptist Mission in Shaanxi to the North, but communications were so poor it was three weeks before he heard the news.[5] Neither was able to offer comfort by their presence. Letters came from Australia, New Zealand, Canada – places where Clifford's presence and personality had made an impression – and from missionary friends in India, Madagascar, and the Belgian Congo. But it was among Friends in Britain that his death was felt most deeply. The day after Clifford's death there was a scheduled Meeting for Sufferings in London – it 'was moved as I have never seen it before and we spent much time in prayer for you – largely in silence', Silcock wrote to Margaret. On the Sunday following 'most of the Meetings in London were thinking of you and Clifford,'[6] and not only in London, as so many had been visited by Clifford during his last furlough, and remembered also his principled stand in refusing a gunboat escort.

The bitter irony, noted by everyone, was that Clifford had been the most pro-Chinese of all the mission community. Joseph Beech wrote that 'Clifford in all his dealings went to the extreme limit to meet the

views of all the Chinese about him, and gave without stint his strength
and affection for them. I cannot conceive of his having an enemy.'[7] One
thing everyone was agreed on was that Clifford had not been singled
out personally for attack. Earlier that evening students had noticed
some shadowy figures with a carrying pole lurking by the hedge, some
distance from Clifford's home, and no one could have known that he
would be going that way. Any foreigner would have sufficed, and he
was just the one who had the misfortune to pass by. But who were the
killers and what was their motive? Given the date of 30th May a
political motive seemed obvious, yet they had also taken his bicycle.
Were they just thieves? Yet they had not taken his watch or ring. In any
case, the degree of violence used suggested a motive beyond robbery.
The debate continues up to the present day; it has been hard for
Chinese to accept that there could have been a nationalist or 'patriotic'
motive behind the murder of such a loved teacher. In newspaper
reports of his death they were described as 'Communists', but this was
a blanket term used by the warlords of Sichuan to demonise any
opposition to their oppressive rule, and to justify their brutality in
maintaining it; the word was then readily taken up by the foreign press.
It was the University itself which decided to make a statement that
Communists were suspected, not because they had any evidence but in
order to absolve the authorities of any blame.[8]

The murderers were caught thanks to Yang Guoping's son Yang
Zhenhua (Stephen Yang). Eighteen years old, he was in his final year at
the Middle School and only a few days before he had been discussing
his future with Clifford. He had helped carry the coffin to the graveyard. The following Sunday he was on his way to Meeting in Qinglonggai when he recognised Clifford's Raleigh bicycle in a repair shop.
He told Fang Shuxuan, and it was not long before the killers had been
rounded up.[9] They confessed their guilt, and admitted they had no
quarrel with Clifford personally. With little ado they were taken out and
shot; the authorities wanted the embarrassment of the murder cleared
away as soon as possible. They were described as 'young men of the
shopkeeper class', and were said to have shouted patriotic slogans as
they were led out to execution. However vocal and offensive nationalist

students could be, direct and random violence of this kind was not their way; theft was also involved, and the killers were probably discontented, semi-employed youths latching on to a political idea, and not part of any wider conspiracy. At the same time the authorities took the opportunity to arrest a number of left-wing students and close down three colleges.[10]

The news of the executions was kept from Margaret out of consideration for her feelings. She and John went to stay with Irene Hutchinson, who would now become the only English Friend in Chengdu, responsible both for the Mission at Qinglonggai, and for the Friends' College. Margaret wanted to get home to her daughters as soon as possible, and in three weeks she had to bring her life in Chengdu to an end, and get rid of or pack up all her furniture and possessions. 'I used to look at her and wonder how she kept so quiet under such distressing, heart-breaking days. "I think Clifford will never leave this place, he loved it so," she said to me one day after the house was all torn up. Again she exclaimed, "However can I leave this place! All of you have gone through this with me, anywhere else no one will know." With the assistance of loving hands she was able to go through the heartbreaking breaking-up of the home, sell off and pack up, leave the campus with the first tears I had seen in her eyes, on the 24th.'[11]

She and John were accompanied as far as Chongqing by 'Uncle Leonard', the father of the Friends' Mission Leonard Wigham, gentle, diffident and now white-bearded, who counted it a great privilege. 'I shall always remember how good and kind you were on the voyage from Chengdu,' he wrote to her, 'and the lessons that your loving peaceful spirit taught me.'[12] From Chongqing they went downriver to Shanghai, then to Vancouver and across Canada, at every stage meeting and being comforted by those who had known Clifford. From there they sailed to Liverpool, then on to Birmingham and Saffron Walden.

Back in Chengdu, the University Senate had met on 5th June, and expressed its deep sense of loss and its sympathy for Margaret and the children. Part of the minute ran, 'His relations with his students were friendly and sympathetic. In his attitude towards problems of the modern world he was far in advance of his age. Real friendship, based upon a generous justice in all relationships – personal, industrial, international, racial – was his ruling passion. Save in his own simple mode of living, he did not neglect the material side of life, yet he ever emphasised the spiritual needs of men. It was this, and the fact that he was living exemplar of what he taught that has made his life so valuable to his students and friends, to the University and the church, to all of which he gave unstinting service.'[13]

The University had asked the authorities for a military guard on the campus, and General Xiang quickly sent a detachment of thirty soldiers. The remaining Friends (now only Simkin and Hutchinson) were 'inclined to resist this proposal, but tacitly accepted it, since it affected the whole community.'[14] Then the Senate turned its attention to the urgent need for a wall around the University. The students wanted it, and the city authorities also claimed they could not protect the University unless it was built. A wall was built during the summer – and initially had the effect they had feared. The sobering effect of Clifford's death had evaporated, the Chengdu press ran a campaign against the creation of a foreign concession on Chinese soil, and a protest march was organised which led to an invasion of the campus and tearing down of the wall. A further invasion led to more vandalism and destruction, although most of the staff were up in the mountains for the summer. Zhang Lingao received a flood of death threats, and was attacked in the press as a 'foreign slave'. Then, as so often, it all calmed down, and by the autumn the wall was in place.[15]

Filling the gap left by Clifford was not going to be easy, and there were fears that the Chemistry Department might have to close down. Family illness would prevent the Sewells returning until 1933; and the whole Science Faculty now had only one foreign teacher, Dan Dye the head of the Physics Department. A Miss Payne was soon brought from Peking to teach inorganic chemistry, but much of the burden was taken over by the young Chinese teachers. A recent graduate, Gao Yulin, had to pick up Clifford's teaching, and quickly made a favourable impression. In November he wrote to Margaret, and told her that before starting his work he had visited Clifford's grave. 'Because I knew I want his help more and more hereafter, and I still believe he is living among us every second as you told me when we three graduate Chemistry students came to say goodbye to you in Miss Hutchinson's house. This is true! ... Dr Stubbs has trained the students of 521 very well so when they come to my class they are so good in every way and I never meet any trouble now, but I only feel busy because I have 28 hours in class per week.' William Sewell described Gao as 'probably the best chemist WCUU ever trained'. He went on the study at the Massachusetts Institute of Technology, and seems never to have returned to China. He kept in touch with Margaret, however, and a letter survives from 1969, when he was about to retire from his work in a company in New Jersey. His memories of Clifford were 'still vivid, warm and fresh. His personal interest in me during those wonderful years has been my guide post, technically as well as spiritually.'[16]

In the autumn of 1930 a picture of Clifford sent by Margaret to members of the Science Club was hung in the entrance hall of the Science Building, in a black wooden frame to harmonise with the architecture, and with a Chinese inscription. It was then ceremonially unveiled.[17] From 1931 there is a letter from Irene Hutchinson[18] passing on the good wishes of the Monthly Meeting, letting Margaret know the University was planning a memorial service for Clifford on 30th May and keeping her up to date with old friends in Chengdu. She gives news of Clifford's servant Leng Jiaxin, who had been with him since his arrival in China. At the funeral he had been one of the pallbearers, doubtless at Margaret's insistence. Now he and his family were unable to settle; they had gone to work at the Canadian School, but had been dismissed for laziness, and decided they could not continue as servants – unless it was with Friends! So they opened a small shop selling rice and firewood, and disappear from view. The cook Pen Si could also only work with Friends it seems: when the Simkins left on furlough, he went off to Tongliang to cook for the mission family there, Leonard and Laura Walker.

As the years passed at Huaxi, Clifford was not forgotten. With the outbreak of war in 1937, and the Japanese occupation of East China, three Christian universities were evacuated to the Huaxi campus, and among others a new science building was put up to house the increased number of students. It was named the Clifford Stubbs Memorial Building 'to commemorate his great contribution to China … and a symbol of faith in the China-to-be – after the war.' The opening ceremonies were accompanied, as they must be in China, with the writing of poems and calligraphic scrolls. It was a final-year student who wrote:

Beautiful and firm rises the Stubbs Memorial Building in the midst of the University campus.
On the right is the Clock Tower, in front the flowing stream. What a surpassing location!
A memorial raised to a former sage, whose spirit endures for ever, his mental strife, his weighty thought.
Famous teachers and brilliant students crowd into the hall cherishing the same ideals.[19]

Back in England, Margaret had taken a post as junior house matron at Saffron Walden School, where Ruth and Jean continued to study. She would stay there until her retirement in 1946, while Ruth went on to qualify as a doctor and Jean as a teacher of French. John, always fragile, had a difficult adolescence, and eventually settled into a clerical job on the railways. After retirement Margaret continued to live in Saffron Walden, where eventually Jean would rejoin her, teaching at her old school. During the 1960s they sorted and transcribed Clifford's letters and other papers, in the hope that a biography could eventually be written, and Jean continued this work alone after her mother's death in 1976.

In 1949 the Communists came to power in China, and the era of missionaries was suddenly over. William Sewell was still at Huaxi, and stayed on until 1952, later writing a lightly fictionalised version of his experience in his book *I Stayed in China*. Fang Shuxuan was now University President, and had the task of negotiating the handover of the University to the new government. Soon it was renamed the People's West China University; all foreigners had left, and in 1953, with a reorganisation of Chinese Higher Education into specialist institutions along Soviet lines, it became the Sichuan Medical College and lost all its non-medical faculties. By now the name of Huaxi, and its missionary connections, were erased everywhere except from people's memories. The Clifford Stubbs Building became Teaching Building No. 2. But despite this apparent downgrading, it was still recognised as a leading centre of medical education in China, and its reputation was passed on to later generations. In 1984 I was walking with two students, who would have been born in the 1960s, past the campuses of the two big state universities in the south-east of Chengdu – Sichuan University and the Science University. I commented that this must be the 'university quarter' of the city. No, they said, the university quarter is by the Medical College. They might have known little or nothing about its mission origins, but it still had unique prestige in their minds. Their contemporaries from old Christian families, however, would have had the problem of somehow reconciling what they heard from their parents about their missionary friends, and what they were told in school about missionaries as agents of imperialism blinding the eyes of the Chinese people with their superstitious preaching.

In 1978 China began to open itself up to the outside world once more, and contacts were quickly renewed between British Friends and Huaxi. In the 1980s British Friends sponsored three grandchildren of Chinese Friends to come and study in England for a year each, and a succession of Quakers, partly sponsored by the Society of Friends, were invited to Huaxi to teach English. In 1985 came the seventy-fifth anniversary of the founding of the University, and it became 'Huaxi' once more, as it was renamed the West China University of Medical Sciences (*Huaxi Yike Daxue*). Jean Stubbs, and John Rodwell's son Henry, were among those invited to the celebrations, and they spent over a week in Chengdu cared for by Stephen Yang and his wife Ruth, the daughter of Zhang Lingao. Jean was able to exchange memories with some of her father's old students on the staff of Huaxi, whose affection for him 'had not dimmed'. They were also taken to the lower slopes of Mount Emei, and to Guanxian.[20] It was no doubt the influence of Clifford's old students which led to Teaching Building No. 2 becoming once again the Clifford Stubbs Memorial Building. In the

1990s Jean Stubbs set up a Clifford Stubbs Memorial Trust, which for ten years provided financial assistance to teachers from Huaxi studying in England, and to Quaker teachers of English in Chengdu.

In 2000 China was seized briefly by a fad for creating mega-universities, and Huaxi, together with other Chengdu institutions, became part of a gigantic Sichuan University; it was renamed once more as the West China Centre for Medical Sciences. To what extent it will retain its individual identity within the larger institution remains uncertain, but it is a positive sign that, when the major historic buildings on the campus were damaged in the 2008 earthquake, a decision was made to restore rather than demolish. Friends in London were asked to send a photograph of their architect Frederick Rowntree, so that a statue or plaque could be made to commemorate him. In 2006 a collection of old photographs was published under the title *Memory of West China Union University*, which includes glowing tributes to its missionary teachers. This would have been unthinkable a decade or two earlier. One of the authors was the Communist Party Secretary of the University.

Above all, Clifford Stubbs's influence on his students was that of his warm, modest and selfless personality. He combined a scientifically trained intelligence with an empathy, which gave him the ability to understand and transcend differences of culture and belief. When he became a Quaker he saw no need to reject his former beliefs and practices; likewise his urge to identify himself with the Chinese people in their struggle for a more just world did not lead him to renounce any of his Christian heritage. He did not just preach racial equality, he lived it. He combined a deep seriousness with a playful humour; wherever Clifford was, laughter was not far away, which did as much as anything to dissolve barriers between Westerner and Chinese. It was this combination of qualities which had led a fellow student at Liverpool to 'realise what an attractive person a real Christian could be', and Joseph Beech to recall him as 'our lovable Clifford Stubbs'. Henry Hodgkin summed up his character authoritatively: 'Few men have been so near to my ideal of what a missionary should be in these days. Quiet strength, a deep sense of mission, a steady persistence in well-doing with no show and seeking no recognition, a self-effacing love and a willingness to cooperate at every point with the Chinese, a great confidence in them and a vision of their possibilities ... From his first application to the FFMA in every contact with Clifford I found my appreciation of him deepened. I have never heard a syllable breathed against him ...'[21]

But we should end, as Clifford would surely have wished, with tributes from Chinese. Towards the end of his long life (he died in 2007), mostly spent as a Professor of Surgery at Huaxi, Stephen Yang wrote down his schoolboy memories of Clifford: 'His lectures were not only easy to understand, but full of Confucius' wisdom. We all respected and admired him as a good teacher and friend. Whenever we asked him a question, there was such patience in the explanation. His manners won our love, and many students would like to follow his path.' He then records a tribute from Zhang Lingao: 'He really loved the Chinese. Whatever he was dealing with, he always thought first about the interests of the Chinese from a Chinese point of view. In our years of working together there were never big differences in our opinions. We understood each other well and developed a good friendship.'[22]

Notes

The following abbreviations are used in the Notes:

AML   Margaret Lees (later Stubbs)
AMS   Margaret Stubbs
CMS   Clifford Stubbs
COM   Committee of Missionaries
FHL   Friends' House Library
FO   Foreign Office Papers in the National Archive
FSC   Archive of the Friends' Foreign Mission Association/
          Friends' Service Council, in the Library of Friends' House,
          London
HHP   Herbert Hodgkin Papers, in the Library of Friends' House
HTH   Henry Hodgkin
HTS   Harry Silcock
JSP   Jean Stubbs Papers, in Durham University Library
RJD   Robert Davidson
WCMN *West China Missionary News*
WCUU   West China Union University
WGS   William Sewell

Chapter 1

[1] FSC/CH/13/10, W.B. Albertson, 11/6/30
[2] JSP/OBIT/2, Esther Lewis, circular letter, 5/6/30
[3] JSP/OBIT/2, Mrs Starrett to Dr and Mrs Kirk, 4/6/30
[4] Translations in JSP/OBIT/4

5   JSP/OBIT/2, Esther Lewis, circular letter, 5/6/30
6   JSP/OBIT/3, Alice Lindsay to AMS, 30/6/30
7   JSP/OBIT/2, D.S. Dye to HTS, 6/6/30
8   FSC/CH/13/10, R.L. Simkin to FSC, 3/6/30
9   JSP/OBIT/4, Wu Xuanxi to AMS

Chapter 2

1   Information about Frederick Stubbs is mainly from typescript notes written by his younger son Eric in 1967, in JSP/MISC/2
2   A copy is in JSP/MISC/2
3   JSP/AMS/7, Ruth Gauden (née Silk) to Jean Stubbs, 11/2/69
4   Keith Sinclair, *A History of New Zealand*, Rev.Ed. 2000, pp.194–5
5   JSP/CMS/4, CMS to AML, 19/7/14
6   JSP/AMS/7, Kathleen Stubbs to AMS, 9/6/69,
7   Ibid., C.I. Jennings to J. Johnson, 1/3/32
8   Ibid., Kathleen Stubbs to Jean Stubbs, 28/4/69,
9   JSP/CMS/21, CMS to Frederick Stubbs, 14/8/04
10 Ibid., CMS to Frederick Stubbs, October 1904
11 JSP/AMS/7, Frederick Stubbs to AMS, Dec. 1931
12 Ibid., Kathleen Stubbs to AMS, 28/4/69, 9/6/69
13 JSP/OBIT/5, Winifred Kirk (Stubbs) to AMS, 6/6/30
14 JSP/CMS/4, CMS to AML, 29/3/14
15 JSP/AMS/7, N.M. Bell to J.A. Brailsford, 3/1/31,
16 *Canterbury College Review*, No.34, p.21 (I am grateful to Bill Willmott for this information)
17 Ibid., C.I. Jennings to J. Johnson, 1/3/32
18 JSP/OBIT/7, J.P. Gabbatt to AMS, 6/6/30
19 JSP/OBIT/3, Mary Pearson to AMS, 4/8/30
20 First Annual Report of the Liverpool Presbyterian Young Men's Bible Class Union, 1912, in JSP/CMS/12
21 *Canterbury College Review*, No.35, p.57
22 JSP/AMS/7, N.M. Bell to J.A. Brailsford, 3/1/31
23 JSP/CMS/2, Journal p.4
24 Clifford Stubbs' Scientific Papers are in JSP/CMS/13
25 JSP/CMS/1, CMS to AML, 30/1/12, 13/2/12
26 FSC/CH/ M4 China Committee Minutes 4/4/12, 30/4/13

27 JSP/CMS/1, CMS to AML, 4/7/13
28 Ibid., 13/8/13
29 JSP, CD2
30 Clifford's letters are in JSP/CMS/1; Margaret's in JSP/CMS/21

Chapter 3

1   JSP/CMS/2, Journal pp.16, 4, 14
2   Journal p.13
3   Journal pp.3, 26
4   JSP/CMS/4, CMS to AML, 21/10/13
5   JSP/CMS/1, CMS to AML, 4/7/13
6   Journal pp.18, 26; JSP/CMS/4, CMS to AML, 8/4/14
7   Journal pp.18, 11, 15
8   Journal pp.22, 10
9   Journal p.29; JSP/CMS/4, CMS to AML, 3/11/13
10 Journal p.53
11 Journal p.51
12 Journal p.54
13 Journal p.60
14 Journal p.64
15 Journal p.61
16 Journal p.72
17 Journal p.56
18 Journal p.78
19 Journal p.78
20 Journal p.81
21 Journal pp.79–80
22 For the early history of the Friends' Mission, see Charles Tyzack, *Friends to China*, 1988
23 JSP/CMS/4, CMS to AML, 27/1/14

Chapter 4

1   JSP/CMS/4, CMS to AML, 31/5/14
2   F.O. 228/1870, Consular Report, May 1913

[3] See Charles Tyzack, *Friends to China*, 1988, Chapter 13

[4] Joseph Beech, 'History of WCUU', in *Journal of the West China Border Research Society*, 1934

[5] The designs were reproduced in *The Builder* for 1924

[6] WCUU Board Executive Committee, Minute 647, May 1927, in FSC/CH/14/6

[7] Journal, 11/10/14, Clifford's Journals are in JSP/CMS/2 (1913 – Jan 1914) and JSP/CMS/3 (Jan 1914 – Jan 1915)

[8] Journal, 28/1/14

[9] Journal, 31/1/14

[10] JSP/CMS/4, CMS to AML, 15/2/14

[11] Ibid., 20/1/14

[12] Ibid., 8/2/14, 15/2/14, 1/3/14, 27/4/14.

[13] Ibid., 28/6/14, 5/7/14, 8/4/14

[14] P.D. Coates, *The China Consuls,* 1988, pp.395–6; F.O. 228/1904, Consular Report, June 1914

[15] JSP/CMS/4, CMS to AML, 27/4/14, 4/5/14, 31/5/14

[16] Journal, 31/1/14

[17] JSP/CMS/10, Report for 1914

[18] Journal, 6/2/14

[19] WCMN, June 1920

[20] Journal, 31/1/14

[21] Journal, 27/12/14; JSP/CMS/4, CMS to AML, 20/12/14

[22] Journal, 12/4/14

[23] WCMN, January 1914

[24] Journal, 28/1/14

[25] FSC/CH/2/9, RJD to HTH, 3/3/19

[26] Journal, 2/2/14

[27] Copy in HHP, Box 1, File 2

[28] Journal, 23/5/14

[29] FSC/CH/13/8, W.G. Sewell's Journal, 5/8/28

[30] JSP/CMS/4, CMS to AML, 14/6/14

[31] Journal, 8/6/14

[32] Ibid., 20/9/14

[33] Ibid., 29/11/14

[34] Ibid., 13/10/14, 27/12/14

[35] Ibid., 19/7/14

[36] Ibid., 26/7/14

[37] Ibid., 9/8/14

[38] *Our Missions*, 1916, p.33

[39] JSP/CMS/4, CMS to AML, 29/9/14; Journal, 6/12/14

[40] Journal, 11/10/14, 13/10/14, 25/10/14, 13/9/14

[41] Ibid., 6/12/14

[42] Ibid., 22/12/14

[43] JSP/CMS/4, CMS to AML, 24/1/15

[44] JSP/CD/2

[45] Journal, 10/1/15, 24/1/15

[46] JSP/CMS/4, CMS to AML, 17/1/15

[47] Journal, 24/1/15

[48] JSP/CMS/4, CMS to AML, 10/1/15

[49] Ibid., 8/1/15

[50] Ibid., 4/2/15

[51] JSP/AMS/8, Alice Deane to Mrs Lees, 4/4/15

[52] JSP/CD/1

[53] JSP/CD 2

[54] JSP/AMS/8, M. Silcock to Mrs Lees, 23/5/15

[55] Ibid., Order of ceremony

[56] Ibid., M. Silcock to Mrs Lees, 2/6/15

[57] JSP/CD 1

[58] JSP/CMS/21, Extract from 'C&M Diary'

[59] FSC/CH/4/1, CMS to J.E. Clark, 20/8/23

[60] Journal, 6/12/14

[61] FSC/CH/14

[62] FSC/CH/3/3(a), HTH to HTS 7/2/21

[63] For details of Simkin's relationship to the FFMA., see FSC/CH/3/1; also CH/3/3(a), HTH to HTS, 7/2/21

[64] Benjamin Elman, *A Cultural History of Modern Science in China*, 2008, p.111

[65] James Reardon-Anderson, *The Study of Change: Chemistry in China 1840–1949*, 1991, p.38. Much of the material in the following paragraphs is taken from this book

[66] Reardon-Anderson, op.cit., p.60

[67] Journal, 5/7/14, 2/8/14

[68] Reardon-Anderson, op.cit., p.93

[69] Quoted in Reardon-Anderson, op.cit., p.109

[70] FO 228/1904, Consular Report, December 1913

[71] Journal, 15/11/14

[72] W.G. Sewell, 'A Chemist in China', *Chemistry in Britain*, Vol.8 (12), 1972

[73] FSC/CH/14/2, WCUU Board Minutes 1920, Minute 420

[74] William Sewell, op.cit.; also, *China through a College Window*, 1937, p.50

[75] FSC/CH/4/3(c), WGS Journal, p.42; JSP/MISC/4, WGS to AMS, 11/3/75

[76] JSP/CMS/6, CMS to AMS, 6/9/25

[77] JSP/CMS/5, CMS to AMS, 20/7/24; FSC/CH/3/4, Leonard Walker to HTS, 17/11/21

[78] FSC/CH/4/3(c), WGS Journal, p.1

[79] Journal 5/1/14

[80] Journal 6/9/14, 10/1/15

[81] JSP/CMS/6, CMS to AMS, 15/2/25

[82] Ibid., 12/4/25

[83] J. Taylor, *History of the West China Union University*, in FSC/CH/14

[84] JSP/CD1

[85] JSP/CMS/21, CMS to Mr and Mrs Lees, 2/8/14

[86] FSC/CH/2/4, account by Kathleen Davidson

[87] Ibid., RJD to HTH 12/7/17; FSC/CH/2/5, HTS Report for 1917

[88] February 17th, p.197

[89] JSP/CD 1

[90] WCMN, May 1918

[91] FSC/CH/2/5. Clifford's reports for 1915 and 1916 have not survived

[92] WCMN, April 1919

[93] FSC/CH/2/6, CMS Report for 1918

[94] FSC/CH/2/8, HTS to J. Beech

[95] FSC/CH/2/5, CMS report for 1917

[96] Ibid.

[97] Note by AMS in JSP/CMS/6, CMS to AMS, 6/1/26

[98] Account by Fang Shuxuan, in C.G. Naish, *Robert John Davidson*, 1943, pp.23–4

[99] FSC/CH/2/7, CMS to HTH, 9/3/19

[100] FSC/CH/10/1, COM Minutes 1919, 1921

[101] FSC/CH/2/9, RJD to HTH, 28/6/19

[102] In JSP/MISC/5

[103] FSC/CH/11, HTS to International Friends Institute, Chongqing, 16/3/25

Chapter 5

1   JSP/CMS/21, CMS to AMS, 19/2/19; FSC/CH/2 /7, CMS to HTH, 9/ 3/19
2   Ormerod Greenwood, *Quaker Encounters 3: Whispers of Truth*, 1978, p.195
3   FSC/CH/M5, China Committee Minutes 24/3/20; this seems excessive, and perhaps inflation played a part. See also FSC/CH/3/2a, HTS to HTH, 26/4/20
4   Ibid., China Committee Minutes, 6/11/19, 3/12/19
5   FSC/CH/11, HTH to H. Morrison, 6/6/20
6   FSC/CH/2/7, CMS to HTH, 30/10/19
7   FSC/CH/3/4a, CMS to HTS, 17/2/22
8   FSC/CH/2/7, CMS to HTH, 9/3/19
9   FSC/CH/2/8, Irene Hutchinson to HTH, 10/11/18
10 FSC/CH/11, HTH to Ernest Sawdon, 11/3/20
11 WCMN, June 1916, July 1918, February 1919
12 FSC/CH/2/8, HTS to HTH, 4/12/19
13 FSC/CH/M5, China Committee Minutes, 5/12/17, 30/1/18
14 For an account of this period see Thomas Kennedy, *British Quakerism 1860–1920*, 2001
15 JSP/CMS/17
16 *The Friend*, 1926, pp.878–9; JSP/CMS/6, CMS to AMS, 3/5/25
17 Thomas Kennedy, op.cit., pp.375, 395
18 JSP/CMS/21, CMS to AMS, 22/3/20, 28/3/20
19 JSP/MISC/4, W.G. Sewell to Winifred White, 21/10/68
20 JSP/CMS/7, 23/10/27
21 JSP/AMS/7, Richenda Scott to AMS, 8/4/69
22 FSC/CH/14/2, WCUU Board Minutes 1920, minute 420; Report of Senate to the Board.
23 FSC/CH/3/3a, RJD to HTS, 4/12/20
24 FSC/CH/3/4a, CMS to HTS, 30/1/22

Chapter 6

1   A. Warburton Davidson in *The Friend*, August 1915, p.765
2   WCMN, February 1920

[3] FSC/CH/4/3c, R.L. Simkin to 'Friends', 20/8/25

[4] See Jessie Lutz, *China and the Christian Colleges 1850–1950*, 1971, p.215 ff.

[5] FSC/CH/3/3b, CMS to 'Friends', 14/7/21

[6] FSC/CH/2/8, HTS to Beech, 7/7/19, 13/7/19; HTS to HTH, 12/8/19, 1/9/19

[7] FSC/CH/3/2a, Ernest Sawdon to HTH, 6/1/20

[8] FSC/CH/3/3b, CMS to 'Friends', 14/7/21

[9] See L. Wigham's 1923 Report in FSC/CH/4/3c

[10] H.G. Wood, *Henry T. Hodgkin: A Memoir*, p.183

[11] Ibid., p.188

[12] FSC/CH/3/3a, HTH to William Nicholson, 13/1/21

[13] Ibid., RJD to HTS, 4/12/20

[14] Ibid., RJD to HTS, 17/1/21

[15] Ibid., HTH to William Nicholson, 13/1/21

[16] Ibid., HTH to Nicholson, 5/4/21; L. Walker to HTS, 17/11/21

[17] Ibid., Mira Cumber to HTS, 14/2/21

[18] FSC/CH/11, HTS to L. Wigham, 11/5/22

[19] The others were Fang Shuxuan, and Yang Fangling from Chongqing

[20] FSC/CH/10, COM Minutes 1923

[21] FSC/CH/4/1a, CMS to HTS, 28/2/23

[22] In FSC/CH/10

[23] See Lutz, op.cit., p.224

[24] In FSC/CH/14

[25] FSC/CH/3/3a, HTH to William Nicholson, 13/1/21

[26] FSC/CH/3/2b, W.H. Davidson to Committee of Missionaries, 9/11/20

[27] FSC/CH/3/3b, W.H. Davidson to HTS, 16/10/21

[28] WCMN, January 1921; FSC/CH/11, HTS to W.H. Davidson, 21/12/21

[29] Jerome Ch'en, *China and the West*, 1979, p.149

[30] JSP/CMS/6, CMS to AMS, 4/11/25; FSC/CH/4, 1925, J.P. Rodwell to HTS, 9/9/25; JSP/CMS/7, CMS to AMS, 22/12/27

[31] JSP/OBIT/1, Memorial Service notes 10/6/30

[32] 18/7/30, p.667

[33] JSP/CMS/10, CMS Report for 1924

[34] FSC/CH/5/4e, Daniel Dye to CMS, 28/6/27

[35] FSC/CH/5/4d, WGS Journal

[36] FSC/CH/4/3c, WGS Journal, p.70

[37] FSC/CH/4/1b, CMS to J.E. Clark, 20/8/23

[38] FSC/CH/13/8, WGS Journal, 5/8/28

[39] JSP/CMS/6, CMS to AMS, 5/8/25, 15/8/25

[40] FSC/CH/4/1a, CMS to HTS, 28/2/23; FSC/CH/4/2a, CMS to HTS 6/4/24

[41] JSP/CMS/5, CMS to AMS, 4/4/24, 10/4/24

[42] HHP, Box 1/9 Rodwell to L.Wigham, 8/3/20

[43] JSP/CMS/6, CMS to AMS, 2/6/25

[44] FSC/CH/11, HTS to L. Wigham, 21/12/23

[45] FSC/CH/3/3b, Henry Davidson to HTS, 16/10/21

[46] FSC/CH/14/4

[47] JSP/CMS/10, 1924 Report

[48] FSC/CH/11, HTS to CMS, 7/2/22, 12/9/23, 28/9/23, 5/10/23, 31/7/25

[49] FSC/CH/3/3b, CMS to 'Friends', 14/7/21

[50] JSP/CMS/10, CMS and AMS, Annual Report for 1923

[51] FSC/CH/14/4

[52] FSC/CH/3/4a, CMS to HTS 17/2/22

[53] JSP/CMS/5, CMS to AMS 7/7/24, 20/7/24, 31/7/24, 15/8/24, 24/8/24

[54] Ibid., 13/7/24, 20/7/24

[55] WCMN, April 1924, January 1925; FSC/CH/4/2a, J.P. Rodwell to HTS, 16/5/24

[56] JSP/CMS/6, CMS to AMS 9/1/25, 2/6/25, 23/8/25

[57] Margaret Simkin, *Letters from Szechwan 1923-1944*, (1978), p.39

[58] FSC/CH/4/3a, S.H. Fang to H.T. Silcock, 12/3/25

[59] JSP/CMS/6, 23/3/25; Robert Kapp, *Szechwan and the Chinese Republic*, 1973, p.29, 148n

[60] Margaret Simkin, op.cit., p.27; FSC/CH/4/2b, 1924, Beech to Sir Joseph Flavelle, 29/3/24; Beech to HTS, 6/10/24

[61] FSC/CH/4/3c, WGS Journal, p.55; JSP/CMS/6, CMS to AMS, 12/4/25, 13/9/25, 27/9/25

[62] FSC/CH/3/4a, Beech to HTS, 14/3/22

[63] FSC/CH/14/4, Senate Report 1923; Executive Committee of Board, December 1923

[64] Ibid, Report of Board of Governors to Cooperating Missions, 1924–5

[65] Quoted in Lutz., op.cit., p.236

[66] FSC/CH/5/2a, J.P. Rodwell to HTS, 5/7/26

[67] FSC/CH/4/2b, Beech to HTS, 6/10/24

[68] Kapp, op.cit., p.69; FSC/CH/14/4, Senate Report 1923; FSC/CH/5/2a, CMS to HTS, 16/12/25

[69] JSP/CMS/5, CMS to AMS, 25/10/24
[70] FSC/CH/14/4
[71] WCMN, Feb 1925; JSP/CMS/6, CMS to AMS, 13/1/25, 8/2/25; JSP/CMS/10, 1925 Report
[72] H.G. Wood, op.cit., p.204; FSC/CH/2/8, R.L. Simkin to HTS, 15/2/19; WCMN July 1922; JSP/CMS/6, 13/1/25
[73] JSP/CMS/6, CMS to AMS, 4/3/25; FSC/CH/10, COM Minutes 1924
[74] JSP/CMS/6, CMS to AMS, 9/6/25; FSC/CH/5/2a, J.P. Rodwell to HTS, 13/2/26
[75] JSP/CMS/10, 1925 Report
[76] FSC/CH/4/3b, J.P. Rodwell to HTS, 13/7/25
[77] JSP/CMS/6, CMS to AMS, 3/7/25, 19/7/25
[78] Margaret Simkin, op.cit., p.45
[79] JSP/CMS/6, CMS to AMS, 21/6/25, 29/6/25, 12/7/25
[80] FSC/CH/5/2a, J.P. Rodwell to HTS, 8/6/26
[81] FSC/CH/4/3b, Chengdu MM to HTS, 30/8/25; K.P. Yang to HTS, 29/9/25
[82] Ibid., from 'China Press', 25/9/25; J.P. Rodwell to HTS, 9/9/25;
[83] *The Friend*, 1/1/26, p.11
[84] JSP/CMS/10, 1925 Report; JSP/CMS/6, CMS to AMS, 24/11/25
[85] JSP/CMS/6 CMS to AMS, 27/12/25
[86] JSP/CMS/10, 1925 Report; JSP/CMS/6, CMS to AMS, 13/9/25, 1/11/25, 8/12/25
[87] FSC/CH/4/3b, J.P. Rodwell to HTS, 29/10/25
[88] JSP/CMS/10, 1925 Report. FSC/CH/14/4/4, Senate Report 1926

Chapter 7

[1] FSC/CH/4/1b, CMS to C.E. Jacob, 6/8/23
[2] JSP/CMS/5, CMS to AMS, 8/6/24
[3] JSP/CMS/6, CMS to AMS, 15/1/26
[4] R.J. Davidson and I. Mason, *Life in West China*, 1905, has a map showing how the Province was divided
[5] JSP/CMS/8, CMS to AMS, 12/2/28
[6] *The Friend*, 1926 p.453
[7] FSC/CH/4/2a, HTH to Herbert Hodgkin, 21/4/24

8   *The Friend*, 1926, pp.931–2; FSC/CH/M6, China Committee Minutes, 19/1/27
9   *Analects*, VI, 23
10 *The Friend*, 1926, pp.948, 969
11 Ibid. p.969; FSC/CH/5/2a, 1926, J.P. Rodwell to HTS, 5/7/26
12 *The Friend*, 1926, p.302
13 Ormerod Greenwood, *Quaker Encounters, Vol.3 Whispers of Truth*, Chapter 8
14 *The Friend*, 1926, pp.878–9
15 H.G. Wood, *Henry T. Hodgkin: A Memoir*, pp.212–5; *The Friend*, 1926, p.13
16 H.T. Silcock, 'China and the Quakers', 1964, typescript in Friends' House Library, describes the establishment of the Universities China Committee
17 FSC/CH/11, HTS to J.P. Rodwell, 23/10/26
18 Ibid., HTS to Irene Hutchinson, 31/8 /26
19 H.T. Silcock, 'China and the Quakers'
20 FSC/CH/11, HTS to HTH, 24/11/26
21 FSC/CH/5/2b, cutting from *Shanghai Times*, 29/11/26
22 Ibid., cutting from *Shanghai Times*, 11/10/26; J.P. Rodwell to HTS, 10/9/26, 10/10/26; WGS to HTS, 24/9/26
23 Ibid., J.P. Rodwell to HTS, 29/10/26
24 FSC/CH/M6, China Committee Minutes, 2/2/27
25 FSC/CH/11, HTS to HTH, 23/10/26
26 *Manchester Guardian*, 26/11/26
27 Ibid., 10/1/27, 1/8/27
28 *The Friend*, 1926, pp.1065, 1137
29 JSP/CMS/19, CMS to AMS, 31/1/27
30 JSP/OBIT/1, anonymous speaker at Memorial Service for CMS at Friends House, 10/6/30
31 *The Friend*, 1927, pp.302, 323; JSP/CMS/19, CMS to AMS, 1/4/27, 24/6/27
32 *News Bulletin 162* of the National Council for the Prevention of War, FHL reference 051.56
33 *Manchester Guardian*, 17/2/27
34 For more information on Gilbert, see Robert Bickers, *Britain in China*, 1999, pp.28ff.
35 FSC/CH/5/4a, WGS to HTS, 16/3/27
36 *The Friend*, 1927, p.362
37 Ibid., pp.449, 418–9
38 Ibid., pp.1070, 1021

[39] FSC/CH/11, HTS to HTH, 30/3/27
[40] Ibid., HTS to Henry Davidson, 10/11/26
[41] *The Friend*, 1927, p.854; JSP/AMS/7, Richenda Scott to AMS, 8/4/69
[42] Ibid., pp.743–4
[43] CMS undated letter to AMS in JSP/CMS/19
[44] *The Friend*, 1927, pp. 1156–7
[45] FSC/CH/5/4a, WGS to HTS, 8/6/27; Harold Brown to CMS, 28/6/27
[46] FSC/CH/5/4b, CMS to HTS, 30/7/27

Chapter 8

[1] JSP/CMS/7, CMS to AMS, 18/9/27, 24/9/27
[2] FSC/CH/13/5
[3] FSC/CH/M6, China Committee Minutes, 30/11/27
[4] JSP/CMS/7, CMS to AMS, 30/9/27
[5] FSC/CH/14/6, Report of Special Meeting of Board, 22/10/27
[6] FSC/CH/5/3, HTH's circular letters, 14/3/27, 5/9/27
[7] Robert Bickers, *Britain in China*, 1999, p.28
[8] A copy is in HHP File 34
[9] FSC/CH/5/3, HTH to HTS, 17/8/27
[10] *The Times*, 11/4/27
[11] FSC/CH/11, HTS to HTH, 30/3/27
[12] FSC/CH/5/3, W.H. Davidson to P.H. Butler, 3/8/27; FSC/CH/3/3a, HTH to HTS, 7/2/21
[13] CMS, 'Missionaries and Armed Defence', *The Chinese Recorder*, February 1929 (copy in JSP/CMS/15)
[14] JSP/CMS/11, CMS Circular letter, 10/11/27
[15] FSC/CH/5/4b, Dsan Da-Jin to CMS, 20/10/27
[16] JSP/CMS/7, CMS to AMS, 6/11/27
[17] JSP/CMS/11, CMS Circular letter, 10/11/27
[18] Ibid.
[19] *Manchester Guardian* 28/12/27, 2/1/28; CMS Circular letters in JSP/CMS/11 and FSC/CH/5/4b. Quotations on following pages are all from the latter, except where otherwise referenced
[20] JSP/CMS/7, CMS to AMS, 11/11/27
[21] JSP/CMS/11, 20/11/27

22 Ibid., 21/11/27
23 Ibid., 29/11/27
24 JSP/CMS/7, CMS to AMS, 30/11/27
25 JSP/CMS/11, 29/11/27
26 JSP/CMS/7, CMS to AMS, 30/11/27
27 JSP/CMS/11, 29/11/27
28 JSP/CMS/7, CMS to AMS, 5/12/27
29 JSP/CMS/11, 23/1/28
30 JSP/CMS/8, CMS to AMS, 15/1/28
31 JSP/CMS/11, 23/1/28
32 JSP/CMS/7, CMS to AMS, 2/12/27
33 FSC/CH/3/3b, 1922, CMS to 'Friends', 14/7/21
34 JSP/CMS/7, CMS to AMS, 22/12/27
35 JSP/CMS/11, 23/1/28
36 JSP/CMS/8, CMS to AMS, 30/4/28; Margaret Simkin, op.cit., pp.74–6
37 JSP/CMS/11, 23/1/28; JSP/CMS/7, CMS to AMS, 22/12/27
38 JSP/MISC/4, WGS to AMS, 11/3/75; private information
39 JSP/CMS/8, CMS to AMS, 1/1/28
40 For Sichuan politics in this period, see Kapp, op.cit.
41 Kapp, pp.79–80
42 JSP/CMS/8, CMS to AMS, 19/2/28
43 Ibid., 17/3/28
44 Margaret Simkin, op.cit., p.65
45 FSC/CH/13/8, WGS Journal, 5/5/28; JSP/CMS/8, CMS to AMS, 15/4/28; R.L. Simkin in WCMN, July 1930
46 JSP/CMS/8, CMS to AMS, 4/4/28
47 JSP/CMS/11, CMS Circular Letter, 23/1/28
48 JSP/CMS/8, CMS to AMS, 1/1/28
49 Ibid., 12/2/28
50 Ibid., 26/2/28
51 FSC/CH/14, Senate Report, June 1927; Deng Hong (ed.), *Memory of West China Union University*, 2006, p.79
52 JSP/CMS/8, CMS to AMS, 15/4/28, 19/4/28
53 Ibid., 11/5/28
54 Quoted in Kapp, op.cit., p.28
55 JSP/CMS/8, CMS to AMS, 4/4/28, 16/5/28; FSC/CH/13/8, WGS Journal, 4/11/28, 3/3/29
56 JSP/CMS/8, CMS to AMS, 25/5/28, 20/6/28

57 Ibid., 7/10/28; FSC/CH/13/8, WGS Journal, 10/7/28
58 JSP/CMS/8, CMS to AMS, 21/10/28
59 Ibid., 12/2/28, 25/5/28
60 JSP/MISC/6, Yang Zhenhua, Memories of Clifford Stubbs (in Chinese); extracts translated by Sam Li Zhou
61 JSP/CMS/8, CMS to AMS, 9/7/28, 13/7/28
62 Ibid., 13/7/28
63 Ibid., 5/8/28
64 Ibid., 21/8/28. 24/8/28; FSC/CH/14, Board Minutes 13/10/28. The Vice-Presidents' Report is in FSC/CH/14/6
65 JSP/CMS/8, CMS to AMS, 27/6/28; JSP/MISC/3, CMS to Consul Handley Derry, CMS to Irene Hutchinson, 25/6/28
66 JSP/AMS/3, AMS to CMS, 4/5/28
67 Ibid., 4/5/28, 8/5/28
68 FSC/CH/13/11, AMS to HTS, 29/6/28; FSC/CH/13/8, WGS Journal, 10/7/28
69 JSP/CMS/8, CMS to AMS, 1/7/28
70 Ibid., 18/6/28, 20/5/28
71 Ibid., 14/10/28; FSC/CH/13/11, CMS's address at Confucian Shrine, received 8/12/28
72 FSC/CH/14/6, Vice-Presidents' Report for 1927–8; Correspondence in FSC/CH/13/11; FSC/CH/15/1, Constitution.
73 FSC/CH/13/11, CMS to Board of Governors, 5/12/28
74 Ibid., CMS to HTS 5/4/29; FSC/CH/13/8, WGS Journal, 10/7/28; FSC/CH/15/1, President's Annual Report, 3/10/29; FSC/CH/12, HTS to CMS, 11/2/29
75 The Chinese Recorder, February 1929 (copy in JSP/CMS/15)
76 Ibid.
77 FSC/CH13/11, CMS to HTS, 28/9/28, 5/4/29; JSP/MISC/3, 'Resolution on resignation …', 5/12/29
78 Margaret Simkin, op.cit., p.80
79 JSP/AMS/5, AMS to Ruth Stubbs, 13/1/29, 21/4/29, 5/5/29, 20/10/29, 17/11/29
80 Ibid., 30/6/29
81 In JSP/CMS/18; see also JSP/AMS/5, AMS to Ruth Stubbs, 29/7/29, 31/7/29
82 JSP/CD 1
83 JSP/AMS/2, AMS to CMS, 18/9/27

84 JSP/AMS/3, AMS to CMS, 7/7/28; JSP/CMS/5, CMS to AMS, 24/8/24
85 FSC/CH/13/8, WGS Journal, 13/10/29
86 Margaret Simkin, op.cit., p.84
87 See anonymous account in WCMN, Jan 1930
88 JSP/AMS/5, AMS to Ruth Stubbs, 14/7/29
89 FSC/CH/13/11, CMS to HTS, 28/8/28; HTS to CMS, 12/6/29
90 JSP/MISC/3, CMS to Musgrave Woodman, CMS to HTS, 30/7/29; FSC/CH/M6, China Committee Minutes, 30/4/30
91 FSC/CH/13/11, HTS to CMS, 29/10/29, 15/5/30; JSP/MISC/3, Mrs Lees to AMS

Chapter 9

1 JSP/OBIT/3, Annie Thaxton, Jane Dye, to AMS; *The Friend*, 18/7/30, p.667
2 JSP/OBIT/ 5, Winifred Kirk to AMS, 6/6/30
3 In JSP/OBIT/2
4 FSC/CH/6, Alfred Davidson to Harriet Newman, 2/7/30
5 JSP/OBIT/5, Alec Lees to AMS, 22/6/30
6 JSP/OBIT/6, HTS to AMS, 6/6/30, 10/6/30
7 JSP/OBIT/3, Joseph Beech to AMS, 13/7/30
8 FSC/CH/13, statement from W.B. Albertson [Bursar] on behalf of university, 11/6/30
9 Patrick Wood, *Time Will Make Things Clear: The Story of Stephen Yang, Chinese Quaker*, 2000, p.15
10 FSC/CH/6, Irene Hutchinson to HTS, 22/7/30
11 JSP/OBIT/2, Esther Lewis's Circular letter, 12/7/30
12 JSP/OBIT/6, Leonard Wigham to AMS, 27/7/30
13 FSC/CH/15, Univ. 1929–32, Senate Minutes, 5/6/30
14 Report of Vice-Consul G.V. Kitson, in FO 371/14680
15 Margaret Simkin, op.cit., pp.91–2
16 JSP/AMS/7, AMS's narrative of 1927–8, p.14; JSP/MISC/4, WGS to AMS, 11/3/75; JSP/OBIT/4, Y.L. Kao (Gao Yulin) to AMS, 16/11/30
17 JSP/AMS/9, Dan Dye to AMS, 2/10/30
18 JSP/AMS/9, Irene Hutchinson to AMS, 10/5/31
19 JSP/AMS/9, typed article by Roy C. Spooner

20 *The Friend*, 1985, pp.1527–9
21 JSP/OBIT/6, HTH to AMS, 6/7/30
22 JSP/MISC/6, Yang Zhenhua, *Memories of Clifford Stubbs* (in Chinese); extracts translated by Sam Li Zhou

Index